THE ASSESSMENT AND TREATMENT OF WOMEN OFFENDERS

WILEY SERIES IN
FORENSIC CLINICAL PSYCHOLOGY

Edited by

Clive R. Hollin
Clinical Division of Psychiatry, University of Leicester, UK

and

Mary McMurran
School of Community Health Sciences, Division of Psychiatry, University of Nottingham, UK

COGNITIVE BEHAVIOURAL TREATMENT OF SEXUAL OFFENDERS
William L. Marshall, Dana Anderson and Yolanda M. Fernandez

VIOLENCE, CRIME AND MENTALLY DISORDERED OFFENDERS:
Concepts and Methods for Effective Treatment and Prevention
Sheilagh Hodgins and Rudiger Müller-Isberner (*Editors*)

OFFENDER REHABILITATION IN PRACTICE:
Implementing and Evaluating Effective Programs
Gary A. Bernfeld, David P. Farrington and Alan W. Leschied (*Editors*)

MOTIVATING OFFENDERS TO CHANGE:
A Guide to Enhancing Engagement in Therapy
Mary McMurran (*Editor*)

THE PSYCHOLOGY OF GROUP AGGRESSION
Arnold P. Goldstein

OFFENDER REHABILITATION AND TREATMENT:
Effective Programmes and Policies to Reduce Re-offending
James McGuire (*Editor*)

OFFENDERS WITH DEVELOPMENTAL DISABILITIES
William R. Lindsay, John L. Taylor and Peter Sturmey (*Editors*)

NEW PERSPECTIVES ON AGGRESSION REPLACEMENT TRAINING:
Practice, Research and Application
Arnold P. Goldstein, Rune Nensén, Bengt Daleflod and Mikael Kalt (*Editors*)

SOCIAL PROBLEM SOLVING AND OFFENDING:
Evidence, Evaluation and Evolution
Mary McMurran and James McGuire (*Editors*)

SEXUAL OFFENDER TREATMENT:
Controversial Issues
William L. Marshall, Yolanda M. Fernandez, Liam E. Marshall
and Geris A. Serran (*Editors*)

THEORIES OF SEXUAL OFFENDING
Tony Ward, Anthony Beech and Devon Polaschek

THE ASSESSMENT AND TREATMENT OF WOMEN OFFENDERS:
An integrative perspective
Kelly Blanchette and Shelley L. Brown

THE ASSESSMENT AND TREATMENT OF WOMEN OFFENDERS

An integrative perspective

Kelley Blanchette, Ph.D.
Correctional Service of Canada

Shelley L. Brown, Ph.D.
Correctional Service of Canada and *Carleton University, Ottawa, Ontario*

John Wiley & Sons, Ltd

Telephone   (+44) 1243 779777

Email (for orders and customer service enquiries): cs-books@wiley.co.uk
Visit our Home Page on www.wiley.com

Other Wiley Editorial Offices

John Wiley & Sons Inc., 111 River Street, Hoboken, NJ 07030, USA

Jossey-Bass, 989 Market Street, San Francisco, CA 94103-1741, USA

Wiley–VCH Verlag GmbH, Boschstr. 12, D-69469 Weinheim, Germany

John Wiley & Sons Australia Ltd, 42 McDougall Street, Milton, Queensland 4064, Australia

John Wiley & Sons (Asia) Pte Ltd, 2 Clementi Loop #02-01, Jin Xing Distripark, Singapore 129809

John Wiley & Sons Canada Ltd, 22 Worcester Road, Etobicoke, Ontario, Canada M9W 1L1

Wiley also publishes its books in a variety of electronic formats. Some content that appears in print may not be
available in electronic books.

Library of Congress Cataloging-in-Publication Data

Blanchette, Kelley.
   The assessment and treatment of women offenders : an integrative perspective / Kelley Blanchette, Shelley L.
Brown.
      p. cm. -- (Wiley series in forensic clinical psychology)
   Includes bibliographical references and index.
   ISBN-13: 978-0-470-86461-6 (cloth : alk. paper)
   ISBN-10: 0-470-86461-3 (cloth : alk. paper)
   ISBN-13: 978-0-470-86462-3 (pbk. : alk. paper)
   ISBN-10: 0-470-86462-1 (pbk. : alk. paper)
   1. Female offenders. 2. Female offenders–Rehabilitation. 3. Women prisoners. 4. Feminist criminology.
   I. Brown, Shelley L. (Shelley Lynn)   II. Title.   III. Series.
   HV6046.B565 2006
   365'.66–dc22   2006009320

British Library Cataloguing in Publication Data

A catalogue record for this book is available from the British Library

ISBN-13   978-0-470-86461-6 (hbk) 978-0-470-86462-3 (pbk)
ISBN-10   0-470-86461-3 (hbk)   0-470-86462-1 (pbk)

Thank you,
Mark, Spencer, Charlie
and
Murray, William and Lydia

CONTENTS

About the Authors   ix

Series Editors' Preface   xi

Preface   xv

Acknowledgements   xix

1   The Extent and Nature of Female Offending and Incarceration Patterns   1

2   Theories of Female Offending   15

3   Assessment for Classification of Women Offenders   41

4   Assessing Women's Risk   53

5   Assessing Women's Needs   83

6   Responsivity, Treatment and Women Offenders   115

7   Conclusion   137

References   149

Index   171

ABOUT THE AUTHORS

Kelley Blanchette   completed her doctorate in forensic psychology at Carleton University, Ottawa, in 2005. Her dissertation was focused on the development and field validation of a gender-informed security classification scale for women offenders. The scale has subsequently been implemented into national practice within the Canadian federal correctional system.

Dr Blanchette has been working with the Research Branch, Correctional Service of Canada, since 1993. She is currently the Director of Women Offender Research, and she has published extensively in this area.

Shelley Brown   completed her doctorate in forensic psychology at Queen's University, Kingston in 2002. Her dissertation focused on understanding the criminal recidivism process with a specific interest in exploring how changes in dynamic risk factors influence criminal recidivism.

Dr Brown has over ten years' experience working with the Research Branch, Correctional Service of Canada. During this time her research with women focused primarily on developing gender-informed assessment strategies. Currently, she is the Research Advisor to the National Parole Board of Canada. She is also an adjunct professor with Carleton University and teaches a criminology research methods course.

SERIES EDITORS' PREFACE

ABOUT THE SERIES

At the time of writing it is clear that we live in a time, certainly in the UK and other parts of Europe – if, perhaps, less so in other areas of the world – when there is renewed enthusiasm for constructive approaches to working with offenders to prevent crime. What do we mean by this statement and what basis do we have for making it?

First, by 'constructive approaches to working with offenders' we mean bringing the use of effective methods and techniques of behaviour change into work with offenders. Indeed, this view might pass as a definition of forensic clinical psychology. Thus, our focus is the application of theory and research in order to develop practice aimed at bringing about a change in the offender's functioning. The word *constructive* is important and can be set against approaches to behaviour change that seek to operate by destructive means. Such destructive approaches are typically based on the principles of deterrence and punishment, seeking to suppress the offender's actions through fear and intimidation. A constructive approach, on the other hand, seeks to bring about changes in an offender's functioning that will produce, say, enhanced possibilities of employment, greater levels of self-control, better family functioning, or increased awareness of the pain of victims.

A constructive approach faces the criticism of being a 'soft' response to the damage caused by offenders, neither inflicting pain and punishment nor delivering retribution. This point raises a serious question for those involved in working with offenders. Should advocates of constructive approaches oppose retribution as a goal of the criminal justice system as a process that is incompatible with treatment and rehabilitation? Alternatively, should constructive work with offenders take place within a system given to retribution? We believe that this issue merits serious debate.

However, to return to our starting point, history shows that criminal justice systems are littered with many attempts at constructive work with offenders, not all of which have been successful. In raising the spectre of success, the second part of our opening sentence now merits attention: that is, 'constructive approaches to working with offenders *to prevent crime*'. In order to achieve the goal of preventing crime, interventions must focus on the right targets for behaviour change. In addressing this crucial point, Andrews and Bonta (1994) have formulated the *need principle*:

> Many offenders, especially high-risk offenders, have a variety of needs. They need places to live and work and/or they need to stop taking drugs. Some have poor self-esteem, chronic headaches or cavities in their teeth. These are all 'needs'. The need principle draws our attention to the distinction between *criminogenic* and *non-criminogenic* needs. Criminogenic needs are a subset of an offender's risk level. They are dynamic attributes of an offender that, when changed, are associated with changes in the probability of recidivism. Non-criminogenic needs are also dynamic and changeable, but these changes are not necessarily associated with the probability of recidivism. (p. 176)

Thus, successful work with offenders can be judged in terms of bringing about change in non-criminogenic need *or* in terms of bringing about change in criminogenic need. While the former is important and, indeed, may be a necessary precursor to offence-focused work, it is changing criminogenic need that, we argue, should be the touchstone in working with offenders.

While, as noted above, the history of work with offenders is not replete with success, the research base developed since the early 1990s, particularly the meta-analyses (e.g. Lösel, 1995), now strongly supports the position that effective work with offenders to prevent further offending is possible. The parameters of such evidence-based practice have become well established and widely disseminated under the banner of *What Works* (McGuire, 1995).

It is important to state that we are not advocating that there is only one approach to preventing crime. Clearly there are many approaches, with different theoretical underpinnings, that can be applied. Nonetheless, a tangible momentum has grown in the wake of the 'What Works' movement as academics, practitioners and policy-makers seek to capitalize on the possibilities that this research raises for preventing crime. The task now facing many service agencies lies in turning the research into effective practice.

Our aim in developing this Series in Forensic Clinical Psychology is to produce texts that review research and draw on clinical expertise to advance effective work with offenders. We are both committed to the ideal of evidence-based practice and we will encourage contributors to the Series to follow this approach. Thus, the books published in the Series will not be practice manuals or 'cook books': they will offer readers authoritative and critical information through which forensic clinical practice can develop. We are both enthusiastic about the contribution to effective practice that this Series can make and look forward to continuing to develop it in the years to come.

ABOUT THIS BOOK

Over the years of its emergence, criminological psychology has focused largely upon white, male offenders of lower socio-economic status. Women offenders figure among the disregarded groups that are the focus of relatively little research. As a result, services for women offenders have often been adaptations of those developed for men. This hand-me-down approach assumes that what is known about male offenders applies equally to women. There are assumptions that pathways into crime are similar for both sexes, that risk factors are virtually identical, and that treatments that work for men will also work for women. This lazy, unscientific and dismissive approach to women offenders has had its day.

In recent years, we have seen a growth in gender-specific research. A meta-analysis of what works specifically with women offenders was conducted at the end of the last decade (Dowden & Andrews, 1999). One early longitudinal study of delinquency, the Cambridge Study in Delinquent Development, focused exclusively on boys, but now the data have been revisited to examine criminal careers of the girls in this study's families (Farrington & Painter, 2004). More recent longitudinal studies of antisocial behaviour have included girls alongside boys from the outset as a focus of research (e.g. Fergusson & Horwood, 2002). These studies are signs of a developing interest in a criminological psychology that includes girls and women.

This growing body of knowledge has not been collated and commented upon until now. In this landmark text, Kelley Blanchette and Shelley Brown put a gender-informed criminological psychology firmly on the map. Embedded in a theoretical context, the evidence on risk, needs and responsivity to treatment for women offenders is presented with an impressive degree of scholarship, academic integrity and eloquence. This work will shape correctional services for women offenders in the short term, by presenting policy-makers and practitioners with the evidence on which services should be configured and developed, and in the longer term, by directing researchers towards the gaps in our knowledge that still need to be filled. We are delighted to include this text in our Forensic Clinical Psychology Series.

Mary McMurran and Clive Hollin

References

Andrews, D. A. & Bonta, J. (1994). *The psychology of criminal conduct*. Cincinnati, OH: Anderson Publishing.

Dowden, C. & Andrews, D. A. (1999). What works for female offenders: A meta-analytic review. *Crime and Delinquency*, **45**, 438–452.

Farrington, D.P. & Painter, K. (2004). *Gender differences in offending: Implications for risk-focused prevention*. Home Office, Research, Development, and Statistics Directorate, Online Report. http://www.homeoffice.gov.uk/rds/pdfs2/rdsolr0904.pdf

Fergusson, D.M. & Horwood, L.J. (2002). Male and female offending trajectories. *Development and Psychopathology*, **14**, 159–177.

Lösel, F. (1995). Increasing consensus in the evaluation of offender rehabilitation? *Psychology, Crime and Law*, **2**, 19–39.

McGuire, J. (Ed.) (1995). *What works: Reducing re-offending*. Chichester: John Wiley & Sons.

PREFACE

We can now unabashedly proclaim that women and girls no longer constitute 'correctional afterthoughts'. Female-centred theory, research and correctional practice are proliferating. Although encouraging, correctional knowledge specific to girls and women is infinitesimal in comparison to the male-dominated *What Works* literature.

In brief, the 'What Works' repository of knowledge has conclusively demonstrated that correctional intervention can reduce criminal recidivism (Andrews, Bonta & Hoge, 1990; Andrews, Dowden & Gendreau, 1999; Izzo & Ross, 1990; Lipsey, 1995; Lipton, Pearson, Cleland & Yee, 2002). Indeed, the 'average' correctional treatment results in a 10% reduction in recidivism (Andrews et al., 1990b; Lösel, 1995). Moreover, treatment approaches that follow empirically validated principles of effective intervention (Andrews et al., 1990b) yield substantially higher reductions in criminal recidivism, ranging from 26% to 40% (Andrews et al., 1999; Andrews et al., 1990b; Lösel, 1996).

Current correctional practice is decidedly evidence-based; and this is apparent in the post-Martinson proliferation of the 'What Works' literature. Regrettably, the majority of both primary studies and meta-evaluations has either focused exclusively on male offenders, or failed to disaggregate the data by gender. As such, the question remains: Do effective female-specific correctional services differ from effective correctional services in general? If so, how?

These questions are central to this book. Chapter 1 contextualizes the discussion by reviewing the nature and scope of adult female offending. Next, an overview of contemporary theories of female offending is provided in Chapter 2. Specifically, gender-neutral, female-centred, and hybrid theoretical paradigms are described, followed by a review of the corresponding empirical evidence. Chapter 3 provides a description of general issues germane to female offender classification including a discussion of static and dynamic risk, actuarial versus clinical assessment, an introduction to the *Risk–Need–Responsivity (RNR) model of offender rehabilitation* along with contemporary critiques and competing rehabilitation frameworks – the *Good Lives Model*. Throughout, gender assumes a preeminent role in the discussion. Chapters 4, 5 and 6 form the nexus of the book. Each chapter is devoted exclusively to one of three principles of effective offender classification: risk (Chapter 4), need (Chapter 5) and responsivity (Chapter 6). A critical examination of the applicability of each principle to adult female offenders is provided. In doing so, current knowledge gaps as well as promising research and practices pertaining to women offender classification and rehabilitation are highlighted. Concluding remarks are provided in Chapter 7.

It is important to underscore that our primary focus is women, rather than girls. However, issues pertaining to both girls and women are noted when relevant. Moreover, in the relative absence of research specific to adult females, we rely on the extant literature pertaining to girls. This will become particularly apparent in Chapter 2, *Theories of Female Offending*.

While we have chosen to focus on three specific areas – risk, need and responsivity – we acknowledge that the principles of effective correctional treatment are manifold. For example, Andrews (2001) has outlined 18 specific principles that should be adhered to in order to yield the greatest reductions in criminal recidivism. Similarly, Gendreau, French and Gionet (2004) have identified many of the same principles but have organized them somewhat differently, generating eight, as opposed to 18, specific principles. While we incorporate other principles of effective rehabilitation throughout the discussion, our selected focus is one of both convenience (more research evidence for review) and practical utility – most correctional researchers and practitioners are familiar with the tenets of the risk, need and responsivity principles, and guidelines for their application are straightforward.

We recognize that gender is but one component of diversity. Many of the issues and problems concerning the lack of research (and therefore appropriate practice) pertaining to girls and women could equally be applied to various other groups outside the white male normative standard. We emphatically concur that *one size does not fit all* and that studies must be devoted to various specific offender subpopulations. Considerations include, although are not limited to, culture, ethnicity and disability. Nonetheless, we highlight that the focus of this book is gender and the development of best practices for women within the criminal justice system. While we recognize the heterogeneity within the female offender population, we cannot purport to address all diversity considerations simultaneously. This publication is not a panacea; rather, it aims to provide a starting point for prospective research endeavours and for the provision of correctional intervention for girls and women in a manner that is informed by gender.

Writing this book presented us with, what seemed at times, an insurmountable challenge. As self-identified feminist authors, it seems prudent to disclose at the outset our potential biases. We have both completed our doctoral degrees in experimental forensic psychology. We have each spent over a decade working as researchers in the public sector at the Correctional Service of Canada. Although our day-to-day work is, to some extent, governed by political influences, public policies and the demands of working in an applied setting, this was not the case for the writing of this book. In that sense, this authorship was a truly liberating experience. We could explore several novel areas of interest typically not available to us during our daily work lives. While the book is consistent with our applied research efforts to date, it is nonetheless important to emphasize that the opinions expressed in this publication are our own and do not necessarily reflect those of the Correctional Service of Canada or Canada's National Parole Board.

While our predilection is the scientific method, we acknowledge that there are biases in science and so-called 'objective' methods. We concur that traditional criminology and forensic psychology are best described as sciences conducted by men and about men. Thankfully, this is now changing, in large part due to vocal feminist advocates who tirelessly challenge the status quo.

We believe in the self-correcting nature of science. We believe that the most effective way to improve the lives of all humans, including girls and women entangled within the criminal justice system, is through the thoughtful consideration and application of empirical evidence. By definition, 'empirical' means 'to be amenable to our senses in some way' (Champion, 2006, p. 23). Thus, empiricism incorporates both quantitative and qualitative research methods.

Consequently, this book incorporates both quantitative and qualitative research results. Notwithstanding that, we acknowledge that our academic training and research experience is primarily quantitative; it is therefore natural that we will inherently favour such approaches. Notably, quantitative research strategies are also the preferred method of most policy decision-makers. More and more, particularly in times of scarce resources, decision-makers continually demand that researchers demonstrate how the results of project 'x' impact the bottom line: How many lives saved? How many dollars spent?

Despite our acknowledged potential biases, we underscore the tremendous benefits of using a multi-method approach; particularly when studying small, diverse, marginalized populations. Each methodology carries with it unique strengths and weaknesses, but the combination of methods yields the greatest dividends in terms of practical research results. Indeed, some of our most rewarding research efforts have been those that have adopted a combined approach (e.g. Blanchette & Taylor, 2005; Brown & Motiuk, 2005).

Although our academic training and professional backgrounds are firmly entrenched in psychology, we similarly concur that there is tremendous value in the integration of diverse theories and practical offender management strategies. Moreover, a comprehensive review of the literature suggests that there are several commonalities among supposedly opposing paradigms. The writing of this book has provided us with an opportunity to integrate and reconcile alternative approaches against the backdrop of traditional psychological thought. In the process, there were certainly some epiphanic moments.

It merits reiteration that we self-identify as feminist researchers. Some may perceive this as an oxymoron, given that we align ourselves with the 'Psy-Sciences' (Kendall, 2000). As others before us have argued (e.g. Naffine, 1987), we believe feminism and empiricism can (and should) be integrated. What is perhaps a greater challenge is the consideration of feminist theories and implementation of feminist remedies within the paradox of an inherently oppressive (prison) environment. Despite this challenge, we maintain that it is the integration of various schools of thought that will facilitate the provision of the best gender-informed correctional interventions for girls and women. Accordingly, we believe that we have made a significant contribution to feminism, as well as criminological and psychological science, through the reconciliation of various paradigms in this book.

ACKNOWLEDGEMENTS

We would like to express our sincere thanks to everyone who helped make this book possible. First and foremost we would like to thank the publishers not only for providing us with the opportunity to write this book but for their immeasurable patience when it came time to request extensions. We would also like to thank Kelly Taylor and Mark Nafekh for their helpful comments and insights. As well, the editorial staff at John Wiley provided invaluable feedback that greatly enhanced the quality and readability of the book. We are particularly indebted to Dr Mary McMurran, Series Editor, and Claire Ruston, Assistant Editor.

Lastly and most importantly, we would like to thank our families for their patience and unwavering support.

Chapter 1

THE EXTENT AND NATURE OF FEMALE OFFENDING AND INCARCERATION PATTERNS

INTRODUCTION

There is one universally accepted fact about crime – men commit more crime than women. This finding persists regardless of time, culture, criterion measure (e.g. official versus self-report) or scholarly orientation (e.g. feminist or evolutionary). This chapter addresses three main areas. First, female offending patterns are described relative to those for males. Conclusions are based on research findings derived from multiple sources, including official arrest statistics, self-report crime surveys and victimization studies. Some studies that have examined trends in crime rates over time are also included. Second, historical and contemporary incarceration trends are discussed. Third, qualitative and quantitative research that has examined the nature or 'gestalt' (Steffensmeier & Allan, 1996) of female crime is reviewed. Throughout the chapter we also provide international and ethno-cultural comparisons when available.

FEMALE OFFENDING PATTERNS

Recently compiled statistics from various countries have demonstrated that females are three to five times less likely than males to be arrested, charged or detained in police custody. In Canada, women accounted for 17% of all adults charged with a criminal offence in 2003 (Canadian Centre for Justice Statistics, 2004). Likewise, in England and Wales, 17% of all arrests in 2003/2004 were attributed to females (girls and women) (Murray & Fiti, 2004). Moreover, a national Australian survey also illustrated that females (girls and women) were less likely (17%) than their male counterparts (83%) to be placed under police custody (Taylor & Bareja, 2002). Lastly, in the United States, females (girls and women) accounted for 23% of all arrests in 2002 (Federal Bureau of Investigation, 2002). Thus, while American females were markedly less likely than American males to be arrested, they still accounted for a greater share of their country's overall arrest rate relative to their counterparts in Canada, Australia or England and Wales.

Not only does the recent statistical portrait support the position that females engage in crime less frequently than males, but a number of reviews have reached the same conclusion (Belknap, 2001; Campbell, 2002; Ellis, 1988; Gottfredson & Hirschi, 1990; Steffensmeier, 2001a). For example, Ellis' (1988) comprehensive review revealed that males committed more crime than females in virtually all of the 77 studies that were examined. This conclusion was based on a heterogeneous group of studies from around the world that employed a variety of different outcome measures. Similarly, self-report studies derived primarily from non-adjudicated samples of youths have also confirmed that young females commit less crime relative to their male counterparts (Canter, 1982; Cernkovich & Giordano, 1979). However, self-report methods have illustrated that the 'gender gap' in crime, particularly less serious crime, is markedly less when juxtaposed against the official portrait. For example, two American studies (Canter, 1982; Cernkovich & Giordano, 1979) demonstrated that, compared to girls, boys were only twice as likely to self-report criminal conduct. Furthermore, the gender differences virtually disappeared when the analyses were restricted to the least serious forms of crime (e.g. minor drug use and shoplifting). Conversely, the gender gap widened considerably (i.e. an average male to female ratio of 5:1) when the analyses focused on more serious types of crime such as burglary, robbery and car theft. Also noteworthy, Cernkovich and Giordano (1979) showed that non-white girls were significantly more likely than their white female counterparts to self-report violent offences that were relational or interpersonal in nature (e.g. fist fighting, using a weapon to attack someone, gang fighting, extortion and carrying weapons).

It is important to highlight that the American findings are consistent with results obtained from a prospective cohort study that examined the criminal trajectories of children ($N = 1037$, 52% male, 48% female) born in Dunedin, New Zealand (Moffitt & Caspi, 2001). This study collected multiple waves of data on 91% of all children born between April 1972 and March 1973. In sum, Moffitt and Caspi (2001) reported that the male-to-female ratio for individuals classified as adolescent-limited (i.e. criminal conduct begins during adolescence, is relatively minor and short-lived) was only 1.5:1. In contrast, the male-to-female ratio for individuals described as 'life-course persistent' (e.g. antisocial conduct begins during childhood, is serious, diverse and persistent) was considerably higher at 10:1.

Moffitt and Caspi's (2001) conclusion that gender disparities in criminal conduct are greatest for serious crime has also been observed in regards to violent criminal conduct. In particular, Ellis (1988) observed that the gender differential in criminal conduct was always strongest for aggressive crime. The author defined aggressive crime as the intentional harming or threatening of another person. In brief, his review of 37 studies revealed that the male-to-female ratio for aggressive crime was substantial, ranging from 5:1 to 10:1. Unfortunately the results were not reported separately for adolescent and adult offenders.

Official statistics have reported similar gender differences in regards to violent crime. For example, in Canada, women account for only 16% of all violent charges brought against adult offenders (Canadian Centre for Justice Statistics, 2004). However, they account for a relatively higher percentage of property charges (23%). Similarly, females in England and Wales are arrested most frequently for theft (41%) followed by violence against the person (24%) (Murray & Fiti, 2004). Lastly, Steffensmeier's research has also demonstrated that females are substantially less likely to be arrested for violent crime in comparison to their male counterparts. Moreover, this finding has persisted across time (e.g. 1965 to 1995) and has been found to exist in 'adult only' female cohorts (Steffensmeier, 1980, 1993, 2001b).

Evidence that further corroborates the gender disparity in violent criminal conduct can be gleaned from victimization surveys, notably Greenfeld and Snell's (1999) research. Greenfeld and Snell analysed five years of data (1993–1997) from the National Crime Victimization Survey (NCVS) conducted annually in the United States. In brief, the NCVS collects information about crime (regardless of whether or not it was reported to the police) from a nationally representative sample of US residents age 12 or older. Overall, their analysis was derived from approximately 40 000 interviews with individuals who reported experiencing some form of violent victimization. A number of noteworthy results emerged. Of the identified violent offenders, 14% (or 1 in 7) were female. Not surprisingly, the gender disparity was greatest for violent sexual offences (1 in 50) and least for simple assault (1 in 6). Moreover, the victims reported that the vast majority of female perpetrators were adults (72%). Similar trends emerged for the male perpetrators (74%).

In sum, evidence gleaned from official statistics, self-report surveys as well as victimization studies has illustrated that females are markedly less likely than males to engage in physically violent behaviour. Interestingly however, another body of literature has illustrated that when 'aggression' is broadly defined to include both overt and covert forms of violence, gender disparities disappear (Quinsey, Skilling, Lalumière & Craig, 2004). Briefly, overt or physical aggression is defined as harm to others through damage or threats of damage to physical well-being. Thus, expressions of overt aggression are likely to attract legal attention. In contrast, covert or *relational* aggression harms others through damage or threat of damage to relationships, and can be direct or indirect, as well as verbal or non-verbal. Examples include threatening to end a friendship unless a peer complies with a request, gossiping and spreading disparaging rumours, and using the 'silent treatment' to punish or control others (Crick, Ostrov, Appleyard, Jansen & Casas, 2004). While covert forms of aggression are generally perceived as less serious than overt forms, it has been persuasively argued that relational violence causes significant short- and long-term harm (Putallaz & Bierman, 2004). Although the study of relational violence is relatively new, it has garnered considerable momentum in regards to young girls and pre-schoolers. For example, the term *relational violence* is referenced in almost every chapter in a recent multi-authored, edited book (Putallaz & Bierman, 2004) entitled *Aggression, Antisocial Behaviour, and Violence among*

Girls. Nonetheless, there is a paucity of research pertaining to adult female offenders.

A fair body of longitudinal research has been devoted to describing female offending patterns over time. Steffensmeier and colleagues, for example, have conducted the most exhaustive and statistically sophisticated analysis in this area. This research spans almost two decades and has been instrumental in dispelling the notion that females have somehow 'caught up' with males in terms of offence frequency and severity and that the Women's Movement was causally related to the narrowing gender gap in crime (i.e. Emancipation Theory).

Building on his previous works in 1978 and 1980, Steffensmeier (1993) examined female arrest statistics reported in the Federal Bureau of Investigation's (FBI) Uniform Crime Report (UCR) data during the period from 1960 to 1990. In brief, his analysis indicated that changes in offending were similar for both genders over the 30-year period of study. For example, Steffensmeier (1993) reported large increases in the following offence categories: larceny, fraud, driving under the influence, drug violations and assault. Conversely, decreases were observed in arrest rates for public drunkenness, sex offences, vagrancy, suspicion and gambling. More recently, Steffensmeier (2001b) extended the time frame to 1995, and similar trends were noted.

The cross-gender stability in patterns of arrest rates over time has also been reported in Canada. Boritch and Hagan (1990) demonstrated a number of similarities between the genders in regards to arrest rates incurred in one Canadian city (Toronto) between 1859 and 1955. Not only did male and female arrest rates decline but there were striking similarities in the long-term patterns for different offence categories. In particular, while males evidenced higher violent arrest rates throughout the study interval, violent arrest rates declined in both genders, although the decline was somewhat more acute for females. Interestingly, crimes of public disorder (e.g. drunk and disorderly, vagrancy) accounted for the largest percentage of arrest rates in both genders.

Campbell's (2002) review of the extant literature has revealed similar patterns. In particular, she reported that male and female crime rates co-vary at exceedingly high levels (e.g. correlations in excess of 0.95). Moreover, Campbell's conclusions are based on research conducted in England and Wales and the United States, as well as research that was conducted by the International Criminal Police Organization. Lastly, Beattie (1975) and Hanawalt (1979) have observed that male and female crime rates in England have risen and fallen together as far back as the thirteenth century.

Thus, the existing trend analyses involving arrest rates have revealed overwhelming similarities between the genders that have persisted across time. However, one noticeable difference has emerged. Specifically, Steffensmeier (1978) has illustrated that female arrest rates (girls and women) for property crime have increased at a faster rate relative to males, specifically from 1960 to 1975. He also demonstrated that the increase was primarily due to minor property crimes perceived as traditional 'female' crimes (e.g. shoplifting, theft of services, fraudulent cheques/credit cards) – a finding he later replicated with an independent adult female sample (Steffensmeier, 2001a). Belknap (2001) has reached similar conclusions; specifically she posited that 'women's offending rates appear to be "catching up" to men's in the area of larceny/theft' (p. 117). Similarly, Campbell (2002) also concluded that women's involvement in petty property crime has demonstrated a marked increase relative to that for men during the last 30 years.

Collectively, the trend analyses stand in stark contrast to conclusions reached by other influential authors (e.g. Adler, 1975) who, at one time, emphatically argued that women were 'catching up' with men in the criminal underworld. Theories that emerged from this erroneous conclusion (e.g. the liberation hypothesis) are discussed at length in Chapter 2. Perhaps one of the most important implications of these findings is that they strongly support the hypothesis proposed by some authors (e.g. Campbell, 2002) that similar aetiological factors account for both male and female criminality. The validity of this hypothesis is also explored at length in Chapter 2.

INCARCERATION TRENDS

A number of reviewers have provided historical accounts of female incarceration patterns (e.g. Dobash, Dobash & Gutteride, 1986; Feinman, 1983; Heidensohn, 1985; Morris, 1987). Based on these collective works, Belknap (2001) has traced the evolution of female incarceration patterns from the sixteenth century through to the present day. In brief, she has made the following observations. While imprisonment became a regular form of punishment during the late sixteenth century, it was not until the late nineteenth century that society readily accepted and endorsed its use. Importantly, this trend did not vary as a function of gender. Additionally, Belknap (2001) has noted how historical accounts have underscored some notable differences between male and female incarceration experiences. Specifically, the practice of housing females in male prisons, a practice that persisted until the 1850s in England and the 1870s in the United States, resulted in a number of harsh consequences unique to women. In particular, although women were housed in separate living units, they were still highly disadvantaged relative to their male counterparts in terms of vulnerability to rape, restricted access to women-specific services and the absence of female guards.

Next, Belknap (2001) described how prison reformers in the United States and England were instrumental in transforming the prison environment for women. Most notable among these reformers was Elizabeth Fry. Elizabeth Fry, who commenced her work in the UK in 1816, was the first prison reformer to focus exclusively on women. Along with countless other reformers (e.g. Quakers, charity workers, early-day feminists), Elizabeth Fry worked throughout the nineteenth century to improve the incarceration experience of women. The most notable changes brought on by these reformers were: (1) a paradigm shift from punishment to rehabilitation, including the need to provide women-specific treatment; (2) a recognition that viable employment options must be provided to women; and (3) the creation of female-only reformatories that resembled cottages and were staffed with female guards.

The final segment of Belknap's (2001) review focuses on changes that occurred in the twentieth century. In brief, she describes how the twentieth century ushered in the 'progressive era', a period characterized by the professionalism of female prison administrators as well as the establishment of offender classification, largely the purview of physicians, psychiatrists and psychologists. However, she argues that little in the way of 'reform' occurred throughout most of the twentieth century. She concludes by outlining contemporary problems still faced by female inmates, specifically: (1) sizeable geographic distance between incarcerated women and their loved ones due to the sporadic and isolated location of female prisons; (2) limited options available to women in the areas of education and employment; (3) absence of specialized treatment programmes for women; and (4) failure to segregate the more serious and mentally ill offenders from the less serious offenders. Thus, from a historical vantage point, female incarceration experiences have improved; however, some problems persist in contemporary settings.

Recent estimates indicate that women comprise approximately 5% of the world's prison population (Lemgruber, 2001). More specifically, women comprise only 5 to 7% of the incarcerated adult populations in the following Western countries: Canada (5.0%), the United States (6.9%), Australia (6.9%) and England and Wales (5.9%). However, women account for a relatively higher share of the incarcerated population in Hong Kong (21.6%) and in Thailand (18.4%) (International Centre for Prison Studies, 2004).

While women constitute a small proportion of the incarcerated population relative to men, the evidence indicates that the proportion of females incarcerated is growing and, in some countries, at a faster pace than that for men (Lemgruber, 2001). For example, in the United States, Harrison and Beck (2005) recently reported that the female incarceration rate increased almost 34% between 1995 (47 per 100 000) and 2004 (63 per 100 000). Although the national incarceration rate for males also increased during the same time period (i.e. 789 per 100 000 to 923 per 100 000), the relative increase was substantially smaller (17%). Similarly, in Australia, Cameron (2001) illustrated that the female incarceration rate has outpaced the male incarceration rate. For example, between 1991 and 1999, the female incarceration rate (per 100 000) grew from 9.2 to 15.3, representing a relative increase of 66%; and although the male incarceration rate also grew (194 per 100 000 to 241 per 100 000), the relative increase was markedly less (24%).

Additionally, Cameron (2001) compared indigenous and non-indigenous incarceration rates for women. She demonstrated that the incarceration rate almost doubled from 1991 to 1999 for Indigenous women (from 104 per 100 000 to 207 per 100 000, representing a 99% relative increase). In comparison, the increase for non-indigenous women was substantially lower (from 8 per 100 000 to 12 per 100 000, representing a 50% relative increase). She concluded by noting that while the absolute number of incarcerated indigenous women was small in 1999 (273), the rate per 100 000 (207 per 100 000) was comparable to that of men in the same year (241 per 100 000). Similarly, in the United States, black women (359 per 100 000) were almost 4½ times more likely to be incarcerated in 2004 compared to white women (81 per 100 000). A relative disproportion was also noted for Hispanic women (i.e. incarceration rate: 143 per 100 000) (Harrison & Beck, 2005).

In Canada, parallel trends have emerged. For example, between 1981 and 2002, the incarceration rate for federally sentenced women[1] increased at a faster pace relative to the federal male incarceration rate. Specifically, the female incarceration rate increased 27.2% during this time period (from 2.2 per 100 000 to 2.8 per 100 000). Although the male incarceration rate also increased during this time period (from 96 per 100 000 to 110 per 100 000), the relative increase was markedly less (14.5%) (Sinclair & Boe, 2002). Finally, similar trends have been observed in England – for example, between 1993 and 1999 the female incarceration rate rose 100% relative to a 43% rise in the male prison population (Home Office, 2000). In brief, while incarceration rates for females have increased at a faster pace relative to male incarceration rates, men still significantly outnumber women in prison populations world wide.

Given that a corresponding increase in female arrest rates has not been observed, there is consensus in the literature that procedural factors have been largely responsible for the observed increase in female incarceration rates rather than an actual increase in female crime. Proposed procedural factors have concentrated primarily on changes in sentencing practices such as the implementation of harsher penalties for drug-related crimes (Belknap, 2001; Chesney-Lind, 1997; Home Office, 2000; Lemgruber, 2001; Mauer, Potler & Wolf, 1999; Owen, 2001). For example, Owen (2001) states: 'Quite simply, the war on drugs has become a war on women and it has contributed to the explosion in women's prison populations' (p. 245). Lastly, it is necessary to emphasize that the incarceration data mirrors the arrest data, at least to some extent. In general, women are being incarcerated primarily for property, non-violent and drug-related offences (Canadian Centre for Justice Statistics, 2001; Home Office, 2000; Lemgruber, 2001; Owen, 2001).

Virtually every profile analysis has revealed one consistent finding: incarcerated female offenders are poor, young, uneducated and lacking in employment skills. Moreover, this finding has been reported world wide (Bloom, Owen & Covington, 2005; Cameron, 2001; Canadian Centre for Justice Statistics, 2001; Her Majesty's Prison Service, 2004; Lemgruber, 2001). Additionally, there is evidence that visible minorities and indigenous or Aboriginal peoples are disproportionately represented within female prison populations. Further, the data suggest that while this disproportionate representation is observed for both genders, it is even more evident among female inmates. For example, in England and Wales, 24% of the incarcerated male population belongs to a visible minority group. Unfortunately, an even higher proportion (31%) of the incarcerated female population belongs to a visible minority group (Her Majesty's Prison Service, 2004). Similar trends have been observed in Canada (Canadian Centre for Justice Statistics, 2001), the United States (Harrison & Beck, 2005) and Australia (Cameron, 2001).

---

[1] In Canada, offenders sentenced to periods of imprisonment of two years or more fall under federal jurisdiction. Those sentenced to less than two years are the responsibility of the provinces.

As Lemgruber (2001) aptly noted, 'being poor, uneducated and unemployed' is not a uniquely female problem. Male inmates are also likely to be poor, uneducated and unemployed. However, it is important to emphasize that a number of reports from various countries have illustrated that female inmates do evidence different, albeit not necessarily criminogenic, needs in comparison to their male counterparts. For example, Her Majesty's Prison Service (2004) reported that women are more likely to demonstrate certain mental health problems such as depression, anxiety or phobia (66%) relative to their male counterparts (20%). Similarly, women inmates are more likely to require medical intervention. Specifically, about 20% of the incarcerated female prison population asks to see a medical professional each day, a figure that is twice as high as that of men. Moreover, women prisoners account for a disproportionate number of self-harm incidents. For example, while females only comprise about 6% of the prison population they account for 25% of self-harm incidents. Also 55% of the adult female prison population consists of primary caregivers responsible for children and elders (Her Majesty's Prison Service, 2004). Similar trends have been reported in the United States (Bloom et al., 2003) and Australia (Willis & Rushforth, 2003). Lastly, it is important to note that the prevalence of physical and sexual abuse in women is typically higher relative to that reported for males (Bloom et al., 2003; Morash, Bynum & Koons, 1998; Task Force on Federally Sentenced Women, 1990).

OFFENCE GESTALTS

It is a commonly held belief that the context of female offending is markedly different from that of male offending. Research that has examined the situational context or the 'gestalt' (Steffensmeier & Allan, 1996) of female offending has focused primarily on motivational factors and the nature of the relationship between the offender and the victim. This section examines the current information on the 'gestalt' of women's offending patterns, both violent and non-violent.

Official statistics world wide confirm that less than 1% of all arrests or charges are for homicide-related crimes (Corrections Statistics Committee, 2004; Greenfeld & Snell, 1999; Steffensmeier & Allan, 1996). However, females are still relatively less likely than males to commit homicide, particularly premeditated homicide (Canadian Centre for Justice Statistics, 2004; Steffensmeier & Allan, 1996).

Greenfeld and Snell (1999) examined the characteristics of all homicide offences that occurred between 1976 and 1997 in the United States. In brief, their analysis was based on 60 000 homicides committed by females and 400 000 homicides committed by males, and the following observations were noted. Females (60%) were markedly more likely to have murdered an intimate partner or family member compared to their male counterparts (20%). In contrast, females were substantially less likely to have murdered a stranger (1 in 14) in comparison to their male counterparts (1 in 4). These findings have been replicated by other researchers who have used data from the

United States and Canada, as well as England and Wales (Gauthier & Bankston, 1997; Mann, 1996; Wilson & Daly, 1992). For example, researchers have found that approximately two-thirds of lethal violence by males is levied against non-familial victims. Conversely, less than 50% of lethal violence by females occurs outside the family. Greenfeld and Snell (1999) also reported that mothers and fathers accounted for roughly the same proportion of homicides against children (both biological and step-children). However, mothers were more likely to have killed children during infancy while fathers were more likely to have murdered children over the age of 7. Lastly, while Greenfeld and Snell (1999) did not disaggregate the data by offender age, they did report that the vast majority (approximately 94%) of female-perpetrated murders were committed by adult females. A comparative analysis of male homicide offenders was not reported.

Interestingly, Kruttschnitt (2001) has noted some motivational similarities between males and females in regards to non-familial homicide. Specifically, she described how males are likely to kill acquaintances as a result of disputes over status competition and 'face-saving' (Daly & Wilson, 1988). Similarly, she observed that females who commit non-domestic assault appear to be doing so for the same reasons as males, specifically vindication and/or an attempt to restore personal integrity. Kruttschnitt's (2001) interpretation was based largely on Daly and Wilson's (1988) evolutionary explanation of homicide offending as well as Anne Campbell's (1984) ethnographic research that involved female gang members in New York. In sum, while the existing evidence is scant, it does suggest that gender does not moderate the motivation underlying non-familial homicide or assault.

In contrast, motivational factors appear to diverge with respect to intimate homicide. For example, there appears to be consensus in the literature that when females murder intimate partners, it is largely in response to years of domestic abuse (Belknap, 2001; Owen, 2001). Conversely, jealousy, infidelity, desertion and control appear to be the catalysts motivating males who murder their intimate partners (Daly & Wilson, 1988).

Daly and Wilson (1988) identified youthfulness, poverty and single parenthood as key risk factors in the explanation of maternal infanticide. In the case of mothers who kill older children, they assign a central role to depression. In contrast, they posit that fathers are more likely to kill children in response to uncertain paternity. This hypothesis was supported by Wilczynski's (1995) research conducted in England and Wales. Wilczynski examined the factors that motivated 20 fathers and 28 mothers who had murdered their children. In brief, he found that male-perpetrated child-killings were motivated by one of three reasons: (1) retaliation (e.g. anger against spouse redirected towards the children); (2) jealousy or rejection by the victim (e.g. believes the child is not his; feels that the mother gives too much attention to the child); and (3) discipline killings (e.g. child killed during the course of punishment). In contrast, the motivational patterns of the mothers were strikingly different. Specifically, the following motives were identified: (1) killing of unwanted or unplanned children (e.g. usually occurring within the first 24 hours of birth); (2) altruistic killing (e.g. 'mercy killings'); (3) psychotic killing; and (4) Munchausen Syndrome by Proxy (i.e. when the parent induces an illness in the child and repeatedly seeks medical attention).

Researchers have also investigated women's participation in other forms of violent offending, specifically in the context of robbery and assault. Sommers and Baskin (1993) conducted 65 in-depth interviews with violent female offenders who had been arrested and/or incarcerated for a variety of violent street crime (e.g. robbery, burglary, arson, homicide, kidnapping and weapons-related offences) in the United States. The study revealed that 89% of the robbery incidents were economically driven. Further, the vast majority (81%) of women who were financially motivated reported needing the money to support a drug habit. Furthermore, the victim was usually a stranger (72%). Lastly, two-thirds of the robberies occurred during the commission of other crimes such as prostitution, drug-dealing or theft. In regards to assault, the motivations and circumstances were varied, and often described as impulsive, disorganized, frequently involving weapons and related to intoxication. Moreover, the authors reported that the majority of assaults (72%) were characterized by situations in which the victim precipitated the assault to some degree.

Miller (1998) compared the motivational and situational factors in a small sample of female ($n = 14$) and male ($n = 23$) robbery offenders. In brief, two notable findings emerged. First, the motivations associated with robbery were gender invariant – males and females both reported committing their offences primarily for financial reasons (e.g. to obtain material goods). Other motivations (e.g. support a drug habit, thrill-seeking or revenge) were less frequently reported in both genders. Second, the strategies used to commit robbery varied as a function of gender. Men were more likely to use direct forms of violence (e.g. gun). Women, on the other hand, were more likely to use varied approaches that were typically less violent in nature – for example, they often targeted other women as victims, or promised to exchange sex for money but did not comply with their part of the agreement. Lastly, they often reported working with male co-offenders. In sum, it would seem that when women commit non-familial violent crime the 'gestalt' is markedly similar to that of men. However, the paucity of research in this area, particularly research that includes male comparison groups, precludes the formulation of firm conclusions.

Qualitative and quantitative evidence suggests that female offenders are less likely to use weapons in comparison to males. As noted, female robbers are less likely than their male counterparts to use weapons during the commission of a robbery offence (Sommers & Baskin, 1993). Similarly, Greenfeld and Snell's (1999) quantitative analysis also revealed that violent female offenders are less likely to use weapons relative to violent male offenders. In particular, Greenfeld and Snell's five-year analysis (1993–1997) of the National Crime Victimization Survey (NCVS) data in the United States revealed that, of the estimated 2.1 million female violent offenders identified in the survey, only 15% had used a weapon (e.g. blunt object, knife, firearm). In contrast, 28% of the identified male violent offenders (13.1 million) had used a weapon (Greenfeld & Snell, 1999).

The 'gestalt' literature has also attempted to describe the nature of non-violent crime in women relative to men. In short, this body of literature suggests that women commit property crime out of economic necessity (e.g. to feed and clothe children) (Belknap, 2001; Campbell, 2002; Carlen, 1988; Chesney-Lind, 1986; Gilfus, 1992; Hunnicutt & Broidy, 2004; Miller, 1986a). In contrast, it is argued that men commit property crime as a means of adventure and status enhancement. Campbell's (2002) vivid description accurately captures this position:

> Unlike the low-profile, mundane involvement of women, men use their criminal profits to furnish a conspicuous and lavish lifestyle. For men, the aim is not simply to pay the rent but to broadcast their over-the-top lifestyle in the local community and thereby to gain indebtedness, prestige and respect. (p. 220)

> Relative to men's property crime, women's is more responsive to personal or family need (rather than desire for a hedonic lifestyle), is viewed as a form of work (rather than adventure), involves more frequent offences with smaller returns and is characterized by concealment (rather than advertising) of their criminal activities. Women need resources as an end in themselves. Men use resources as a means to status and respect. (p. 222)

Three studies (Daly, 1989; Goldstraw, Smith & Sakurai, 2005; Zietz, 1981) have specifically examined the nature of white-collar crime in females. While Daly and Goldstraw et al. included a male comparison group, Zietz's analysis did not. Zietz studied embezzlement and fraud in a sample of women incarcerated in a correctional institution in California. Based largely on the in-depth analysis of six women incarcerated for embezzlement (breach of trust offences), Zietz (1981) devised a 'typology' of female embezzlers: (1) the obsessive protectors (motivation: children); (2) the romantic dreamers (motivation: to preserve the love of a husband); (3) the greedy opportunists (motivation: originally do it for children or to secure the love of a husband, but continue doing it because they are now accustomed to the 'good life'); and (4) the victims of pressure or persuasion (motivation: do it out of fear that they will lose a significant other). The belief that women commit property crime, specifically white-collar crime, 'out of love for family' is also supported by Campbell (2002):

> Lest we fall into the trap of imagining a female executive busily transferring funds and stocks into her account on a computer, these offences encompass passing bad cheques, defrauding an innkeeper, other thefts of service, credit-card fraud, welfare fraud, stealing from an employer and shoplifting. Criminal women are more likely to be lying to welfare agencies or stealing tonight's dinner than transferring funds to offshore accounts. (p. 219)

Daly's (1989) study of white-collar crime in the United States noted several gender differences in convicted men and women. Specifically, women were more likely to have worked alone and were more likely than men to have identified 'family need' as a driving motivational factor. Additionally, women were typically employed in clerical roles (e.g. bank tellers) whereas men were more often employed in managerial or administration positions. Lastly, the convicted men in the study garnered larger financial gains in comparison to the women.

The final and most recent study was conducted by Goldstraw et al. (2005). The researchers examined the nature of serious fraud in a sample of 155 separate cases brought before either the Australian or New Zealand court system. Cases met the definition of serious fraud if a financial loss over $100 000 was incurred, if there was evidence of sophisticated planning and formal organization and if the offenders were considered to be professionals. In brief, the authors concluded that, despite popular belief, women do commit sophisticated and well-thought-out cases of serious fraud. Moreover, while greed was the most frequently cited primary motive in both genders, women were twice as likely to cite 'please others' as a primary motive. Examples within this category included: 'not being able to refuse their families anything', 'supporting children after the break up of a relationship' or 'wishing to buy gifts for partners as a means of demonstrating affection'. Interestingly, half of the women committed the crime with a male co-offender while the remaining half acted alone. Similar to Daly's findings the average loss was substantially lower among the female offenders (average cost of the fraud: $165 505 excluding one case involving $80 million) in comparison to their male counterparts (average cost of the fraud: $1 340 532). Further, while both genders were highly educated, 16% of the male offenders belonged to professional associations or possessed statutory registration in their respective professions. In comparison, none of the female offenders possessed either of these two characteristics.

The nature or 'gestalt' of drug-related crimes committed by females has also been explored. Belknap's (2001) review of the extant literature examined gender differences pertaining to drug use and drug dealing. In terms of drug dealing, she suggests that the greatest gender difference revealed in the literature is that women are typically relegated to the lower echelons of the drug trade (e.g. courier) relative to their male counterparts who typically wield the greatest power. In terms of drug use, she cites Inciardi, Lockwood and Pottieger's (1993) research, which has shown that female drug users are more likely than male drug users to have been indoctrinated into drug use by an intimate partner. However, she also cites Maher's (1995) research illustrating that a multitude of factors, not just the negative influence of an intimate partner, contribute to female drug use, including same-sex peers, opportunity, cost and past drug experience. Lastly, in regards to maintenance, there is evidence that while females continue to use drugs as a coping mechanism, males are more likely to continue their drug use as a result of peer pressure and pleasure (Inciardi et al. 1993).

Research pertaining to drug use has examined its linkage to other forms of crime, namely, prostitution. Chesney-Lind's research (e.g. Chesney-Lind & Rodriguez, 1983; Chesney-Lind & Sheldon, 1998) has described how childhood victimization, running away, prostitution and drug use are inextricably linked. These linkages have been organized into a theoretical framework, *feminist pathways research*, that is described in Chapter 2.

Lastly, the final 'gestalt' component deals with the role men play in female offending patterns. Steffensmeier and Allen (1996) have concluded that 'the role of men in initiating women into crime – especially serious crime – is a consistent finding across research' (p. 467). While this suggestion has been supported by some researchers (e.g. Brownstein, Spunt, Crimmins & Langley, 1995; Covington,

1985), others have challenged this contention. In particular, Kruttschnitt (2001) has recommended that this statement be qualified. Specifically, she notes that while women may be more likely to commit robbery with an accomplice, the accomplice is not necessarily male. Moreover, she emphasizes that women are more likely to act alone in the commission of an assault or homicide. Likewise, Sommers and Baskin (1993) have demonstrated that while female robbers often acted with accomplices (63%), the accomplices were either female (38%) or male (25%).

Perhaps the greatest challenge to the commonly held belief that males are the primary instigators in female crime can be garnered from Greenfeld and Snell's (1999) five-year analysis (1993–1997) of the National Crime Victimization Survey (NCVS) data conducted in the United States. Specifically, among the estimated 2.1 million female violent offenders included in their analysis, most (53%) acted alone. Thus, over 1 million female violent offenders committed their violent crimes in the absence, or at least in the apparent absence, of men. Moreover, 40% of the female violent offenders acted with a *female* accomplice. In contrast, only 8% were in the company of at least one male co-offender. Interestingly, only 1% of the male violent offenders (there were 13.1 million male violent offenders in the study) committed the crime with a female co-offender. Thus, the belief that men play a pivotal role in the initiation of female crime has not been fully supported in the literature.

CONCLUSIONS AND RECOMMENDATIONS

In this chapter, which reviewed the nature and extent of female offending – in particular, adult female offending – a number of notable trends emerged. First, women commit less crime than men. Moreover, the gender disparity is greatest for violent and serious offending. In general, the 'gender gap' in crime, particularly violent and serious crime, has persisted across time, across countries and across studies published by varied scholarly orientations, using various methodologies. However, the magnitude of the gender difference does vary as a function of the outcome measure employed, with self-report strategies yielding the smallest differentials and official statistics generating the largest differences. Additionally, while the gender gap is widest in reference to overt forms of aggression – a finding confirmed in both official and self-report studies – it virtually disappears when relational or covert forms of aggression are considered. In brief, research focusing on self-reported crime in adult women as well as relational aggression in incarcerated adult women is noticeably absent.

On average, women comprise 5% of incarcerated populations world wide. However, statistical analyses have indicated that, in the last two decades, the female incarceration rate is growing at a faster rate than that of males. This finding is consistent across a number of countries including Canada, the United States, England and Wales and Australia. Most importantly, however, there is consensus that the observed increase has most likely resulted from changes in judicial processes (e.g. sentencing practices) rather than true differences in female criminal behaviour. Moreover, world wide, the average female offender is poor, uneducated and lacking in employment skills.

Lastly, this chapter examined the 'gestalt' of female offending and the following observations were noted. Women's violence does appear to be more relational and directed against familial members, particularly intimate partners. Moreover, the motivational factors that contribute to familial female violence appear to differ from those of their male counterparts. There are also similarities and differences in terms of the motivational factors that contribute to male and female drug and property offending.

In sum, women commit less crime, particularly less serious crime, than men, their incarceration rates are increasing at a faster rate relative to men and they evidence similarities as well as differences relative to men in terms of the contextual factors that characterize their crime. Future research must continue to explore gender differences in offending and incarceration patterns as well as the offence 'gestalt'. We now turn our attention to understanding female offending patterns through the lens of various theoretical perspectives.

Chapter 2
THEORIES OF FEMALE OFFENDING

INTRODUCTION

Since the publication of Lombroso and Ferrero's *The Female Offender* (1895), scholars from multiple disciplines have proposed varied theoretical explanations of female offending. These perspectives have converged as well as deviated from one another on a number of key factors including basic assumptions, questions posed, the level of explanation provided (e.g. proximal versus distal explanations) and, most importantly, the variables that have assumed central and causal significance. A perennial question in this body of literature is whether mainstream or 'gender-neutral' theoretical perspectives provide sufficient explanations of female offending, or whether female-specific theories are required.

This chapter reviews contemporary theories of female offending. Each theoretical perspective is described and followed by a review of corresponding empirical evidence as well as existing criticisms. While both direct and indirect evidence are considered, greater emphasis is placed on direct or intentional tests of a particular theory given that a detailed review of indirect evidence is provided in the forthcoming chapters. Briefly, indirect evidence includes research that does not purposefully set out to test a theory but nonetheless examines theoretically relevant variables.

From the outset, it should be noted that the greatest challenge in writing this chapter was determining its organizational structure. As will become evident, the existing theoretical paradigms are not easily classified into mutually exclusive categories. In part, this is due to disciplinary 'turf wars' and intradisciplinary isolation. But it is also due to the existence of thoughtfully integrated perspectives that readily cross disciplinary boundaries. Consequently, the theoretical review is not organized according to disciplinary ownership; rather, it is structured according to the extent to which gender is afforded pre-eminence. Gender-neutral theories (androgynous) are described first, followed by female-centred paradigms, which, in turn, are followed by perspectives that intentionally incorporate elements of both: hybrid paradigms.

GENDER-NEUTRAL THEORIES

Gender-neutral theories include mainstream or general criminological perspectives that either explicitly state or implicitly assume that the theory applies to both genders. While a gender-neutral theory may directly address issues pertaining to females, gender is not afforded central significance. Control theories, social learning perspectives, the personal–interpersonal community reinforcement model, life-course theory as well as evolutionary and biological explanations are among the most influential gender-neutral theories of criminal conduct in the contemporary literature.

Control Theories

Early control theorists such as Nye (1958), Reiss (1951) and Reckless (1967) greatly influenced contemporary models of control. Currently, there are three distinct control theories in the extant literature: self-control (Gottfredson & Hirschi, 1990; Hirschi, 2004); social control (Hirschi, 1969, 2002, 2004) and informal social control (Laub & Sampson, 2003; Sampson & Laub, 1993). While each perspective is unique, each seeks to answer the same fundamental questions: Why do individuals abstain from committing crime? Or: why do they eventually desist?

Self-control theory

In 1990, Gottfredson and Hirschi published *A General Theory of Crime*, which describes a theory also known as self-control theory. In sum, the theory asserts that two factors explain why individuals engage in crime: *low self-control* and *opportunity*. Low self-control is defined as the tendency to pursue short-term, immediate gratification while ignoring the long-term consequences. Individuals with low self-control are defined as 'impulsive, insensitive, physical (as opposed to mental), risk-taking, short-sighted, and non-verbal' (p. 90). The authors further indicate that low self-control results in an enduring propensity to engage in criminal conduct and analogous behaviour over the life course. In brief, the theory asserts that individuals with low self-control will engage in criminal conduct and/or analogous behaviour when afforded the opportunity to do so. The authors further assert that individual differences in low self-control emerge during childhood as the result of child-rearing practices. Specifically, it is suggested that poor parental supervision coupled with parental failure to recognize and punish inappropriate behaviour results in low self-control.

In regards to gender, Gottfredson and Hirschi (1990) assert that their perspective is a general theory that can explain individual differences in criminal conduct irrespective of gender, race or social class. Additionally, they argue that observed gender differences in crime exist because males are more likely than females to exhibit low self-control. They also hypothesize that gender differences in self control are the product of differential socialization practices (e.g. owing to the tendency of parents to supervise girls more closely than boys, girls have fewer opportunities to engage in criminal behaviour).

The empirical evidence supports the contention that low self-control is related to criminal conduct in male offenders (Andrews & Bonta, 2003; Brown & Motiuk, 2005; Pratt & Cullen, 2000; White et al., 1994). Parallel research involving female samples has demonstrated a similar relationship. For example, a recent meta-analytic test of self-control theory illustrated that poor self-control was correlated with crime in both genders (Pratt & Cullen, 2000). Interestingly, the magnitude of the effect was stronger for females relative to males. In contrast, a recent study involving non-adjudicated youths reported that the correlation between low self-control and self-reported crime was stronger for males relative to females (Vazsonyi & Crosswhite, 2004). Indirect evidence in support of the theory can also be gleaned from two independent studies: a meta-analytic review (Dowden & Andrews, 1999) and a large-scale Canadian recidivism study (Brown & Motiuk, 2005). More specifically, Dowden and Andrew's (1999) meta-analytic review of the female offender treatment literature demonstrated that programmes targeting 'self-control deficits' reduced re-offending by 22%. Similarly, Brown and Motiuk's (2005) three-year recidivism study, which included 765 female offenders released from correctional facilities across Canada, demonstrated that a single, dichotomous 'impulsivity' indicator was moderately predictive of recidivism ($r = 0.18$).

While it has been established that low self-control is related to female criminal conduct, another body of research has sought to examine the extent to which gender adds incrementally to the explanation of female crime above and beyond self control. In sum, the research to date has produced inconsistent results. First, some studies (e.g. Burton, Cullen, Evans, Alaird & Dunaway, 1998; Keane, Maxim & Teevan, 1993; Tittle, Ward & Grasmick, 2003) have demonstrated that low self-control correlates with mild forms of antisocial behaviour (e.g. driving drunk) in the general population. Moreover, these studies have shown that gender does not provide any additional explanatory power above and beyond self-control. In contrast, other studies have demonstrated that gender does in fact add incremental variance above and beyond low self-control. For example, LaGrange and Silverman's (1999) Canadian study involving secondary school students found that gender contributed unique variance in outcome after self-control variables were statistically controlled for. Moreover, the research demonstrates that the relationship between self-control, gender and delinquency is complex, varying as a function of (1) offence type, (2) how self-control is operationalized and (3) whether or not variables from other theoretical perspectives are incorporated (e.g. Blackwell & Piquero, 2005; Burton et al., 1998; Nagin & Paternoster, 1993; Tittle et al., 2003).

Although self control theory has been criticized for failing to assign a pre-eminent role to gender (Miller & Burack, 1993), the evidence to date supports the contention that low self-control plays a role in understanding female criminal conduct. However, there remains a dearth of direct tests of the theory involving prospective designs that compare adjudicated males and females.

Social control theories

Unlike self-control theory, Hirschi's social control theory (1969, 2002, 2004) focuses on external rather than internal controls. Specifically, the theory posits that individuals commit crime as a result of weakened or broken bonds to society. The bond is conceptualized as a multi-dimensional construct comprising four elements: *attachment, commitment, involvement* and *belief*. While *attachment* refers to the emotional bond and the degree of love or respect an individual has for conventional people and institutions (e.g. parents, teachers, friends, institutions and pets), *commitment* refers to the extent to which one is currently invested or hopes to become invested in conventional aspirations such as employment and education. *Involvement* considers the extent to which an individual is engrossed in conventional activities, including leisure pursuits, employment and community involvement. Lastly, the construct of *belief* considers the extent to which an individual rationalizes or justifies criminal conduct. In sum, the theory asserts that individuals who are strongly attached to conventional people and institutions, committed to work and/or education, involved in conventional pursuits, and do not rationalize or justify crime, are substantially less likely to engage in criminal conduct.

Hirschi's theory does not address gender. Moreover, while Hirschi's original empirical test of the theory was derived from a community sample comprised of male and female adolescents, virtually all of the reported analyses were derived exclusively from the male sample. Similarly, Hirschi only collected information pertaining to official criminal records for the male sample.

Sampson and Laub (1990, 1993) have developed an age-graded informal social control theory[1] to explain childhood antisocial conduct, adolescent delinquency and criminal conduct during early adulthood. In sum, the theory asserts that both static (i.e. immutable, won't change with time) and dynamic (i.e. have the potential to change over time) factors are necessary to understand criminality. Specifically, the theory posits that while early childhood experiences and individual traits help explain stability in criminal conduct, experiences during adolescence and adulthood, labelled 'turning points', can alter criminal trajectories for better (e.g. complete desistence) or worse (e.g. escalation in offending). 'Turning points' refer specifically to how attached an individual becomes to a marital partner, school or employment. It is hypothesized that these 'turning points' or attachments are the primary causal mechanisms that alter one's criminal trajectory. Thus, individuals who demonstrate strong marital attachment and employment stability are more likely to desist from criminal activity than those who do not.

Sampson and Laub derived their theory from a re-analysis of data originally collected by Sheldon and Eleanor Glueck (1950). Briefly, Glueck and Glueck (1950, 1968) compared 500 delinquent males with a matched sample of 500 non-delinquent males using a three-wave prospective design. A number of variables were collected at three different age intervals: 14, 25 and 32. Sampson and Laub's (1993) re-analysis demonstrated that employment stability and marital attachment were strongly related to desistence from criminal activity in adulthood.

---

[1]Sampson and Laub's perspective is also a life-course theory given that it uses longitudinal designs to study how changes over the life course impact desistence. However, we included the theory here given that it focuses primarily on the relationship between *societal bonds/controls* and desistence.

Considerable empirical evidence, both direct and indirect, has amassed to support the applicability of social control theories to male offenders (Andrews & Bonta, 2003; Brown & Motiuk, 2005; Farrington & West, 1995; Gates, Dowden & Brown, 1998; Gendreau, Goggin & Gray, 2000; Gendreau, Little & Goggin, 1996; Hirschi, 1969, 2002; Laub, Nagin & Sampson, 1998; Laub & Sampson, 2003; Sampson & Laub, 1990, 1993). In regards to women and/or girls, fewer studies have been conducted and the research that does exist has yielded mixed findings. While some studies have found that the theory is equally valid for both genders, others, particularly more recent research, suggest that the theory may require modification in order to explain observed gender differences. This evidence is now reviewed.

A number of Canadian researchers have found indirect support for both Hirschi's and Sampson and Laub's social control theories in the context of validating offender assessment protocols with women offenders (e.g. Brown & Motiuk, 2005; Gendreau, Goggin & Smith, 2002a). Similarly, Covington (1985) directly tested the applicability of Hirschi's social control theory in a sample of male ($n = 202$) and female ($n = 170$) heroin users. She reported that social control variables accounted for a significant portion of the explained variance in self-reported crime in both genders.

In contrast, the results of four recent studies suggest that gender may indeed moderate the relationship between social control variables and criminal activity. For example, Alarid, Burton and Cullen (2000) conducted a cross-sectional test of Hirschi's social control theory in a sample of 17- to 25-year-old male ($n = 1,031$) and female ($n = 122$) offenders admitted to a residential court-ordered boot camp programme in the United States. In sum, the results suggested similarities as well as differences between men and women. While marital attachment was uncorrelated with self-reported crime in men, it was strongly correlated with self-reported crime in women, but not in the hypothesized direction. Specifically, married/attached women were *more likely* to self-report crime than their non-married counterparts. Moreover, while not being attached to parents and not being involved in conventional activities were correlated with self-reported crime in both genders, the effects were particularly strong for women. Lastly, both peer attachment and belief (measured by two indicators: 'respect for police' and 'it's OK to do crime if you can get away with it') did not emerge as meaningful correlates for either gender.

Similarly, Spencer and MacKenzie (2003) reported that marital attachment, employment and education stability reduced the risk of future re-offending in a Virginia sample of adult male probationers ($n = 94$). However, the same factors actually *increased* the likelihood of re-offending in a comparison sample of adult female probationers ($n = 31$).

In a similar vein, Benda (2005) also demonstrated that gender moderated the relationship between a number of social bonding variables and criminal conduct. Benda's study compared adult male ($n = 300$) and adult female ($n = 300$) boot camp graduates in a midwestern American state over a five-year follow-up period. A number of notable findings emerged that supported the moderating function of gender. For example, education level did not predict outcome for women but it did so for men. Similarly, while number of children, positive relations with family of origin and a friendship variable significantly predicted desistance among the female sample, these variables demonstrated no relationship with outcome in the male sample. Moreover, while job satisfaction, partner satisfaction, criminal peers and criminal partner predicted outcome in men and women, the magnitude of the association varied as a function of gender. In particular, job satisfaction and criminal peers were more strongly related to outcome among males than females. In contrast, partner satisfaction and having a criminal partner were more strongly related to outcome for the females relative to their male counterparts.

Lastly, Giordano, Cernkovich and Rudolph (2002) tested social control theory in a sample of adjudicated youths, both male ($n = 101$) and female ($n = 109$). The authors utilized a methodologically rigorous design that was not only long-itudinal in nature (participants were followed over an approximate 13-year period from adolescence through to adulthood) but also incorporated data from multiple sources (e.g. open-ended life history narratives, structured interviews, self-reported criminal activity, official arrest rates). Surprisingly, neither marital attachment nor job stability predicted desistence for the males or the females.

In sum, there is still a paucity of women-specific tests of social control theory. Nonetheless, the existing research does suggest that the explanatory power of social control theories could be enhanced by incorporating women-specific bonding factors (e.g. children). However, whether or not the apparent moderating effect of gender on the relationship between marital attachment and criminal conduct is best explained by a female-centred theory, or by an existing gender-neutral perspective such as social learning theory, requires further investigation.

Social Learning Theory

In 1966, Burgess and Akers combined Sutherland's differential association theory (1947) with the principles of psychological behaviourism resulting in the creation of social learning theory (SLT). As Akers and Jensen (2003) note, SLT was derived in a large part from parallel work conducted by psychologists (i.e. Andrews & Bonta, 1998; Bandura, 1977; Patterson, Reid, Jones & Conger, 1975). In brief, the theory asserts that crime is learned. Specifically, individuals learn *'definitions'* that support crime (beliefs, attitudes, justifications, orientations) and the necessary skill set for engaging in crime through the learning principle of differential reinforcement. Differential reinforcement is comprised of two elements: (1) instrumental learning or operant conditioning (the psychology of how rewards and punishers shape behaviour) and (2) imitation (the psychology of how behaviour is learned via observational learning and modelling). Differential reinforcement learning mechanisms operate in a process of differential association. Differential association refers to the extent to which an individual is either directly or indirectly exposed to criminal others. The theory asserts that an individual is more apt to commit crime when (1) he or she differentially associates with others who commit, model and support criminal conduct (differential association); (2) the criminal act is differentially reinforced (rewards exceed costs); (3) he or she is exposed to more criminal than prosocial behaviour (imitation); and (4) his or her own learned definitions (attitudes, rationalizations) are favourable to committing crime. Thus, criminal attitudes and criminal associates are central to SLT.

Akers (1998) suggests that the relationship between gender and criminal behaviour is largely mediated through social learning variables. Specifically, he hypothesizes that 'variations and stabilities in the behavioural and cognitive variables specified in the social learning process account for a substantial portion of individual variation and stabilities in crime and deviance and mediate a substantial portion of the relationship between most of the structural variables [including gender] in the model and crime' (p. 340). Further, he postulates that gender may evidence a particularly strong effect relative to social learning variables in regards to violent behaviour. However, he also speculates that other socio-demographic variables such as class may play a significant role.

Ample evidence involving both adjudicated and non-adjudicated samples exists to support the role of social learning theory in explaining male criminal conduct (Akers, 1998; Akers & Jensen, 2003; Andrews, 1980; Andrews & Bonta, 2003; Pratt & Cullen, 2000). However, there is a paucity of research, particularly direct tests of the theory involving women offenders. Nonetheless, as will become evident shortly, the existing evidence, both direct and indirect, supports the role of SLT in the explanation of female criminal conduct.

Simons, Miller and Aigner's (1980) cross-sectional study of Iowa youths in the United States (2012 male and 1913 female) revealed that social learning variables (e.g. criminal support from friends, criminal attitudes) were not only correlated with self-reported delinquency in both genders but that the magnitude of the correlations did not vary as a function of gender. Moreover, the study revealed that the higher frequency of self-reported crime among the male participants could be explained by social learning variables. Specifically, females were significantly less likely than their male counterparts to possess definitions favourable towards law violations. Similarly, based on the results of a cross-sectional survey of non-adjudicated Boston youth, Morash (1986) concluded that the correlation between gender and self-reported crime is largely, though not completely, mediated by delinquent peer activity.

More recently, Alarid et al. (2000) employed a cross-sectional design to test the applicability of social learning theory on a sample of male ($n = 1031$) and female ($n = 122$) offenders admitted to a residential court-ordered boot camp programme in the United States. The results revealed that social learning variables (i.e. criminal attitudes and criminal friends) were correlated with self-reported delinquency in both samples and to the same degree. Moreover, Sellers, Cochran and Winfree (2003) examined the extent to which social learning variables mediated the relationship between gender and self-reported courtship violence in a sample of Florida university students ($N = 1826$). Their study revealed that social learning variables could partially but not fully account for observed gender differences in the prevalence of courtship violence. Lastly, in a recent, direct test of the theory, Piquero, Gover, MacDonald and Piquero (2005) examined how gender mediates the effects of peer association on self-reported delinquency in a sample of high school students. Although the study reported both similarities and differences between males and females, one of the most pertinent findings was that peer association was a stronger predictor of self-report delinquency among the males than the females. In brief, direct tests of SLT involving female samples appear to support Aker's (1999) hypothesis that social learning variables can explain most, but not all, of the observed gender differences in crime. Nonetheless, additional research is required before firm conclusions can be reached.

Indirect support for the SLT can be gleaned from the correctional literature. Dowden and Andrews' (1999) meta-analytic review of 26 female offender treatment studies revealed that treatment programmes grounded in social learning principles reduced re-offending by 26% to 38%. Moreover, Brown and Motiuk (2005) recently demonstrated that criminal attitudes and criminal associates were among the strongest predictors of readmission in a sample of Canadian offenders (765 females, 15 479 males) – a finding that was upheld irrespective of gender. Lastly, Benda's (2005) five-year recidivism study comparing adult male ($n = 300$) and adult female ($n = 300$) boot camp graduates in a midwestern American state revealed the following. First, having a criminal partner was strongly related to recidivism among females but was either unrelated or only weakly related to recidivism among the males. Second, while criminal peers predicted recidivism in both genders, the magnitude of the result was noticeably higher among the male sample. Thus, Benda's research suggests that marital attachment to a criminal partner is a particularly salient factor in understanding female criminal conduct.

In sum, while some feminist scholars (e.g. Morash, 1999) continue to criticize social learning theory for failing to assign central significance to gender, others (e.g. Belknap, 2001) acknowledge that the theory may potentially contribute to the explanation of gender differences in crime. Moreover, despite the absence of direct tests of the theory involving adjudicated female samples, the existing evidence does support the applicability of SLT to female offenders. However, we concur with Morash (1999) that further research must take a female-centred approach and, for example, examine how gender moderates the relationship between social learning variables such as differential association and criminal conduct. For example, future research should test the hypothesis that having a criminal partner is more problematic for women than for men, as well as the hypothesis that criminal peers are more problematic for men relative to women. Moreover, the extent to which differential prevalence rates (e.g. women are more likely than men to be married to a criminal partner) account for observed gender differences merits investigation (Farrington & Painter, 2004).

Personal, Interpersonal and Community-reinforcement Theory

The personal, interpersonal, community-reinforcement (PIC-R) theory (Andrews, 1982a; Andrews & Bonta, 2003) is a multi-disciplinary perspective that integrates biological, sociological, cultural, familial, interpersonal, personal and situational variables. Grounded heavily in social learning and self-control theories, PIC-R posits that individuals commit crime when the rewards for doing so exceed the costs. Various factors influence the balance of rewards and costs ranging from highly proximal factors located in the immediate situation (e.g. opportunity) to more distally orientated factors (e.g. political/economic/cultural influences). The theory categorizes these factors along four dimensions: *situational, personal, interpersonal* or *community. Situational factors* include opportunities/ temptations, stressors (e.g. negative affect), facilitators (e.g. psychotic state) and inhibitors (e.g. substance abuse) while *personal factors* include antisocial cognitions, history of antisocial behaviour, antisocial personality and biological factors. *Interpersonal factors* include variables such as antisocial associates and family while the *community* dimension encompasses factors such as neighbourhood and criminal justice influences. Although each category differs as a function of temporal proximity to the immediate situation, each one influences the probability that some individuals will find themselves in a situation conducive to committing crime. Additionally, each category also determines whether or not an individual will develop an internal dialogue consistent with definitions favourable towards criminal conduct (e.g. rewards exceed the costs) and consequently, commit the criminal act.

PIC-R concurs with sociological perspectives that suggest that broad-based societal/structural factors are important, however, only to the extent that they control the distribution of rewards and costs within a social system. Further, the theory is primarily concerned with explaining individual differences in criminal conduct. With this in mind, Andrews and Bonta (2003) have identified those risk factors (derived from the empirical evidence) that account for the greatest individual variation in criminal conduct.

Each risk factor has been assigned to one of three predictive accuracy levels. The first and most powerful set includes (1) antisocial cognition (attitudes, beliefs, values that support criminal conduct), (2) antisocial associates, (3) a history of antisocial behaviour and (4) antisocial personality (including indicators such as restless energy, adventuresomeness, impulsiveness, poor problem-solving skills, hostility and callousness). Risk factors placed in the middle range include (1) substance abuse, (2) family, (3) parenting, (4) school/employment achievement and (5) leisure/recreation. Lastly, risk factors in the low range of predictive validity include (1) lower-class origins, (2) low verbal intelligence and (3) personal distress.

PIC-R is presented as a general theory that can account for individual differences in criminal conduct irrespective of gender, class or ethnic origin. While gender is classified as a distal, personal variable that shapes both the person and the immediate situation, it is not central to the model.

One of the most practical and influential outputs of the theory was the development of the risk, need and responsivity principles. Briefly, the risk principle states that offenders who evidence the highest potential for re-offending should receive the most intensive levels of intervention. While the risk principle focuses on *who* should be treated the need principle addresses *what* should be treated. Specifically, the need principle asserts that treatment should prioritize dynamic needs that have been empirically linked to reductions in criminal recidivism. Lastly, the responsivity principle focuses on *how* the intervention should be delivered. Specifically, the responsivity principle asserts that treatment is most effective when the mode of service delivery is matched to the offender's learning style, motivation, aptitude and abilities (Andrews, 2001; Andrews & Bonta, 2003; Andrews et al., 1990b). These principles form the basis of effective correctional programming and are practised world wide in several correctional jurisdictions.

An extensive amount of research has been amassed to support the applicability of the PIC-R perspective, particularly in regards to adult male offenders (Andrews et al., 1990b; Brown & Motiuk, 2005; Gendreau et al., 1996; Lösel, 1995; McGuire, 2002; Motiuk & Serin, 2001). However, the extent to which PIC-R – specifically the principles of risk, need and responsivity – apply to female offenders has not been examined in depth. Moreover, various scholars have been critical about the application of these principles to women (Hannah-Moffat, 2004; Sorbello, Eccleston, Ward & Jones, 2002). Given that one important objective of this book is to explore the applicability of these principles to women offenders, an empirically-based critique will be deferred to later chapters.

Life-course Perspectives

Developmental or life-course perspectives have emerged independently within sociology (e.g. Sampson & Laub, 1990, 1993) and psychology (Farrington, 2005; Loeber & Leblanc, 1990; Moffitt, 1993; Patterson, 1992; Patterson & Yoerger, 1997). Life-course theorists assert that risk factors vary as a function of age or developmental stage. Specifically, during childhood, parental factors play a pre-eminent role in explaining criminal conduct whereas adolescent peer association and school attachment assume greater importance during adolescence. Finally, factors such as employment stability and marital attachment become increasingly relevant during adulthood. Life-course theorists are also recognized by their reliance on longitudinal research designs that examine how changes in developmentally salient risk factors translate into changes in criminal conduct. To date, only one of the developmental theorists (i.e. Moffitt) has explicitly addressed theoretical issues pertaining to female offending. Consequently, only Moffitt's work is reviewed.

In 1993, Terrie Moffitt published a seminal article positing the existence of two distinct offender groups or developmental taxonomies: life course persistent and adolescent limited. Each group has unique aetiological pathways as well as differential antisocial trajectories that vary in terms of onset, severity and desistence. According to Moffitt, antisocial behaviour in life-course-persistent offenders emerges early in life. It results from both internal and external factors. Specifically, individuals considered high risk (i.e. inherited or acquired neuropsychological deficits resulting in mild cognitive impairment, difficult temperament or hyperactivity) and who are also raised in a high-risk social environment are likely to become life-course-persistent offenders. The high-risk social environment initially includes factors such as inadequate parenting and poverty but also incorporates additional developmentally relevant risk factors (e.g. peers and teachers) as the child begins to age. The theory argues that a series of negative, bidirectional interactions occurring between the high-risk child and high-risk environment eventually culminate in the development of a 'disordered personality' characterized by persistent physical aggression and antisociality.

In contrast, Moffitt asserts that the onset of antisocial behaviour in adolescent-limited individuals coincides with the onset of puberty. For this group, the primary causal factor accounting for the onset of antisocial behaviour is the maturation gap, defined as a period '...when otherwise healthy youngsters experience dysphoria during the relatively roleless years between their biological maturation and their access to mature privileges and responsibilities...' (Moffitt & Caspi, 2001, p. 356). The theory asserts that it is the norm rather than the exception for youths during this period to mimic the behaviours of life-course-persistent offenders as a means of achieving respect from peers and autonomy from parents. Eventually, adolescent-limited individuals desist when they reach real maturity and are able to successfully pursue conventional ambitions. Unlike life-course-persistent individuals, they are able to successfully transition back to a prosocial lifestyle, given that their behavioural repertoire already contains the necessary skill set to function in a prosocial world (e.g. educational attainment, positive interpersonal functioning). However, severe addiction or the existence of criminal records may impede the successful transition. Lastly, few individuals will meet the life-course criteria. However, those that do will account for a significant amount of crime, particularly serious crime, well into adulthood. In contrast, the theory asserts that crime committed as a result of adolescent-limited behaviour is commonplace, minor, non-violent and relatively temporary – typically ending before early adulthood.

Moffitt (1994) hypothesizes that this developmental typology applies to both genders. She further asserts that observed gender differences in antisocial behaviour exist largely because boys are more likely than girls to become life-course-persistent offenders. This, she suggests, is because boys are more likely to be high-risk children (e.g. hyperactive, cognitive deficits, delayed speech, learning disabilities). The theory does not speculate in terms of whether or not environmental risk factors vary as a function of gender.

In regards to adolescent-limited behaviour, Moffitt and her colleagues suggest that boys and girls experience the same dysphoria associated with the maturation gap. Consequently, both genders are expected to mimic life-course-persistent offenders as a means of achieving independence from parents and respect from peers. While the theory posits that girls' delinquency will be considerable, it predicts that female delinquency will be less frequent than male delinquency for two reasons. First, girls will have reduced access to antisocial male role models as a consequence of gender-segregated male antisocial groups. Second, girls will be less likely to perceive antisocial behaviour as reinforcing due to the greater possibility of personal risk or injury (e.g. pregnancy, injury from dating violence) and, as a consequence, will be less likely to adopt an antisocial pathway.

Silverthorn and Frick (1999) have questioned the applicability of the typology to girls and, as a result, have proposed an alternative female pathway. Specifically, they assert that all delinquent girls commence engaging in antisocial behaviour post-puberty. Moreover, they hypothesize that all delinquent girls will exhibit the same high-risk causal backgrounds that characterize life-course-persistent offenders.

Interestingly, Belknap (2001) has categorized development perspectives, including Moffitt's research, as 'pro-feminist'. Moreover, with the exception of one study (Kratzer & Hodgins, 1999) the generalizability of Moffitt's typology to females is mounting (Caspi, Lynam, Moffitt & Silva, 1993; Fergusson & Horwood, 2002; Moffitt & Caspi, 2001; Moffitt, Caspi, Rutter & Silva, 2001).

Evolutionary Psychology

Contemporary evolutionary psychology seeks to understand the human mind and consequently, human social behaviour through the lens of Darwinian natural selection. Evolutionary psychologists posit that contemporary human social behaviour including the 'good' (e.g. love, empathy, compassion, altruism), the 'bad' (e.g. jealousy, aggressiveness, lying, impulsivity, crime) and everything in between is largely a consequence of evolutionary adaptation. Specifically, the theory hypothesizes that in the environment of evolutionary adaptation (i.e. hunter–gatherer societies), human social behaviours (initially inherited by chance through genetic mutation) were *adaptive*, in the sense that they imbued the person in question with a reproductive survival advantage such that he or she was more likely to survive, reproduce and consequently transmit his or her genetic material (including the 'adaptive mutation') into the next generation.

Evolutionary psychology posits that genetic and environmental factors are causal determinants of behaviour (Quinsey et al., 2004; Wright, 1995). Consequently, contrary to popular belief, evolutionary theory does not support biological determinism. Not only does the theory assign pre-eminence to the environment, particularly in regards to how humans initially evolved, but it also recognizes the role that today's environment plays in shaping contemporary human behaviour both at the group and individual level. Lastly, it is important to emphasize that the theory does not equate evolutionary adaptations with moral righteousness; to do so would be to commit the naturalist fallacy: 'the belief that what is natural is morally right or desirable' (Campbell, 2002, p. 19).

While the majority of evolutionary theorists have focused on explaining male criminality (e.g. Daly & Wilson, 1988), recent theorists (e.g. Campbell, 1995, 1999, 2002; Campbell, Muncer & Bibel, 2001; Quinsey et al., 2004) have applied the principles of evolutionary psychology to female criminal conduct. Evolutionary theorists such as Anne Campbell posit that risky behaviours (e.g. crime, theft, aggression) were naturally selected in the environment of evolutionary adaptation because they enhanced survival and, consequently, reproductive success under certain environmental pressures, specifically resource scarcity. Campbell's perspective is succinctly described as follows:

> We argue that resource scarcity [e.g. food, money, shelter] drives both property and violent offending in women. Property offenses reflect women's attempts to provision themselves [directly] while violence reflects female–female competition for provisioning males [indirect source of resources]. Evolutionary pressure (the critical importance of maternal survival to females' reproductive success) [dependency of offspring on mother for survival] resulted in females' lower threshold for fear, relative to males, when faced with the same level of objective physical danger. This adaptation inhibits women's involvement in crime, makes them more likely to be involved in property rather than violent crimes and, when direct confrontation is inevitable, causes them to use low-risk or indirect tactics [e.g. verbal aggression]. (Campbell et al., 2001, p. 481)

Campbell (2002) further argues that poverty (the immediate cause of resource scarcity) is a necessary precursor to female criminality. However, it is not necessarily sufficient. Individual differences in fear thresholds among women explain why some poverty-stricken women resort to crime while others do not. Thus, Campbell's perspective incorporates distal as well as proximal risk factors. Moreover, she also recognizes the importance of a number of direct and indirect factors that mediate the relationship between poverty and crime. These factors operate at both the macro (e.g. overcrowding) and individual level (e.g. poor parenting) and are derived from existing criminological theories such as social learning theory, social control theory and life-course perspectives.

Common criticisms levied against the theory include biological determinism, legitimization of existing patriarchal structures (an example of the naturalistic fallacy) and ideological incongruence (Belknap, 2001; Fausto-Sterling, 1992). The latter criticism is best exemplified by Belknap: "...this perspective is ... insulting to girls and women, viewing them as pathetic, needy competitors for male attention..." (p. 57). Chesney-Lind (2001), a prominent feminist scholar, has been more tempered, aptly observing that, while interesting, the theory requires empirical validation. To date, direct tests of Campbell's theory have not been conducted. However, indirect evidence demonstrates that females are more risk-averse than males (e.g. Blackwell & Piquero, 2005; LaGrange & Silverman, 1999) and that poverty (defined as unemployment/employment instability) plays a significant role in female criminal recidivism (Brown & Motiuk, 2005). Thus, the application of evolutionary principles to the explanation of female crime remains promising. However, it requires further empirical validation as well as further theoretical integration with more proximally oriented theories.

Biological Theories

Contemporary biological explanations of criminal conduct have emerged within the fields of behavioural and molecular genetics. Briefly, behavioural genetics considers how genetic and environmental factors account for individual differences in behaviour within a given species. Behavioural geneticists typically utilize adoption and twin studies for hypotheses testing. To date, several reviews in the area have reached the same conclusion: genetic factors can partially account for individual differences in antisocial behaviour (Carey & Goldman, 1997; Quinsey et al., 2004; Rowe, 2002; Van Dusen & Mednick, 1983). As Quinsey et al. (2004) conclude, 'The evidence of a genetic influence on antisocial conduct has become overwhelming' (p. 47). Moreover, behavioural genetics has also confirmed that environment contributes to the development of antisocial behaviour. Specifically, it is aspects of the *non-shared environment* (e.g. factors that differentiate siblings such as exposure to different peer groups or variable parental practices) rather than the *shared environment* (e.g. factors common to all family members such as socio-economic status, neighbourhood) that account for most of the explained environmental variance in antisocial behavior (Quinsey et al., 2004).

Some studies have disaggregated their data by gender. Although scant, the existing research has demonstrated that genetic factors contribute to individual differences in both males and females. However, the extent to which gender may or may not moderate genetic influences or genetic/environment interactions remains unclear. For example, Rowe's (1986) reported heritability estimates (h^2) for antisocial behaviour[2] in a sample of adolescent male and female twins did not vary as a function of gender (43% for males and 47% for females). In contrast, Eley (1998) reported greater genetic influence among females than males but also reported that the influence of the shared environment was greater in males. Similarly, Bohman's (1996) analysis of 913 female and 862 male adoptees also revealed a significantly stronger genetic influence for females relative to males. For example, while 21% of the adopted male criminals had at least one biological parent who was criminal, the percentage was twice as high among the adopted female criminals (50%). Nonetheless, additional research is required before firm conclusions can be reached.

While behavioural genetics partitions the explained variance in antisocial behaviour into genetic and environmental components, molecular genetics seeks to identify the actual genes and/or combinations of genes that are responsible for the genetic variation. In sum, this line of research suggests that certain gene combinations may cause an imbalance between neurotransmitters (e.g. dopamine, serotonin and norepinephrine) that result in impulsive, compulsive, addictive and affective behaviours (Quinsey et al., 2004).

Caspi et al. (2002) have conducted one of the most influential studies in this area. In sum, their research provided compelling evidence in support of a gene/environment interaction. Specifically, they demonstrated that childhood maltreatment was strongly predictive of future aggression but only among boys who possessed a certain genetic predisposition: low activity in the metabolizing enzyme monoamine oxidase A (MAOA) gene. Briefly, the MAOA gene, located on the X chromosome, encodes the MAOA enzyme which in turn regulates other neurotransmitters such as serotonin, dopamine and norepinephrine. A

---

[2]A heritability estimate (h^2) is a statistic that represents the proportion of variance among individuals in a trait that is due to genetic differences. It ranges from 0 to 1 or from 0% to 100%.

parallel analysis involving girls revealed similar trends. Specifically, childhood maltreatment significantly predicted conduct disorder in girls with a low activity MAOA gene (present on both X chromosomes) whereas childhood maltreatment did not predict conduct disorder in the high-activity MAOA group. The authors highlight how the discovery of an X-linked genetic predisposition may help explain gender differences in violence. Specifically, they argue that as a result of having two as opposed to one X chromosome (thus two chances to inherit a normal functioning MAOA gene), females have been afforded extra protection or resiliency potential in comparison to males when exposed to hostile environments. To date, some feminist critics (e.g. Belknap, 2001) have denounced biological explanations of female offending based largely on the premise that earlier theorists used internal factors (biology) to explain female criminality but applied external explanations (society) to account for male offending. In contrast, contemporary biological explanations of criminal conduct underscore the importance of genetic and environmental influences in both genders.

FEMALE-CENTRED THEORIES

Feminist critiques (e.g. Belknap, 2001; Covington & Bloom, 2003; Feinman, 1986; Leonard, 1982; Morris, 1987; Naffine, 1987; Smart, 1976, 1982) have underscored two crucial flaws in the criminological literature. First, some feminist scholars have criticized early theoretical paradigms, specifically the pre-sociological era of criminological thought (e.g. Freud, 1953; Lombroso & Ferrero, 1895; Pollack, 1950; Thomas, 1923) for their inherent sexism and immutable focus on female sexuality, biology and psychology. Second, feminist scholars have aptly noted that the majority of traditional criminological explanations of criminal conduct have either ignored females completely or assumed generalizability across gender without female-specific empirical support.

As a result, female-centred theories have emerged in which gender is afforded pre-eminent status. Moreover, most female-centred theories posit that the onset, maintenance and eventual desistence of female criminal conduct is different from that of their male counterparts (Steffensmeier & Allan, 1996). Similarly, female-specific theories asserting that the oppression of girls and women is causally related to criminality have been traditionally conceptualized as 'feminist'. The following female-centred theories are reviewed: (1) women's liberation, also known as the emancipation hypothesis; (2) economic marginalization perspectives including an integrated liberation/marginalization model; (3) socialization theories; (4) relational theory; (5) power control theory and two feminist perspectives, including (6) power belief theory and (7) feminist pathways research.

Women's Liberation/Emancipation Theory

In 1975, two influential books concerning female crime (Freda Adler's *Sisters in Crime* and Rita Simon's *Women and Crime*) were published. Both authors hypothesized that the women's liberation movement of the 1960s and early

1970s was responsible for the apparent increase in female crime that occurred during the same time period. In brief, the theory argues that as women achieve equal status with men in social, political and economic spheres they will make parallel 'gains' in the criminal world. Specifically, Adler states that, '. . .as the position of women approximates the position of men, so does the frequency and type of their criminal activity' (p. 251). Similarly, Simon asserts that, '. . . women's participation in selective crimes will increase as her employment opportunities expand, as her interests, desires and definitions of self shift from a more traditional to a more "liberated" view' (p. 36). While Adler argued that both violent (excluding murder) and non-violent crime committed by women had substantially increased relative to men, Simon suggested that only non-violent property crime had increased while violent crime had remained relatively constant. Moreover, Adler believed that increased economic opportunity coupled with the tendency of women to take on masculine traits (e.g. aggression, competitiveness) caused the increase in female crime, particularly violence. In contrast, Simon suggested that as women entered the workforce they would gain access to greater criminal opportunities, particularly the chance to engage in work-related crime such as embezzlement.

Liberation/emancipation theory, also labelled role convergence theory (Hart-nagel, 2000) or gender equality theory (Steffensmeier & Allan, 1996), has been criticized both conceptually and empirically. Conceptually, some feminist scholars have underscored the paradoxical nature of the theory itself; that increases in economic equality cause increases in criminal activity when traditional sociological theories (i.e. strain theory) posit the converse; that economic inequality leads to criminality (Belknap, 2001; Chesney-Lind, 1986). Moreover, several feminist researchers (Belknap, 2001; Feinman, 1986; Leonard, 1982; Morris, 1987; Naffine, 1987, 1996) have soundly challenged the theory's fundamental assumption, that the women's movement resulted in equal employment opportunities which, in turn, increased criminal opportunities for women.

Empirically, the theory has been faulted for relying upon exaggerated and misrepresented statistics (Chesney-Lind & Shelden, 1998; Leonard, 1982; Morris, 1987; Naffine, 1987; Smart, 1982). Steffensmeier (1980) thoroughly substantiated this criticism based on a detailed quantitative analysis of FBI Uniform Crime Reports along with an analysis of local studies. In brief, he concluded,

> Females are not catching up with males in the commission of violent, masculine, male-dominated, serious (excluding larceny) or white-collar crimes. Females made arrest gains in the UCR [Uniform Crime Report] categories of larceny, fraud, forgery and vagrancy but localized studies of arrest and court statistics indicate that such gains are due to more women being arrested for traditional female crimes. (pp. 1098–1099)

Lastly, a series of studies involving both adjudicated and non-adjudicated females have found no relationship or a negative relationship between feminist attitudes and criminal conduct (e.g. Bunch, Foley & Urbina, 1983; Giordano & Cernkovich, 1979; James & Thorton, 1980; McCord & Otten, 1983). Consequently, there is consensus that the liberation hypothesis as originally articulated by Adler and Simon is not a viable explanation of female offending. However, the theory has not been abandoned entirely as will be demonstrated shortly within the context of Hunnicutt and Broidy's (2004) integrated liberation and economic marginalization theory.

Economic Marginalization Theory

Economic marginalization theory, also labelled gender inequality theory (Steffensmeier & Allan, 1996) originated as an alternative to the liberation perspective (Hunnicutt & Broidy, 2004; Morris, 1987; Smart, 1982). In sum, the theory postulates that poverty causes females to commit crime. Poverty or, more specifically, female economic marginalization is a multi-dimensional construct comprised of the following female-specific indicators: single, female-headed household, dependent children, children born out of wedlock, divorce and minority status (Hunnicutt & Broidy, 2004; Steffensmeier, 1993).

The economic marginalization hypothesis is strongly supported within the sociological community as evidenced by statements such as, 'there is general agreement among scholars that the economic marginality of women is closely linked to female crime... it is one of the most pervasive explanations for female crime' (Hunnicutt & Broidy, 2004, p. 132). Quantitative analyses have also found a consistent positive relationship between aggregate crime rates and female poverty (Box & Hale, 1984; Chapman, 1980; Hunnicutt & Broidy, 2004; McLanahan, Sorense & Watson, 1989; Simon & Landis, 1991; Steffensmeier & Allan, 1996; Steffensmeier & Haynie, 2000). Additionally, a recent quantitative analysis conducted at the individual level demonstrated that poverty was related to self-reported re-arrest rates in a sample of female offenders ($n = 134$) in the State of Oregon (Holtfreter, Reisig & Morash, 2004). Moreover, using a methodologically rigorous design, Farrington and Painter (2004) reported that poverty indicators (e.g. low social class, low family income, poor housing) evidenced stronger predictive associations with criminal behaviour among a sample of sisters ($n = 519$) compared to their brothers ($n = 494$). Similarly, qualitative ethnographic studies demonstrating that females commit crime largely for economic reasons provide further support for the theory (e.g. Gilfus, 1992; Miller, 1986a; Zietz, 1981). Lastly, theoretical convergent validity (e.g. both evolutionary and economic marginalization perspectives assign central significance to poverty) further bolsters this perspective.

In conclusion, the evidence suggests that poverty contributes to the explanation of female criminal conduct. However, several cautionary notes are in order. First, there is a dearth of quantitative studies at the individual level. Second, the extent to which characteristics of the individual woman mediate and/or moderate the relationship between poverty and aggregate crime requires examination. Third, although ethnographic evidence possesses high face validity, it must be interpreted carefully due to the reliance on small, unrepresentative samples and retrospective research designs and the noticeable absence of control groups. Fourth, the extent to which poverty is a relatively stronger predictor of recidivism among women in comparison to men requires investigation.

Integrated Liberation and Economic Marginalization Theory

Hunnicutt and Broidy (2004) assert that economic marginalization and liberation theories are complementary perspectives that should be integrated. The authors hypothesize that changing gender roles initially brought on by the women's liberation movement have unintentionally increased the 'economically marginal roles' of women by pushing them further into the economic margins of society. Specifically, the women's movement has perpetuated the belief that women are better off financially, a situation that has caused society to overlook evidence to the contrary. Moreover, the authors argue that divorce, a consequence of liberation, has increased the economic instability of women because there are now more single, female-headed households with dependent children. Lastly, the women's movement has increased female expectations in regards to status and wealth such that women may be more likely to adopt illegitimate means to achieve wealth and power.

Hunnicutt and Broidy directly tested the theory using aggregate data pooled across 10 countries. Based on a time series analysis that employed aggregate level independent variables (e.g. the number of divorces per 100 000 married persons) and an aggregate level dependent variable (crime rate per 100 000) they concluded 'that liberation does indeed stimulate crime among women, to the extent that changing roles and expectations of gender equality further marginalize women' (p. 150). However, the extent to which this finding may be explained by other individual level factors remains unknown. In sum, future research questions must ask, 'Why don't all divorced mothers living in poverty resort to crime?' These studies are particularly important because they may elucidate naturally occurring protective factors that insulate women from a life of crime. This information in turn can be used to inform women-centred intervention strategies.

Socialization Theories

Psychological research examining gender differences in development (e.g. Gilligan, 1982; Maccoby & Jacklin, 1974) greatly influenced socialization perspectives. Although socialization theorists (e.g. Chesney-Lind, 1997; Covington, 1998; Dougherty, 1998; Gottfredson & Hirschi, 1990; Grosser, 1952; Hoffman-Bustamante, 1973; Morris, 1964) emphasize different features, they all agree that gender differences in criminal conduct result from differential socialization and child-rearing practices. Specifically, socialization theories argue that the widespread tendency of parents and society to reinforce aggressiveness, physicality and ambition in boys, while simultaneously reinforcing alternative behaviours in girls (e.g. passivity, gentleness and nurturance), is largely responsible for the observed gender differences in crime. Moreover, socialization theories usually assign causal significance to differential supervision practices. For example, it is assumed that because girls are supervised more closely than boys they have less opportunity to engage in crime. Socialization perspectives also assert that the tendency of parents and society to be more permissive of non-conformist behaviour in boys ('boys will be boys') also accounts for observed gender differences in crime. Some feminist scholars have enthusiastically embraced (e.g. Chesney-Lind, 1997; Covington, 1998; Dougherty, 1998) socialization perspectives. However, most feminist interpretations of the theory focus on how *gendered socialization processes* (e.g. Covington, 1998) result in children internalizing and, consequently, accepting existing patriarchal and oppressive power structures.

Campbell (2002) provides a compelling critique of socialization theories. She argues that they are not only guilty of social determinism but that they are based in political ideology rather than empiricism. Her empirically-based criticism is derived primarily from a meta-analytic review (Lytton & Romney, 1991) that examined the results of 172 studies from around the world that specifically examined whether or not parental practices vary as a function of child's gender. In sum, the review concluded that parents did not treat their sons and daughters differently. In contrast, parents treated boys and girls similarly along a number of dimensions including the amount of interaction and warmth they demonstrated, the extent to which they encouraged dependency and achievement, how restrictive they were, how much they used discipline, how often they reasoned with the child and, lastly, how much aggression they tolerated. One difference did emerge: parents gave children sex-appropriate toys – a finding Campbell argues is not sufficient to explain gender differences in crime. She also notes that socialization cannot explain the existence of gender-differentiated behaviours (e.g. differences in aggressiveness, play styles and activity levels) that emerge as early as the age of 2, long before children have the cognitive ability to internalize parental beliefs and gender biases. In sum, Campbell concludes that socialization theories should not be discounted entirely. However, she argues that the more pertinent question is how theory can account for the temporal and cross-cultural stability of gender differences in crime. Specifically, she queries whether or not the gender gap in crime exists because all cultures socialize children similarly or, alternatively, whether it is because men and women are 'hardwired' differently. In sum, we concur with recent reviews that have examined the role of socialization in understanding female aggression (Maccoby, 2004; Susman & Pajer, 2004; Zahn-Waxler & Polanicka, 2004); specifically, that the most comprehensive explanation will only emerge when the bidirectional and reciprocal effects of psychological, biological and sociological factors are considered in tandem.

Relational Theory

Relational theory (Bloom *et al.*, 2003, 2005; Covington, 1998; Miller, 1986b) emerged from within the psychology literature that sought to understand gender differences in moral development (Gilligan, 1982) and interpersonal relationships (Miller, 1976). In sum, relational theory posits that healthy human development requires that individuals feel connected to one another. This need, however, is hypothesized to be particularly important in women. The theory further asserts that the defining features of a healthy relationship are: empathy, empowerment and mutuality (i.e. when individuals respond to and influence each other). Healthy relationships promote zest and vitality, empower individuals to act, enhance knowledge of self and others, increase self-worth and, lastly, increase a desire for more connection (Miller, 1986b).

Relational theory has primarily been used to inform women-centred intervention strategies (see Chapter 6) rather than theoretical explanations of female offending. However, a reasonable hypothesis derived from the theory is that women may be less willing to engage in crime because of the potential threat it poses to important relationships. Moreover, Bloom et al. (2003) posit that situational pressures such as the loss of valued relationships play a greater role in female offending. Benda's (2005) five-year recidivism study, which compared male and female boot camp graduates in a midwestern American State, provided indirect evidence in support of relational theory. Specifically, Benda demonstrated that 'relationship-oriented' variables (e.g. number of children, positive relationship with family of origin, partner satisfaction, friendships) evidenced stronger predictive relationships with desistence in the women relative to the men, or that the variables were only predictive of desistence in women. Prospective research will assist in fully understanding the role that relational factors play in the onset, maintenance and desistance of female offending.

Power Control Theory

Power control theory (Hagan, Gillis & Simpson, 1990) asserts that the distribution of power between parents ultimately explains gender differences in crime. It is argued that the power relationship between one's parents (i.e., patriarchal versus egalitarian) differentially impacts parental supervision practices, which in turn differentially influences risk-taking preferences in sons and daughters. Specifically, the theory posits that patriarchal families (e.g. father works outside the home, mother works within the home or outside the home in a subordinate position) supervise daughters more closely than egalitarian families (mother and father both work outside the home). It further assumes that this socialization practice creates risk-averse girls and risk-taking boys, which in turn results in boys committing more crime than girls. In contrast, children, particularly the daughters of egalitarian families (i.e. working mothers) are supervised less and consequently have more opportunity to engage in criminal activity and develop risk-taking preferences that are commensurate with their brothers.

Empirically, power control theory has received mixed support (see Akers, 1998; Belknap, 2001; Blackwell, 2000 for reviews). Moreover, the theory's implicit assumption, that working mothers increase the delinquency of their female daughters, runs counter to feminist philosophies. Nonetheless, researchers (e.g. Blackwell & Piquero, 2005) continue to investigate and expand upon the theory by incorporating elements of perceived shame and embarrassment as well as by examining its relationship to other mainstream theories such as self-control theory.

Feminist Theories

A monolithic feminist theory of criminal conduct does not exist. This is not surprising given the existence of several schools of feminist thought. For example, Daly and Chesney-Lind (1988) identify four streams of feminism: liberal (supports psychological androgyny and the traditional scientific method), radical (rejects all things 'male'), Marxist (emphasizes the role capitalism plays in the oppression of women) and socialist (adds gender to the Marxist perspective, also emphasizes the role gender and race play in oppression). Campbell (2002) identifies five additional categories of feminism including Afro-American (argues that race, rather than gender, is the primary oppressive force in society), essentialist (considers women as equal if not superior to men), psychoanalytic (grounded in neo-Freudian theory, believes in the unconscious internalization of female powerlessness) and post-modern (believes that there is no objective definition of gender; gender is socially constructed contingent upon the situation at hand). Despite feminist hetero-geneity, Daly and Chesney-Lind define feminism as 'a set of theories about women's oppression and a set of strategies for change' (p. 502). Consequently, it follows that the one common theme that binds feminist theories of female crime is the assumption that the oppression of women plays a central role in the explanation and prediction of female criminal conduct. Two prominent per-spectives that meet this requirement are reviewed here: power belief theory and feminist pathways research.

Power belief theory

Dougherty's (1998) power belief theory asserts that female criminal conduct must be explained within the context of oppression in patriarchal societies. It is argued that adult males hold positions of power and privilege while women and children assume subordinate roles in both public and private spheres. The theory posits that crime is more likely to result when females internalize this power differential in the form of beliefs in powerlessness. Moreover, the theory hypothesizes that childhood maltreatment (e.g. physical, sexual, emotional abuse) increases the probability that a female will internalize feelings of power-lessness. To date, power belief theory has not been tested empirically.

Feminist pathways research

According to Belknap (2001), two features characterize the feminist pathways perspective: (1) the belief that childhood victimization (e.g. abuse, neglect) is the primary, causal factor that leads girls towards a criminal trajectory and (2) the use of ethnographic approaches including in-depth, face-to-face interviews that ensures that the voices of girls and women are heard.

The feminist pathways perspective argues that childhood victimization causes girls to run away from home and/or abuse drugs as a coping mechanism. It further hypothesizes that drug-selling, prostitution and robbery ensue as a means of street survival. Thus, girls and women may be 'criminalized' for their survival strategies (Chesney-Lind, 1998). Moreover, Zaplin (1998) suggests that such cycles of events lead to emotional distress, low self-esteem (or even self-hatred), anxiety, depression and aggressive/impulsive behaviours. The psychological–behavioural sequelae disable the development of 'healthy' empathic or caring attitudes towards the self or others, leading to crime and potential violence.

The feminist pathway model also proposes alternative 'pathways' to female offending. For instance, Belknap and Holsinger (1998) point to research documenting how male batterers coerce or force their spouses into committing crimes such as selling drugs, robbery and prostitution. Numerous scholars including self-identified feminists (e.g. Chesney-Lind & Rodriguez, 1983; Daly, 1992; Shaw, 1991a) as well as researchers to whom Belknap assigned a feminist label (e.g. Widom) are cited as providing evidence in support of the pathways perspective.

Direct tests of the theory are noticeably absent. While early reviews indicted that firm conclusions could not be reached regarding the relationship between childhood victimization and future violence (Widom, 1989) more recent reviews (Widom, 2003) have concluded that early childhood maltreatment does in fact predict delinquency. Widom's (2003) conclusions were based on the results of four methodologically rigorous studies conducted in the United States. All of the studies were prospective, involved large samples and included adequate comparison groups. However, this evidence only provides partial support for the pathways model. Research that demonstrates childhood victimization has more explanatory power among females than males would provide the most compelling evidence for the theory. Unfortunately, the evidence that does exist has produced mixed results.

Widom's (2000) review of two studies that specifically compared gender differences concluded that child abuse was likely to result in stereotypical outcomes: internalizing behaviour in girls (e.g. depression) and externalizing behaviour in boys (e.g. conduct disorder). Similarly, Trickett and Gordis' (2004) review of nine studies that compared sexually abused girls with non-sexually abused girls on a variety of aggression outcome measures yielded inconclusive results. However, Trickett and Gordis' (2004) own independent research study demonstrated that sexually abused females were more likely than their non-sexually abused counterparts to engage in overt forms of aggression in the period immediately following the abuse. However, the differences became less discernible seven to eight years after the abuse. Additionally, the relative importance of childhood abuse in females compared to males could not be ascertained due to the absence of a male comparison group.

Benda's (2005) research supports the feminist pathways model. Benda found that while childhood abuse predicted recidivism in both genders, the magnitude of the effect was stronger for females relative to males. In brief, the empirical evidence does not support the unequivocal conclusion reached by some feminists that childhood victimization plays a central role in the explanation of female criminality. Future research involving prospective studies, and comparison groups that include both abused and non-abused individuals from both genders, are required before firm conclusions can be reached.

HYBRID THEORIES

The final section of this chapter reviews two theories that have explicitly incorporated elements from both gender-neutral and female-specific perspectives. While general strain theory (GST; Agnew, 1992; Broidy & Agnew, 1997) has garnered considerable attention in the literature, Steffensmeier and Allan's (1996) gendered perspective has not. Nonetheless, both are reviewed.

General Strain Theory

In 1992, Agnew reformulated the works of classic strain theorists (e.g. Cohen, 1955; Cloward & Ohlin, 1960; Merton, 1938; Miller, 1958) resulting in the creation of general strain theory. Briefly, classic strain theory states that individuals, particularly the lower class and disadvantaged minority groups, will commit crime when they are unable to achieve middle-class status and/or monetary success through legitimate means. The inability to achieve status and/or wealth through conventional means creates personal strain or pressure. In turn, this causes the individual to resort to illegitimate or non-conformist behaviour (crime) in order to achieve wealth and/or status. Various psychological, sociological and feminist scholars have levied conceptual as well as empirical-based criticisms against classical strain theory (Agnew, 1992; Akers, 1998; Andrews & Bonta, 2003; Leonard, 1982; Morris, 1987; Naffine, 1987).

General strain theory (GST) is heavily grounded in the psychological literature that pertains to aggression, stress, coping and justice/equity. In sum, GST posits that strain or stressful events produce negative emotions, particularly anger which, in turn, results in criminal conduct in the absence of strong, prosocial coping resources. Agnew posits three sources of strain: (1) inability to achieve positively valued goals; (2) the removal of positively valued stimuli; and (3) the presentation of negative stimuli. The first source of strain comprises three sub-components: (a) real or perceived imbalance between aspirations (ideal situation/utopian world view) and expectations or actual outcomes; (b) real or perceived imbalance between expectations and actual achievements; and (c) imbalance between just or fair outcomes and actual outcomes. The second major source of strain (the removal of positively valued stimuli) refers to stressful life events such as job loss, death or divorce. Lastly, the third and final source of stress (the presentation of negative stimuli) includes factors such as abuse and neglect. Thus, strain as originally conceptualized by classic strain theorists is still captured within the theory as the first sub-type of stress within the 'inability to achieve positively valued goals'.

Broidy and Agnew (1997) argue that GST adequately explains the gender gap in crime for the following reasons: (1) males and females experience different *types* of strain, with male strain being more conducive to serious property and violent crime; (2) males and females differ in their emotional response to strain, specifically women are more likely to respond with depression, whereas men are more apt to respond with anger, a response more conducive to crime; and lastly

(3) males differ from females with respect to their coping strategies, social supports, opportunities, social control and the disposition to engage in crime such that they are more likely to exhibit criminal behaviour.

Broidy and Agnew (1997) also assert that the theory can explain why women commit crime. In this regard, they align GST with feminist perspectives by arguing that strain can also be conceptualized as oppression. Specifically, they argue that 'oppressed individuals may turn to crime in an effort to reduce their strain or manage the negative emotions associated with their strain' (p. 288). They present a number of female-specific forms of strain that may be crime-inducing. For example, they note how high rates of divorce and abuse generate relational and financial stress in females. Additionally, they argue that society's tendency to undervalue females at home and in the workplace (e.g. relegated to 'pink-collar jobs', lesser pay relative to male counterparts) results in another source of strain: feelings of injustice. They also identify other forms of strain including death of loved ones, victimization, discrimination, sexual harassment and, more generally, the knowledge that 'the status of female is devalued in our society' (p. 293). Thus, GST is consistent with female-specific theories including relational theory and feminist pathways research.

To date, there have been few gender-specific tests of GST and the research that does exist has produced mixed results. Hoffmann and Su (1997) tested the theory using a longitudinal design on an American sample of non-adjudicated youths. In sum, they concluded that there were few gender differences. Specifically, stressful life events had a similar, short-term impact on delinquency and drug use in both genders. Similarly, Hay (2003) studied the correlation between family strain, negative emotions and self-reported delinquency in an American sample of 182 high school students (95 females, 87 males) using a cross-sectional design. In brief, the researchers reported that while family strain and anger were correlated with self-reported delinquency in both genders, the magnitude of the effect was substantially higher for males relative to females. Lastly, Benda's (2005) five-year recidivism study involving 300 male and 300 female boot camp graduates in the United States demonstrated that while GST variables (e.g. stress, depression, fearfulness, suicidal thoughts) were related to recidivism in both genders, the magnitude of the results was somewhat stronger among the females. Interestingly, 'aggressive feelings' were predictive of recidivism in men but not in women.

In summary, there have been few direct tests of GST, and tests of the complete theory are absent. While some of the research has discerned few significant gender differences, Benda's (2005) research involving adjudicated adult offenders suggests that gender may partially moderate the type of negative emotions that precede recidivism. Regardless, the dearth of prospective tests of GST involving adjudicated offenders precludes firm conclusions.

Gendered Theory

Steffensmeier and Allan (1996) describe *a gendered theory of female offending*. Briefly, the theory postulates that macro-level social factors characteristic of traditional criminological theories (e.g. social learning theory, control theory) causally influence both male and female crime. However, it is gender or rather 'the organization of gender' that moderates how macro-level social factors differentially influence observed gender differences in offence type, offence frequency and the offence gestalt (e.g. nature of offence, victim/offender relationship). The 'organization of gender' construct comprises five elements: (1) gender norms (e.g. female nurturance/obligations, femininity stereotypes), (2) moral development and amenability to affiliation (e.g. greater female empathic concern for others), (3) social control (e.g. greater parental supervision of females relative to males; sanctions more serious for non-conformity among females), (4) physical strength/aggression and (5) sexuality.

The authors also posit that the relationship between 'the organization of gender' and the crime gender gap is mediated by two additional constructs: (1) motivation for crime and (2) opportunity. In regards to motivation, they argue that women are less willing to participate in crime because, in comparison to their male counterparts, they are more risk averse, are more likely to experience shame or embarrassment, have greater self-control, experience higher costs associated with criminal activity and, lastly, experience higher rewards for conformity. Thus, this notion has much in common with Akers' (1998) social learning theory, Moffitt's (1993) developmental perspective as well as Andrews and Bonta's (2003) personal, interpersonal, community-reinforcement (PIC-R) perspective. In terms of opportunity, they argue that men simply have more of it and consequently are more likely to engage in crime. Lastly, the model recognizes that biological factors influence, albeit weakly, all of the constructs in the model. In contrast to other theories, the gendered perspective has received virtually no attention in the literature.

SUMMARY AND RECOMMENDATIONS

In summary, this chapter reviewed several influential contemporary theories of female criminal conduct that were classified as either gender-neutral, female-centred or hybrid perspectives. A number of important themes emerged during the review. First, it became readily apparent that feminist critics were emphatically correct in one important aspect. Many contemporary gender-neutral theories have either explicitly or implicitly overlooked the female gender. For example, even when female-specific data were available it was often disregarded (e.g. Hirschi, 1969; 2002). Similarly, two prominent perspectives – personal, interpersonal, community-reinforcement perspective (PIC-R) and informal social control theory – both of which were heavily grounded in Glueck's (1950) seminal research on delinquent boys, failed to incorporate equally important research involving female delinquents. Ironically, this seminal work was also conducted by Glueck and Glueck (1934): *Five Hundred Delinquent Women*. However, on a positive note, it is important to emphasize that a number of prominent 'gender-neutral' theories are now asking female-centred questions (e.g. evolution, biology, self-control, social learning theory, life-course models). While there is still a dearth of female-specific evidence, we can no longer claim that women constitute 'theoretical afterthoughts'.

Second, while women-specific theorizing is burgeoning, direct tests of a given theory involving samples of adjudicated males and females are still absent. Additionally, as Farrington and Painter (2004) aptly note, future research must carefully consider whether or not observed gender differences are real or simply statistical artifacts. Specifically, Farrington and Painter have demonstrated that using statistical approaches that do not adequately address the base rate differential between men and women may lead to erroneous conclusions.

Third, the evidence to date clearly indicates that gender-neutral theories have a sizeable role to play in the explanation of female criminal conduct. However, it is equally clear that the explanatory power of these theories will only be enhanced when they become 'gender-informed' as opposed to 'gender-neutral'. For example, social control theories have focused primarily on the role of marital attachment and employment. In order to become a 'gender-informed' theory, social control must operationalize its core constructs in such a manner that readily accommodates women-specific bonding factors (e.g. attachment to children and the importance and centrality of positive healthy relationships).

Fourth, while a number of 'female-centred' paradigms have emerged they have not been studied to the same degree as 'gender-neutral' perspectives. Moreover, some of the gender-neutral theories, such as the biological and developmental perspectives, have benefited from methodologically rigorous research designs that permit convincing statements regarding causality. Nonetheless, the extant research suggests that our understanding of female criminal conduct may be enhanced by incorporating elements from 'gender-informed' as well as 'female-centred' perspectives.

Fifth, the review also revealed that each theoretical perspective varied in terms of the extent to which it attempted to translate theory into practice. For example Andrews and Bonta's (2003) PIC-R model is one of the few perspectives that provided clear direction for correctional workers (i.e. risk, need, responsivity principles) in the real world.

Lastly and most importantly, a number of seemingly divergent theoretical perspectives were actually complementary. For example, evolutionary and feminist perspectives, two seemingly opposing perspectives, both identified poverty as a central proximal risk factor in the explanation of female criminality. Similarly, self-control and evolutionary theories assign central significance to risk-taking behaviour. While a number of theories converged in the identification of proximal risk factors, they tended to deviate in terms of distal explanations. For example, some perspectives favoured proximal explanations (occurring within the lifespan of the individual, e.g. socialization) over distal perspectives (occurring within the lifespan of the human species, e.g. evolution). Regardless, a number of thoughtfully integrated perspectives now exist that have readily crossed disciplinary boundaries.

Chapter 3

ASSESSMENT FOR CLASSIFICATION
OF WOMEN OFFENDERS

INTRODUCTION

In the correctional literature, the terms 'assessment' and 'classification' are often used interchangeably. This is perhaps because assessment is a necessary pre-requisite of any organized classification schema. Assessment involves the identification of similarities and differences between individuals in the population of interest, thus allowing the assessor to classify individuals into groups. In this sense, the assessment is the *process*, while the classification is the end *result*. Assessment involves defining and measuring, while the classification refers to groupings or clusters that have resulted from the assessment process.

We acknowledge the importance of using various forms of assessment for many purposes of classification (e.g. clinical or medical assessment for diagnosis) within correctional environments. However, to our knowledge, the pre-eminent concern within all correctional jurisdictions is *risk management*. This chapter is therefore focused primarily on assessment and offender classification for risk management purposes (i.e. security/custody placement, risk of recidivism, potential harm to public). Some esteemed colleagues have expressed discomfort with this approach (e.g. Ward & Brown, 2004), particularly for the classification of women (Hannah-Moffat, 1999; Hannah-Moffat & Shaw, 2001; Sorbello et al., 2002). We acknowledge that quality of care and humanitarian considerations are paramount in the provision of services to offenders. None-theless, we feel that it is important to highlight risk assessment as responsible correctional practice, requisite for *any* offender population. Moreover, we under-score the fact that not only does the practice of 'risk assessment' incorporate consideration of offenders' treatment needs, but it also has the potential to include personal capabilities and protective factors. Also, 'risk assessment' can and should include an evaluation of those personal characteristics that might increase or decrease the offender's ability to productively engage in correctional treatment.

This chapter covers the role of assessment for the classification of offenders. In a broad sense, it aims to underscore the importance – or rather the absolute necessity – of classification for risk management purposes. A description of static and dynamic risk is followed by a discussion of actuarial versus clinical assessment processes. The relevance of gender is incorporated throughout the discussion, concluding with a brief presentation of gender-informed classification for women.

HISTORY OF CLASSIFICATION

Classification of criminal populations has been in use since the 1800s. The earliest offender typologies were influenced by Darwin's theory of evolution and proposed by Lombroso, who suggested that offenders could be classified into five types: the 'born criminal', the 'insane criminal', the 'criminal by passion', the 'habitual criminal' and the 'occasional criminal'. Similar to those for their male counterparts, Lombroso's classification schemas for women were based on the assessment of physical features and purported to distinguish 'women of good life' from 'the fallen class', 'lunatics' and female 'criminals'. It was also argued that 'criminal' women could be further differentiated by cranial–facial criteria according to their offence type: 'prostitution', 'abortion', 'infanticide' and 'complicity in rape', for example (Lombroso & Ferrero, 1895). It has been over a century since empirical testing invalidated Lombroso's criminal typologies. However, offence-based classification has persisted and severity or type of admitting offence(s) is still incorporated as one consideration in many current risk management assessment paradigms.

As noted, social science researchers and practitioners continue to categorize heterogeneous groups of offenders by various criteria and for numerous purposes. Today, classification is aptly lauded as the cornerstone to effective correctional intervention. Classification of offender populations is one of the most important functions of any correctional agency. It is inextricably linked to the management of offender behaviour because it governs access to privileges and resources throughout the course of their sentence.

As a management tool, appropriate classification minimizes the potential for institutional misconduct and violence, mitigates the probability of escape and directs resources to where they are most needed. Accordingly, in practice, offender classification should serve to structure correctional decision-making with respect to custody/security designations, supervision requirements, program placement and the terms and conditions of release (Motiuk, 1997). Austin (1986) appropriately noted that 'a properly functioning classification system is the "brain" of prison management as it governs inmate movement, housing and program participation, which in turn heavily influence fiscal decisions on staffing levels and future budget needs' (p. 304).

Today, the notion of 'effective rehabilitation' is premised primarily on principles of classification first articulated by Canadian researchers (Andrews, Bonta & Hoge, 1990). While the notion of 'what works' in corrections has been expanded and reformulated eloquently in more recent publications (e.g. Andrews & Bonta, 2003; Gendreau, 1996; Gendreau et al., 2004; Ogloff & Davis, 2004), the original article concentrated on four basic principles of offender classification: risk, need, responsivity and professional override. As they will be discussed more comprehensively in forthcoming chapters, these principles are only briefly introduced here.

The risk principle suggests that: (1) with appropriate assessment, risk of recidivism can be predicted and (2) the level of risk should be matched with the level of service provided. Specifically, Andrews and colleagues posit that higher levels of service should be provided to higher risk offenders, while those assessed as lower risk derive better outcomes from less intensive intervention.

The need principle contends that, to reduce criminal recidivism, intervention must focus on the 'criminogenic needs' of the offenders. Criminogenic needs are characteristics of the offender (or his or her social situation) that relate directly to his or her risk of re-offending. Accordingly, changes in levels of criminogenic needs are associated with changes in risk to re-offend. Importantly, the need principle distinguishes 'criminogenic' from 'non-criminogenic' needs; while offenders might have multiple needs, only some will be criminogenic in nature. For instance, Andrews and colleagues (Andrews & Bonta, 2003; Andrews et al., 1990) suggest that attributes of the offender such as psychological distress, low self-esteem, or poor physical health are 'non-criminogenic' in nature. While the need principle does not necessarily denounce the provision of services for non-criminogenic needs, it clearly states that the focus and priority for intervention should be those areas that are criminogenic (e.g. substance abuse, pro-criminal attitudes, anger/hostility).

The responsivity principle posits that treatment services should be delivered in a style and mode that match the learning style and ability of the offender. The responsivity principle subsumes two general types of consideration. The first, commonly called 'broad' or 'general' responsivity, states that for most offenders, optimal treatment response will be achieved when treatment providers deliver structured interventions (e.g. cognitive behavioural strategies) in a warm and empathic manner and using a firm but fair approach. Thus, the general responsivity principle describes attributes of the intervention that are external to the offender (Ogloff & Davis, 2004). The second type of responsivity pertains to internal characteristics of the individual being assessed. These are referred to as 'specific' responsivity considerations and examples include: gender, ethnicity, motivation to change, literacy level and intelligence. The specific responsivity principle also recognizes the need to match individual therapist characteristics with those of the client in order to maximize treatment gain.

The principle of professional override suggests that, after having considered risk, need and responsivity in one's assessment, classification decisions ultimately rest with the professional assessor. To be clear, this does not mean that assessors should not use empirically derived risk–needs measures to assist with their classification decisions. It is quite the contrary; Andrews and colleagues wholeheartedly endorse the use of such tools (Andrews & Bonta, 2003; Bonta, 2002) though they also underscore the role of the professional as an important component of a fair and just system. They note that although the risk, needs and responsivity principles provide an empirical basis to offender assessment, 'sooner or later there will always be a case that does not fit the formula' (Andrews

& Bonta, 2003, p. 265). This means that, on rare occasions, the professional assessor's judgment can (and should) override the principles of risk, need and responsivity to make the classification decision.

STATIC VERSUS DYNAMIC RISK

Obviously, offender classification has evolved considerably since Lombroso's time. Most assessors now incorporate multiple risk factors into their assessment paradigms. This is because the research evidence suggests that the determinants of criminal behaviour are manifold (Andrews & Bonta, 2003; Bonta, 2002). Risk factors that are used to predict criminal behaviour are generally described as either 'static' or 'dynamic'. Static risk factors are constant and unchanging, or change only in one direction (e.g. age, criminal history). Research has demonstrated that some of the most robust static predictors of criminal recidivism include youthfulness, being male, number of previous offences, age at first arrest, criminal versatility, poor parental supervision and early onset of behavioural problems (e.g. lying, cheating, stealing $\leq$ age 12) (Andrews & Bonta, 1998, 2003; Farrington, 1995; Gendreau et al., 1996; Loeber, 1982; Moffitt, 1993). Static factors, although potentially potent predictors, are not amenable to treatment.

Conversely, dynamic risk factors are attributes of the offender (or his/her situation) that are changeable, with changes associated with changes in the likelihood of recidivism. As such, dynamic risk factors (also called 'criminogenic needs') are promising targets for correctional intervention (Andrews & Bonta, 1998, 2003). Dynamic factors such as criminal attitudes, antisocial/criminal associates, lack of employment and substance abuse are among the most robust predictors of criminal recidivism (Dowden & Brown, 2002; Gates et al., 1998; Gendreau et al., 1996; Goggin, Gendreau & Gray, 1998; Law, 2004; Robinson, Porporino & Beal, 1998) and therefore have been identified as promising targets for correctional intervention.

CLINICAL VERSUS ACTUARIAL ASSESSMENT

The most critical changes in offender classification have probably occurred within the past twenty years, as risk assessment technologies evolved from 'first-generation' assessment to 'third-generation' paradigms. In brief, Bonta (1996) described first-generation assessments as subjective clinical judgments. Second-generation assessments, introduced in the late 1980s and early 1990s, are numerically based, consisting of clearly defined criteria that are validated by research. These tools generally comprise static/non-malleable factors such as age and criminal history. While these measures have proven utility in terms of classification for correctional management and risk assessment, they offer little in terms of treatment planning and iterative offender assessment. Third-generation models incorporate dynamic predictors into the actuarial assessment. Many consider these as superior to second-generation paradigms because offenders can be treated and re-assessed to evaluate changes in risk.

It can be unequivocally stated that assessors should incorporate multiple considerations into the evaluative process. There are two principal ways of aggregating static and dynamic criteria to make a classification decision: *clinical* and *actuarial* (the latter sometimes called the 'statistical' method). The clinical method, described by Bonta (1996) as a 'first-generation' assessment approach, relies mostly on professional judgment that is based on informal, subjective techniques, sometimes including case conferencing strategies. In general, there are no strict predefined regulations governing what information should be considered, how it should be measured, which information sources should be used, or how the information should be combined and weighted. With this method, the assessor's professional judgment determines how best to select, combine and weight the information. Thus, the rules vary across decision-makers as well as the individual about whom the decision is being made (Bonta, 1996; Grove & Meehl, 1996; Grove, Zald, Lebow, Snitz & Nelson, 2000; Marchese, 1992).

The actuarial method grounds decision-making in statistical relationships (Silver & Miller, 2002). It involves formal, objective procedures to combine and weight factors that render a score and recommendation for decision. Relevant variables are selected and mathematically combined and weighted such that their statistical association with the criterion of interest is maximized (Grove & Meehl, 1996; Grove et al., 2000). Importantly, the weighting of factors is performed according to a set of objective, predefined criteria that do not vary as a function of the decision-maker. Thus, clear guidelines are established *a priori* in terms of what information should be collected, how it should be collected, the source(s) of information and, lastly, how variables should be combined.

Since the 1920s many authors (e.g. Freyd, 1925; Lundberg, 1926; Viteles, 1925) have evaluated the comparative accuracy of clinical versus actuarial prediction. In 1954, Meehl published the first narrative review of the research (20 studies) and concluded that actuarial prediction was either equal to or better than clinical prediction in every case. Since Meehl's (1954) initial review, numerous studies have emerged resulting in a series of narrative reviews (e.g. Dawes, Faust & Meehl, 1989; Grove & Meehl, 1996; Marchese, 1992; Meehl, 1965; Swets, Dawes & Monahan, 2000) and a quantitative meta-analysis of the relevant literature (Grove et al., 2000). Collectively, more than 80 years of research conducted across a diverse array of assessment realms has clearly demonstrated that actuarial/statistical prediction equals or supersedes clinical judgment in the majority of cases. Thus, Meehl's original conclusion made in 1954 holds true over 50 years later.

As noted, research also suggests that objective actuarial prediction instruments often yield more liberal decisions than professional judgment (Austin, 1983). More specifically, some researchers have shown that actuarial tools tend to significantly lower the average risk classification, as well as the rate of false positive predictions (Buchanan, Whitlow & Austin, 1986). It has been suggested that staff, left to their own professional discretion, will act more conservatively because there are serious potential consequences for under-classification such as institutional violence or criminal re-offending in the event of early release. While over-classification also evokes consequences, especially for the offenders (e.g. being held in higher security than necessary, denial of discretionary release), they are less apparent than those caused by under-classification (Alexander, 1986; Hannah-Moffat, 2004).

In sum, there are clear benefits to using actuarial methods for offender classification: evidence suggests that their use results in more accurate and more liberal (lenient) decisions, relative to clinical methods (Buchanan et al., 1986). Actuarial approaches have other practical advantages (Zinger, 2004); for instance, scoring criteria and decision rules are standardized and transparent, thus providing a clear accountability framework for staff. The reliability (particularly inter-rater reliability) of the assessment is increased with standardized criteria. Moreover, the transparent and clearly defined scoring criteria have the potential to motivate offenders to lower (or prevent an increase in) their risk classifications through behaviour change. Actuarial approaches provide an empirically quantified defensible standard that is available for continuous refinement, validation and amelioration. When used for prediction, these tools reflect the agency's risk-taking policy (risk tolerance) and the effects of policy changes can be simulated in advance.

Systems of assessment vary considerably in terms of statistical sophistication. While clinical methods generally involve no statistical operations, mechanical tools range from simple summative item checklists to complex scoring algorithms. Notwithstanding, all Western correctional organizations use some form of classification system. While traditional models stress the importance of subjective expertise and clinical judgment in decision-making, the 'new generation' of assessment model is statistically derived and hailed as more liberal, equitable, explicit and efficient (Austin, 1983; Austin & Hardyman, 2004; Brennan, 1987). It is therefore not surprising that actuarial risk measures are used in many correctional jurisdictions, including Canada (Andrews, Bonta & Wormith, 2005; Blanchette & Taylor, 2005; Solicitor General Canada, 1987), the United States (Baird, 1981), the United Kingdom (Clark, Fisher & McDougall, 1993), Australia (Daly & Lane, 1999) and New Zealand (Collie, 2003).

APPLYING 'OBJECTIVE' MEASURES TO FEMALE OFFENDERS

Most of the objective classification instruments being used today were originally developed with samples of male offenders and then later implemented for use with females (e.g. Andrews, 1982b; Andrews & Bonta, 1995; Hare, 2003; Solicitor General Canada, 1987). Because they are applied to both men and women, they have been acclaimed as 'gender-neutral'. However, while the 'gender-neutral' appellation implies impartiality, the normative standard is male (Brennan, 1998). In reviewing the first body of literature that emerged specific to female offender classification (late 1970s), Shaw and Hannah-Moffat (2000) noted that it 'consistently concluded that in most countries the small populations of women were classified using . . . systems developed for men' (p. 165). Over a decade later, a US survey of state correctional agencies found that the vast majority of states (40/48) used the same objective classification system for women as for men (Burke & Adams, 1991). A subsequent survey noted few changes in the situation (Morash, Bynam & Koons, 1998). Finally, US research results published more recently indicated that, of 50 state correctional agencies and the Federal Bureau of Prisons, only four have a separate custody classification system for women (Van Voorhis & Presser, 2001). The Canadian and New Zealand systems have been similarly criticized for using a male-based actuarial classification system for the security placement of women (Collie, 2003; Webster & Doob, 2004) and the situation is no different in Western Australia (J. Salomone, personal communication, 23 August 2005).

Although purported 'gender-neutral' measures are applied in everyday correctional practice with men and women, relatively little research has been devoted to their validation specifically for female offenders (Hardyman & Van Voorhis, 2004). Rarer still is research focused on the development of classification measures exclusively for female offenders. Rather, existing measures are used with the implicit assumption that the same classification factors are equally salient for both men and women (Aitken & Logan, 2004; Brennan, 1998; Hardyman, 2001; Hardyman & Van Voorhis, 2004).

There are three courses of action that might be taken to address the lack of gender-specificity (for women) with existing classification measures. The first is actually better framed as 'inaction', as it would suggest that nothing needs to be done because the same principles of classification can be applied, regardless of gender. Regrettably, this is probably the most common approach to women's classification (e.g. Aitken & Logan, 2004). The second option involves the tailoring of existing measures to better reflect women's risk/need factors. This is the approach that has been adopted by many jurisdictions in the US for security classification (Van Voorhis & Presser, 2001) and amendments include the addition or deletion of specific scale items, the re-weighting of existing items and/or changing scale cutoff scores to create different risk categories for women. The third option involves the development of classification measures *specifically* for women, using women-only construction and validation samples and doing so in a manner that is informed by gender. We suggest that, when possible, this is the preferred option; one that has been adopted in Canada for security reclassification of women under federal sentence (Blanchette, 2005; Blanchette & Taylor, in press).

Some researchers suggest that risk-based classification is inappropriate for women (Bloom, 2000; Hannah-Moffat, 1997, 1999, 2000; McMahon, 2000; Shaw & Hannah-Moffat, 2000) and that women are over-classified when systems use tools that were developed primarily for men. More specifically, they argue that when male-based assessment instruments are used for females, they render classifications that are not commensurate with female offender risk. Rather, these measures will categorize women at higher levels of risk (e.g. security, supervision) than necessary. Accordingly, they emphatically stress the importance of considering the context of women's lives and their 'pathways' into the criminal justice system. For instance, the evidence suggests that women are considerably less violent than men and that the circumstances in which they act violently differ; women's violence tends to be directed at a family member or intimate partner. As such, a classification system designed for men may not accurately gauge female risk for violence and therefore may result in the over-classification of women (Brennan, 1998; Hardyman & Van Voorhis, 2004; Harer & Langan, 2001; Van Voorhis & Presser, 2001). Accordingly, Hardyman's (2001) analysis of a large dataset from one US state (Florida District of Corrections) showed that female offenders were routinely over-classified in terms of custody placement: the rate of institutional misconduct by medium security female inmates was similar to that observed for minimum security male inmates. A study by Van Voorhis and Presser (2001) presented results indicating that the review period for reclassification was often inappropriately long for women, who generally serve shorter sentences than their male counterparts. Their survey data also suggested that correctional administrators *want* classification models that better support gender-responsive programming, moving women more quickly through the system (Van Voorhis & Presser, 2001).

Research results have indicated that separate assessment instruments improve risk classifications for females, both in terms of institutional security classification (Blanchette, 2005) and post-release outcome (Funk, 1999). However, while results reported by Funk (1999) indicate that female risk factors differ substantially from those of their male counterparts, that by Blanchette (2005) suggest only minor variability by gender. Importantly, this latter study noted family contact as a variable that was particularly salient for the prediction of women inmates' security classification. Likewise, Hardyman and Van Voorhis (2004) indicated that classification models incorporating 'gender-responsive' variables (i.e. relationships, mental health, child abuse) were more strongly predictive of prison misconduct than the traditional (male-based) model.

Classification for risk management purposes is almost invariably linked to correctional intervention because dynamic factors are changeable. When a woman's criminogenic needs are addressed through appropriate treatment, risk is decreased. While this concept is simple in principle, there are some caveats. First, as will be discussed in detail in Chapter 5, the research evidence supporting the 'criminogenic' nature of particular needs is based primarily on samples of male offenders. There is therefore still debate regarding which areas constitute promising treatment targets to reduce risk for women offenders. Moreover, little is known about the programme elements that promote successful outcomes for women in particular (Koons, Burrow, Morash & Bynum, 1997). The services offered to female inmates have traditionally been based on models derived from their male counterparts. Accordingly, past research examining the adequacy of programming to meet the needs of female offenders suggested that treatment for women was either inappropriate or unavailable (Dauvergne-Latimer, 1995; Gray, Mays & Stohr, 1995; Morash, Haar & Rucker, 1994; Task Force on Federally Sentenced Women, 1990).

GENDER-INFORMED ASSESSMENT MODELS FOR WOMEN

Founded on the premise that risk-based classification is not appropriate for women, some authors argue that women have different treatment needs than men and are more appropriately classified according to both their personal abilities and treatment entitlements. Hannah-Moffat (2004) argues that 'gender-neutral' assessments of risk/need factors have persisted over time 'because they characterize problems and define solutions in ways that fit with the dominant correctional culture and the power structure that narrowly and instrumentally defines risk and need' (p. 245). In brief, authors contributing to this body of literature emphasize the importance of contextualizing women's participation in crime by examining their 'pathways' to criminal offending. In doing so, it is argued that women's *individual* needs can be assessed and treated in a holistic approach (e.g. Hannah-Moffat & Shaw, 2001).

Others, borrowing from positive psychology (Seligman, 2002, as cited in Ward & Brown, 2004), emphasize strength-based approaches to assessing and treating offenders – female offenders in particular (Sorbello et al., 2002; Van Wormer, 2001; Ward & Brown, 2004). In brief, these approaches, variously referred to as 'strengths-based', 'enhancement', or 'good lives', recommend a shift in focus from criminogenic needs/harm avoidance to enhancing offender capabilities. Proponents of the strengths-based approach argue that the best way to lower offenders' likelihood of recidivism is to equip them with the necessary resources to live more fulfilling lives. For instance, Sorbello and colleagues (2002) suggest that risk management models (risk/needs approaches) overlook crucial female-specific non-criminogenic issues. Rather, they argue that 'offender rehabilitation should focus on identifying internal and external obstacles that prevent women from meeting fundamental needs' (p. 199). The examples provided by the authors include personal and vocational skills deficits, maladaptive attitudes and beliefs and inadequate social supports. After identification of the internal and external obstacles, the strengths-based model suggests that rehabilitation should provide women with the necessary conditions to meet basic needs and live stable and rewarding lives. Finally, Sorbello and colleagues argue that 'this "good life" should be realistic for a woman, encompassing her capabilities, temperament, interests, skills, deep commitments and support networks' (p. 199).

The strength-based approach has intuitive appeal, especially for assessment and treatment of women offenders, given that the majority does not represent a significant risk to re-offend. However, this approach does not represent a radical departure from the popular risk–needs–responsivity model proposed by Andrews and colleagues. Rather, it is our contention that the strengths-based model is simply a reframing and moderate shift in emphasis of the core assessment and rehabilitation issues proposed by Andrews and colleagues. The exemplar of 'internal and external obstacles' is notably similar to the notion of criminogenic needs; this point is also acknowledged by Ward and Stewart (2003a). Moreover, Ward and colleagues' (Sorbello et al., 2002; Ward & Brown, 2004; Ward & Stewart, 2003a, 2003b) emphasis on addressing universal *human* needs (e.g. self-esteem, relatedness) aligns well with the traditional approach. Specifically, Bonta and Andrews (2003) underscore the importance of incorporating such factors, which is commensurate with traditional responsivity considerations, also noted recently by Ogloff and Davis (2004).

Ward and Brown (2004) clearly delineate nine classes of primary human goods that, once attained, would provide offenders with a 'good life', ultimately leading to crime desistence: (1) life (e.g. optimal physical functioning, sexual satisfaction),

(2) knowledge, (3) excellence in play and work, (4) autonomy and self-directed-ness, (5) inner peace, (6) relatedness and community, (7) spirituality (finding meaning and purpose in life), (8) happiness and (9) creativity. While these are lofty and virtuous goals, this Utopian model is problematic because it lacks empirical evidence (Bonta & Andrews, 2003) and extends beyond the purview of *any* correctional system's mandate. Ultimately, the fundamental responsibility of the correctional system in any jurisdiction is the protection of society which, of course, includes the person charged/convicted. Nonetheless, Bonta and Andrews (2003) argue that improved quality of life is attained by offenders when they are provided with services to address their criminogenic needs (e.g. dealing with substance abuse issues, finding employment).

As noted earlier, the targeting of criminogenic needs for correctional interven-tion does not preclude assessment of the individual's strengths and capabilities. These can and should be incorporated into the risk assessment (e.g. an offender's risk is assessed as reduced because she has a university education and a solid employment history) in addition to responsivity considerations. In the Canadian federal system, the Offender Intake Assessment (OIA; Brown & Motiuk, 2005; Motiuk, 1997) process incorporates both needs and strengths into the model. In this structured clinical assessment, dynamic factors are globally evaluated along a four-point continuum, ranging from 'considerable need for intervention' to 'asset to community adjustment'. Similarly, the most recent actuarial offender assessment instrument developed by Andrews and colleagues (*Level of Service/Case Management Inventory; LS/CMI*) incorporates the provision for 'strength' notations for each of the eight risk/need areas (Andrews et al., 2004). However, strength notations are not included as part of the LS/CMI quantitative scoring criteria. Since there is a relative lack of empirical evidence supporting the assessment of offender capabilities in terms of predictive utility, they are not routinely incorporated as weighted items into actuarial assessment measures. One notable exception is the Security Reclassification Scale for Women (SRSW), recently implemented in Canada (Blanchette & Taylor, 2005). In addition to static and dynamic risk considerations, the SRSW incorporates two independent strength factors in its scoring algorithm: correctional plan motivation/progress and prosocial family support.

Unlike the assessment of criminogenic needs, the identification of offender strengths and capabilities will not significantly contribute to classification with respect to treatment targets. However, the assessment of offender strengths offers great potential in terms of increasing predictive accuracy and, therefore, risk management. If prospective research concludes that particular offender strengths serve as protective factors, mitigating risk, then those items should be mathematically incorporated into actuarial models accordingly. More specifically, pending more substantiating empirical data, protective factors could and should be incorporated into risk assessment models for women. As such, actuarial methods could include the assessment and scoring of both criminogenic needs and personal strengths/capabilities; while the former would be positively weighted, the latter would be negatively weighted. Such a measure would capitalize on the merits of both the risk–needs–responsivity models of offender assessment, as well as the strength approach articulated by Ward and colleagues.

SUMMARY AND RECOMMENDATIONS

While there is still some debate regarding *how* to best assess and classify women for rehabilitation, there is consensus on one point: assessment is fundamental to effective correctional intervention. Offender classification serves several purposes, ranging from security placement, to treatment planning, release decision-making and supervision standards. Individualized assessment is necessary to establish *risk* (to safely manage offender populations) and to match offenders' *needs* to treatment resources. While some authors suggest that the basic principles of 'what works' in terms of classification for male offenders is also applicable to female offenders (Dowden & Andrews, 1999), results of other studies suggest that additional or unique parameters should be evaluated to optimize correctional treatment outcomes for women (Austin, Bloom & Donahue, 1992; Covington, 1998, 2000; Dougherty, 1998).

Assessment for classification and rehabilitation has advanced considerably over the years, most notably in the last decade. There is an inordinate amount of research suggesting that actuarial approaches are superior to clinical methods, particularly when the principle of professional override is incorporated into the assessment paradigm. The development of a good actuarial classification tool requires a large representative sample: criteria more easily met within the dominant male correctional population. Whether it is because the overwhelming majority of offenders are male, or whether it is because females are viewed as comparatively lower risk, actuarial classification tools for women are virtually absent. This is a point worth highlighting – especially in light of research evidence suggesting: (1) women offenders may be over-classified when systems use actuarial tools developed with a male normative population (e.g. Van Voorhis & Presser, 2001) and (2) actuarial tools tend to lower the average classification (e.g. Buchanan et al., 1986; Blanchette, 2005).

The rapid increase in the number and proportion of women under correctional supervision world wide signals an urgent call to action. While there is indeed evidence that some of the 'gender-neutral' risk assessment measures are valid with samples of women (e.g. Andrews et al., 2004; Blanchette, Verbrugge & Wichmann, 2002), there is also evidence to suggest that actuarial assessment is even more accurate when purpose-built *specifically* for women (Blanchette, 2005).

It is our contention that, in discussing effective assessment for female offenders, it is necessary to consider elements common to evaluations of men, as well as deviations from and supplements to the standard male model. As such, we believe that a gender-informed model of assessment for women offenders should be effective, as follows:

(1) The model should capitalize on the seminal work by Andrews and colleagues through continued validation efforts focusing explicitly on girls and women.

Importantly, this recommendation does not suppose that the *same* risk and need factors should be incorporated into routine assessments for rehabilitative services for girls and women. Rather, it posits that the operational principles of classification set out by Andrews and colleagues could well apply to women. As will be demonstrated in forthcoming chapters of this book, much more research is needed to optimally apply these principles to girls and women in a manner that is gender-informed. That notwithstanding, substantiating evidence is emerging; as will be shown, some practical evidence-based solutions can be implemented immediately.

(2) The model should profit from tenets of strength-based approaches and test the viability of capabilities/protective factors as (negative) predictors of recidivism outcome or, alternatively, (positive) predictors of desistence. Tenets of strength-based approaches might be optimally applicable to women, given their relatively lower risk in comparison to men. There is a good possibility that women's strengths/capabilities could serve as protective factors and thus increase desistence.

(3) The model should incorporate research results from (1) and (2) above into the development of gender-informed actuarial risk management tools for girls and women. We recommend the use of actuarial assessment tools that are gender-informed and built *from the ground up* for the specific population to which they will be applied – in this case, girls and women. We concede that use of the term 'specific population' here is rather nebulous. As noted at the outset, the female offender population is heterogeneous and we cannot purport to address all diversity issues simultaneously. As such, this recommendation to develop actuarial risk management tools for the *specific* populations of interest must be tempered with a note of caution. In particular, the population of interest must be sufficiently large to meet statistical requirements for the development of such a tool and the costs incurred must be balanced with the practical utility of the model. For instance, it would not be fruitful to develop a statistical measure to assess the risk to re-offend for female sex offenders. As such, an important caveat is that all actuarial measures must necessarily include provisions for professional override considerations.

(4) The model should comprehensively include gender as a responsivity issue, building a clear and significant evaluation of the context of the individual's offending into the assessment paradigm.

We believe that it will be in the reconciliation of various approaches that the best model of assessment for girls and women will emerge. Clearly, there is tremendous value in traditional, evidence-based approaches to assessment for classification and rehabilitation. Nonetheless, we concede that the research guiding these principles has focused on the majority (white male) offender population while that including girls and women is virtually absent. The three chapters that follow will offer a comprehensive examination of the research to date on the applicability of the risk, need and responsivity principles to girls and women.

Chapter 4

ASSESSING WOMEN'S RISK

INTRODUCTION

Regardless of the criterion of interest, the term 'risk assessment' necessarily incorporates the notion of prediction. Within the correctional context, outcomes of interest (i.e. what the assessor is attempting to predict) are diverse. Examples include self-injury or attempted suicide, progress in treatment, institutional adjustment and likelihood of re-offending or re-offending violently. We agree entirely with the importance of considering alternative outcomes. However, one aim in this chapter is to examine the applicability of the *risk principle* to women offenders; inherent in the risk principle is the traditional notion of risk to re-offend and severity of re-offence.

Most would concur that offender rehabilitation is best evidenced through the reduction or desistence of criminal behaviour. Given that rehabilitation is the fundamental goal of most correctional systems, our focus is on the assessment of women's risk for recidivism. The term 'risk', both here and elsewhere, carries with it the connotation of harm to others in terms of re-offending and violent re-offending. The classification of the offender into a particular risk category is the ultimate result of the evaluative process; it implies that recidivism can be predicted with accuracy better than chance.

As discussed in the previous chapter, the assessment process can include the application of actuarial tools, clinical assessments, or some combination of methods. As noted, 'third-generation' models of assessment include the evaluation of dynamic factors that are linked to re-offending. As such, criminogenic needs are a subset of offender risk. Nonetheless, there is still some disagreement regarding *whether* women's needs should be incorporated into risk assessments (Hannah-Moffat, 1999; Hannah-Moffat & Shaw, 2001), and, if so, *which* needs are criminogenic for women in particular. These issues will be addressed in detail in Chapter 5.

We recognize that criminogenic needs comprise an integral component of most current models of risk assessment. Nonetheless, this chapter focuses primarily on the research evidence regarding the applicability of many commonly applied risk assessment tools to women. Specifically, we examine the research evidence regarding the application of these tools for women, *in their entirety*. A review of the specific dynamic variables (criminogenic needs) included as items within many of the measures is provided in the following chapter.

This chapter begins with a review of the risk principle and an overview of criticisms and concerns regarding its applicability to female offenders. An extensive review of the evidence regarding the reliability and validity of various mathematical risk assessment tools for women follows. The chapter closes with some conclusions and recommendations regarding the assessment of risk for women.

THE RISK PRINCIPLE

There are two aspects to the *risk principle*. The first asserts that criminal behaviour can be predicted; the second suggests that, to reduce recidivism, the level of treatment should be matched to the assessed risk level of the offender. This is where appropriate classification bridges assessment and effective treatment. Specifically, the risk principle argues that, in order to reduce recidivism, intensive services should be provided to those offenders assessed as higher risk, while those assessed as lower risk fare better with minimal or no intervention (Andrews & Bonta, 1998, 2003).

A significant body of research has provided strong empirical support for the risk principle (Andrews et al., 1990a, b; Gendreau, 1996; Lipsey, 1995) and Andrews and colleagues maintain that the principle is valid across a range of correctional populations. Despite these claims, narrative and meta-analytic reviews supporting the risk principle have either excluded female offender samples, or have failed to disaggregate the data by gender. One exception is a meta-analysis by Dowden and Andrews (1999). To examine the validity of the risk, need and responsivity principles for female offenders, the authors included treatment studies that met the following criteria:

(a) The samples were composed predominantly (at least 51%) or entirely of female offenders.
(b) The study included a follow-up period.
(c) The study compared offenders who had received some form of intervention to a control group who did not receive the primary intervention.
(d) The study included a measure of recidivism (reconviction, re-arrest, parole failure).

Dowden and Andrews tested the risk principle by coding studies as treating 'high-risk' or 'low-risk' women. Specifically, treatment groups were categorized as high risk if 'the majority of those [participants] in the study had penetrated the justice system at the time of the study or had a previous criminal offense' (p. 441). Alternatively, treatment groups comprising individuals with no criminal history and/or those who had been diverted from the justice system were coded as low risk.

Results revealed stronger treatment effects in programmes targeting higher versus lower risk samples. Specifically, the data (45 effect sizes) generated a 19%

reduction in recidivism for high-risk groups and no treatment effect for low-risk groups. Moreover, when the authors narrowed the focus to include *exclusively* female treatment studies (24 effect sizes), this effect was even more pronounced, and a 24% reduction in recidivism was observed for the high-risk group. The authors concluded that these results support the risk principle for effective intervention with female offenders.

While the study by Dowden and Andrews provides preliminary insight into the applicability of the risk principle for women, some important limitations to their research should be acknowledged. First, in comparison to the research on male offenders, there are relatively fewer studies on female offenders. Analyses by Dowden and Andrews included 16 studies comprising entirely female samples. As primary studies continue to accumulate, prospective meta-analytic research will garner larger samples to increase confidence in results.

The second limitation concerns the basic assertion of the risk principle that suggests matching the level of service to the level of risk of the offender. Dowden and Andrews' meta-analysis does not fully address this issue, as treatment 'dosage'/intensity was not reported. Rather, the authors described reductions in recidivism for treated (versus untreated) groups.

Finally, the authors' method of partitioning treatment studies into 'high-risk' and 'low-risk' groups was questionable. Specifically, it is argued that those with a current or past involvement in the criminal justice system (the high-risk groups) are much more likely to demonstrate reductions in recidivism than their low-risk counterparts because they have higher base rates of offending at the outset. While differential base rates at pre-test is problematic to all meta-analytic research, it is particularly salient to the study by Dowden and Andrews because it appears that, at least in some cases, the low-risk groups comprised non-offenders. Clearly, more research addressing some of these limitations is required before it can be confidently declared that high-risk females recidivate less with more intensive treatment, while low-risk females recidivate less with little or no intervention.

Additional criticisms of the risk principle are predicated on the notion that the concept of risk is 'gendered' and 'racialized' and should therefore not be applied to minority groups (Hannah-Moffat, 1999). Specifically, these critics argue that the failure to consider gender and diversity issues in risk assessment results in inequitable practices of classification for women and other minority offender populations. Accordingly, they argue that these biases result in the systemic discrimination of these groups, ranging from over-classification to failure to provide appropriate services (Bloom & Covington, 2000; Hannah-Moffat & Shaw, 2001).

As noted earlier, most Western correctional jurisdictions incorporate actuarial tools into the risk assessment process. There can be no debate that the research guiding the development of these actuarial assessment tools has been based almost exclusively on white male offender populations. While some researchers have included women and other minority groups in their development and validation samples, the results inevitably reflect the male majority, and potential differences for women are lost in the aggregate data.

This was demonstrated well in a recent study by Olson, Alderden and Lurigio (2003). The authors examined the predictors of recidivism in a large sample of adult male ($n = 2636$) and female ($n = 689$) probationers. With a large pool of predictor variables, they ran a full-sample logistic regression analysis, as well as separate analyses by gender. They found that the same factors that predicted re-arrests in the full sample predicted re-arrests for the male-only subsample. These findings were not surprising, given that the full sample comprised predominantly male offenders. When the analyses were generated separately by gender, results showed: (1) fewer variables predicted re-arrests in the female-only samples and (2) the magnitude and even the direction of the effect was different for some variables. These findings support those published by other researchers, suggesting that some factors that predict risk for males are invalid for females (Blanchette, 2005; Farr, 2000; Funk, 1999).

The results presented by Olson and colleagues (2003) underscore the importance of disaggregating the data analyses by gender. However, the failure to consider gender in research, particularly tool development, cannot be fully addressed by data disaggregation. This is because performing separate analyses by gender does not consider variables that are theoretically more salient for women; rather, the same pool of 'candidate' predictor variables is examined, regardless of gender.

Classification of female offenders into high-risk and low-risk groups will continue to present more of a challenge than that for male offenders. Essentially this problem relates to the first tenet of the risk principle, which posits that recidivism can be predicted. Although there is evidence that criminal history variables accurately predict re-offending for women (Loucks & Zamble, 2000; Rettinger, 1998), the incorporation of such static variables into mathematical prediction paradigms has been less reliable. In particular, most offender risk classification schemas, developed on samples of men, decline in predictive validity when applied to women (Blanchette, 1996; Bonta, Pang & Wallace-Capretta, 1995; Hann & Harman, 1989; Salekin, Rogers & Sewell, 1997). The remainder of this chapter will review some of the most commonly used actuarial risk classification tools, with specific focus on their reliability, validity and practical utility for adult female offenders.

STATISTICAL INFORMATION ON RECIDIVISM – REVISED SCALE

The principle pre-release risk assessment instrument used to assess offenders under federal jurisdiction (i.e. those offenders sentenced to two years or more) in Canada is the Statistical Information on Recidivism – Revised (SIR–R1) scale. Originally developed by Nuffield (1982), the measure was modified slightly in 1996 by the Correctional Service of Canada. Employed primarily for parole decision-making, the Statistical Information on Recidivism score provides an estimate of the probability that an individual will re-offend within three years after release. Each offender's total score on the SIR–R1 scale is a simple summation of (15) static item scores, with total scores ranging from -30 (very high risk) to $+27$

(very low risk). In her construction sample, Nuffield clustered the scores to form five risk categories, ranging from 'very good' (84% predicted to succeed) to 'very poor' (32% predicted to succeed). When Nuffield applied this scale to a validation sample, the results showed that the predicted outcomes for each group held up very well. Numerous subsequent studies have shown that SIR–R1 scores accurately predict decisions to grant parole, as well as post-release outcome for non-Aboriginal male offenders (Bonta, Harman, Hann & Cormier, 1996; Hann & Harman, 1988, 1992; Motiuk & Porporino, 1989; Nafekh & Motiuk, 2002; Serin, 1996; Wormith & Goldstone, 1984).

Applying the SIR scale to male federal offender populations yields approximately 20% in each of the five risk categories; this was intentional in the development of the measure (Nuffield, 1982). Research with female offenders suggests that their scores are, on average, lower than those of their male counterparts. Specifically, two independent studies applying the SIR scale to women indicated that just under half (44%) were classified in the 'very good' risk category, while few were rated as 'very poor' risk (Blanchette, 1996; Bonta et al., 1995).

While the SIR scale is reported to be internally reliable (Cronbach's alpha = 0.77; Nafekh & Motiuk, 2002), to date there are no published studies reporting on the reliability of the SIR scale specifically for female offenders. Few authors have examined the validity of the SIR scale for female offenders and studies have been limited to testing the predictive validity of the measure. Hann and Harman (1989) conducted some preliminary analyses on a small sample of female offenders ($n = 59$) released from a penitentiary in 1983–1984. The results were inconclusive; the authors suggested that "the Nuffield Scoring System [SIR scale] does seem to be somewhat indicative of release risk for Female Non-natives – but its value is considerably less than that for Male Non-natives" (p. 14). Based on these preliminary results, Hann and Harman concluded that the SIR scale should not be used for women until a separate scoring system could be developed specifically for that group.

In 1995, Bonta and colleagues published results of their investigation of the applicability of the SIR scale for women. Using a sample of 81 female offenders released in 1983–1984, the authors calculated SIR scores retrospectively from file information. The study included a three-year follow-up period and the recidivism outcome measure was conviction for a new offence or parole revocation. Once again, the results were inconclusive. The total SIR score was moderately correlated with recidivism ($r = -0.25, p < 0.05$). Although there was a significant statistical association between the SIR prognostic categories and recidivism ($\chi^2 = 23.94, p < 0.001$), the relationship was not linear. In fact, the prognostic categories showed very poor discrimination with respect to outcome, with offenders in the 'good' risk category demonstrating the highest rate of recidivism. Based on these results, the authors concluded that there was not enough evidence to support the use of the SIR scale for female offenders.

Blanchette (1996) achieved somewhat similar results. As a part of a larger study, SIR scores were calculated, based on file information, for a sample of 66 women who had been incarcerated at a Canadian federal prison for women in 1989 and had been released in May 1995. Controlling for time at risk, partial

Table 4.1 SIR risk categories and recidivism: female offenders

Risk category	Bonta et al. (1995)		Blanchette (1996)	
	N	% recidivists	N	% recidivists
Very good	36	13.5	29	17.2
Good	20	75.0	12	91.7
Fair	11	18.2	7	85.7
Poor	5	60.0	8	100.0
Very poor	9	44.4	10	90.0

correlations showed a strong relationship between SIR scores and recidivism. This was true whether recidivism was broadly defined to include any return to custody ($r = -0.49, p < 0.0001$), or was narrowed to comprise only new convictions ($r = -0.52, p < 0.0001$). Similar to findings reported by Bonta et al. (1995), chi-square analyses showed a significant statistical association between the SIR prognostic categories and recidivism ($p < 0.001$), regardless of whether the broad or narrow definition was used. However, once again, the relationship was not linear. When the broad definition of recidivism was used, the 'poor' risk group was most recidivistic (100%), followed by the 'good' risk group (92%). While those in the 'very good' risk category were much less likely to recidivate, there was little differentiation between the remaining four prognostic groups. Recidivism rates by SIR prognostic categories from Bonta et al. (1995) and Blanchette (1996) are presented in Table 4.1.

Most studies on the applicability of the SIR scale to female offenders have been limited by small sample sizes. One exception is the psychometric examination provided by Nafekh and Motiuk in 2002. With a large sample ($n = 342$) of adult female offender case files, the authors created a proxy measure of the revised SIR scale (SIR–proxy) using data available through the Correctional Service of Canada's automated Offender Management System (OMS). The sample included all women with information available on OMS, who had been released between 1995 and 1998 and were available for follow-up for three years.

In brief, the SIR–proxy was created by matching each of the 15 items from the revised SIR scale (SIR–R1) with proxy data available through the automated system. Only one scale item could not be appropriately approximated: the number of dependents at most recent admission. The cutoff scores for the SIR–proxy groupings were established to reflect the same sample distribution as the actual SIR–R1 groupings. When the authors measured the SIR–proxy against the SIR–R1, they determined that it very closely approximated actual SIR–R1 scores and groupings. Specifically, Pearson correlation coefficients between the SIR–R1 and SIR–proxy were $r = 0.90$ and $r = 0.85$ for scores and groupings, respectively.

Results of Nafekh and Motiuk's study were somewhat more positive in terms of the SIR–proxy's predictive accuracy for women. The measure was correlated with general recidivism ($r = 0.32, p < 0.0001$) and the area under the Receiver Operating Characteristic curve indicated that scale groupings accurately discriminated between recidivists and non-recidivists (AUC = 0.77).[1] The authors also included a table in the appendix of their report, indicating a clear linear relationship between SIR–proxy risk category and proportion of recidivism. While only about 1% of women in the 'very good' risk category recidivated, 39% of those in the 'poor' risk category were recidivistic. Unfortunately, the authors did not provide the raw numbers of women in each grouping.

Despite the preliminary positive findings published by Nafekh and Motiuk, we do not recommend using the SIR scale (or SIR–proxy) for female offenders. The research results pertaining to women are both inconsistent and inconclusive. Most studies have been limited by small sample sizes and there are no published data examining the reliability or validity of the scale with women serving shorter sentences or those in other jurisdictions. In terms of practical utility, the SIR is critically restricted by its reliance on static (primarily criminal history) items. As such, the measure cannot be used to guide the provision of treatment services, nor as an iterative re-assessment tool to gauge women's progress in key areas.

PSYCHOPATHY CHECKLIST – REVISED

Assessment of 'psychopathy' is also commonly used for the evaluation of risk for offender populations. In brief, psychopathy refers to a constellation of affective, interpersonal and behavioural traits associated with a marked absence of compassion and a lack of personal integrity. The Psychopathy Checklist – Revised (PCL–R; Hare, 2003) is currently the most widely accepted measure of psychopathy. The PCL–R consists of 20 items, each scored on a three-point scale (0, 1 or 2), on the basis of a semi-structured interview with the offender and institutional file information. Items on the checklist are summed to provide a total score and two subscale scores. The first subscale (Factor 1) is defined by interpersonal and affective characteristics and is labelled 'callous, selfish and remorseless use of others'. Factor 2 is defined by behavioural traits indicative of a 'chronically unstable and antisocial lifestyle; social deviance'. In the most recent revision of the PCL–R, each of the two higher order factors is broken down into two facets: Factor 1 includes facet 1 'interpersonal' items and facet 2 'affective' items. Factor 2 includes facet 3 'lifestyle' items and facet 4 'antisocial' items (Hare, 2003). The total PCL–R score could range from 0 to 40, with higher scores suggestive of more psychopathic traits. To use psychopathy as a categorical measure, the recommended cutoff score, and that most commonly used in North America, is 30.

Average PCL–R scores derived from female samples are invariably lower than those obtained with comparable male samples. Using the recommended cutoff score of 30, the prevalence rate in male offender samples typically ranges between 15% and 30% (Vitale, Smith, Brinkley & Newman, 2002), although

---

[1]The Area Under the Curve (AUC) is a measure of predictive accuracy, with a possible range of values from 0.50 to 1.0, where 0.50 reflects accuracy equal to chance, and 1.0 reflects perfect predictive accuracy.

percentages as low as 11% have been reported (Simourd & Hoge, 2000). Various studies have confirmed that the PCL-R rated prevalence of psychopathy in female samples is considerably lower. However, prevalence rates among female samples have varied considerably, ranging from 6% (Jackson, Rogers, Neumann & Lambert, 2002) to 31% (Strachan, 1993). It should be noted that the high prevalence rate reported by Strachan (1993) is probably attributable to the fact that maximum security women were over-represented in her sample. While maximum security women typically comprise less than 10% of sentenced adult female offender populations, they represented almost half (47%) of Strachan's sample. Some authors have therefore suggested that a more accurate reflection of the base rate of psychopathy in female offender samples is between 9% and 23% (Vitale et al., 2002), although the most recent edition of the PCL–R manual noted a base rate of only 7.5% for the pooled female offender samples (Hare, 2003).

Reliability

The PCL–R was developed and largely defined according to the characteristics of male forensic samples. Accordingly, research has demonstrated that the PCL–R provides a reliable and well-validated measure of psychopathy in samples of men (Hare, 1991, 2003; Vitale & Newman, 2001). The most recent technical manual also provides preliminary data regarding the applicability of the construct for adult female offenders (Hare, 2003). Using data pooled across several samples of female offenders, the PCL–R shows very good internal consistency (Cronbach's alpha $= 0.82$), commensurate with that reported for male offenders. Item-to-total correlations were acceptable; with the exception of three items, they ranged from $r = 0.35$ to $r = 0.52$ for the pooled female offender samples. Finally, inter-rater reliability was also very high, the reliability of total scale scores for pooled female offender samples (single ratings, interclass correlation) was $ICC = 0.94$ (Hare, 2003).

Rutherford, Cacciola, Alterman and McKay (1996) examined the one-month test–retest reliability of the PCL–R with a small sample ($n = 51$) of adult female methadone patients. The correlation of baseline and one-month PCL–R total scores was 0.79, which is somewhat lower than that reported for samples of men ($r = 0.94$; Hare, 1991). However, even weaker test–retest reliability was noted when the authors examined the stability of the PCL–R as a categorical construct, using a cutoff score of 25. The results suggested that the PCL–R is a relatively unstable measure in women, with a reported test–retest reliability (kappa coefficient) of 0.40.

Vitale and Newman (2001) suggest that this low test–retest reliability is attributable to the fact that Rutherford et al. (1996) did not use the recommended cutoff score of 30 to designate the psychopathy classification. Because no women in Rutherford et al.'s sample scored above 29 on the PCL–R, the authors used a score of 25 or greater to classify psychopathic individuals. Vitale and Newman argue that the authors' inability to use the recommended cutoff score of 30 may have artificially lowered the test–retest reliability estimate. Rutherford and colleagues also conceded that the poor test–retest reliability was a result of the fact that, even with the lowered categorical demarcation (> 24), only six women scored above the cutoff. Thus, these results should be interpreted with caution until further research, using larger samples of women, is offered.

Construct Validity

With few exceptions (e.g. Jackson et al., 2002), research on the PCL–R with women has supported a two-factor solution. However, it has shown some gender differences in the factor structure; the discrepancy more apparent within Factor 2 (behavioural) items (Bolt, Hare, Vitale & Newman, 2004; Cooke, 1995; O'Connor, 2003; Salekin et al., 1997; Strachan, 1993; Warren et al., 2003). While three studies using samples of women yielded a two-factor solution similar to that described by Hare (1991), the individual PCL–R items did not load on these factors the same way as they do in male samples. See Table 4.2 for a breakdown of items comprising Factors 1 and 2 in studies of male (amalgamated) and female samples.

With a sample of 75 sentenced women in Canada, Strachan's (1993) data supported a two-factor solution, yielding factor compositions similar to those obtained in male samples. However, three items failed to load on either factor: early behaviour problems, failure to accept responsibility and revocation of conditional release. Interestingly, items 11 (promiscuous sexual behaviour), 17 (many short-term marital relationships) and 20 (criminal versatility), which do not load on either factor in samples of men, all had significant loadings on Factor 2. These findings were later replicated by O'Connor (2003), who also found that items 11 and 17 (sexual promiscuity, numerous marital relationships) were strong markers of the antisocial deviance (Factor 2) aspect of psychopathy for women.

Strachan's results were largely supported by Salekin et al. (1997). Similar to data presented by Strachan, the authors noted that items 19 (revocation of conditional release) and 16 (failure to accept responsibility) failed to load on either factor for women. However, item 17 (many short-term relationships) also failed to load on either factor, similar to Hare et al.'s (1990) samples of men. Also in support of Strachan's results, items 11 (promiscuous sexual behaviour) and 20 (criminal versatility) had significant loadings on Factor 2. Hare's updated technical manual (2003) still suggests a two-factor solution. While Factor 1 consists of the same eight items as suggested in the earlier manual (Hare, 1991; see male sample in Table 4.2), Factor 2 now consists of one additional item: item 20, which is criminal versatility. This is notable because all three earlier factor analytic studies using female samples had also indicated that item 20 loads on Factor 2.

Cooke (1995) examined the generalizability of the PCL–R to a sample of offenders in Scotland. Nineteen per cent (n = 61) of the sample comprised women and some analyses were disaggregated by gender. As shown in Table 4.2, PCL–R items loaded very differently on Factors 1 and 2 in Cooke's sample, as compared to Hare's (1991) pooled data for male offenders. Notably, Cooke's results suggest that the dramatically different factor structure is a function of

Table 4.2 Factor structure of the PCL–R: male and female samples

		Hare et al. (1990)		Strachan (1993)		Salekin et al. (1997)		Cooke (1995)	
Sample		998 males		75 females		103 females		61 females	
Item	Item description	F1	F2	F1	F2	F1	F2	F1	F2
1	Glib-superficial charm	0.86	−0.25	0.67	−0.25	0.67	0.10	0.63	0.13
2	Grandiose	0.76	−0.16	0.87	−0.23	0.66	0.21	0.69	0.10
3	Need for stimulation	0.09	0.56	0.24	0.68	0.60	0.38	0.03	0.47
4	Pathological lying	0.62	0.03	0.44	−0.14	0.69	0.24	0.12	0.52
5	Conning/manipulation	0.59	0.10	0.56	0.11	0.75	0.13	0.11	0.47
6	Lack of remorse/guilt	0.53	0.11	0.58	0.39	0.77	0.31	0.28	0.58
7	Shallow affect	0.57	0.10	0.61	0.37	0.47	0.24	0.01	0.61
8	Callous/lack of empathy	0.53	0.22	0.55	0.44	0.79	0.29	0.10	0.54
9	Parasitic lifestyle	0.00	0.56	−0.03	0.78	0.20	0.49	0.34	0.46
10	Poor behavioural controls	0.14	0.44	0.00	0.71	0.47	0.56	0.43	0.55
11	Promiscuous sexual behaviour	0.35	0.08	−0.04	0.62	0.15	0.46	0.14	0.28
12	Early behavioural problems	−0.01	0.56	0.14	0.38	0.13	0.82	0.44	0.77
13	Lacks realistic goals	0.10	0.56	0.04	0.67	0.39	0.40	0.54	0.49
14	Impulsivity	0.01	0.66	0.08	0.72	0.53	0.43	0.52	0.22
15	Irresponsibility	0.16	0.51	0.04	0.72	0.43	0.34	0.19	0.50
16	Failure to accept responsibility	0.47	0.02	0.33	0.21	0.31	0.01	0.37	0.20
17	Many short-term marital relationships	0.18	0.18	−0.08	0.57	0.11	0.10	0.20	0.50
18	Juvenile delinquency	−0.18	0.59	−0.10	0.54	−0.02	0.78	0.22	0.74
19	Revocation of conditional release	−0.00	0.44	−0.02	0.34	0.35	0.11	0.20	0.53
20	Criminal versatility	0.15	0.33	−0.24	0.77	0.29	0.50	0.17	0.58
	Variance accounted for	17%	15%	48%		34%	7.3%	12%	25%

Note: Substantial loadings (>0.39) are shaded grey. Strachan (1993) provided only total variance accounted for. The most recent revision of the PCL–R (Hare, 2003) suggests that item 20 (criminal versatility) loads on Factor 2.

gender, rather than culture. More precisely, the factor structure of the PCL–R for the Scottish male sample was very similar to Hare's (1991) North American samples.

While the pooled North American data for male offenders suggest that eight items comprise Factor 1, only two of those loaded on Factor 1 in Cooke's analysis of female offenders. Similar to results presented by Strachan (1993) and by Salekin et al. (1997), item 16 (failure to accept responsibility) failed to load on either factor. However, unlike results from the other studies of female offenders, item 11 (promiscuous sexual behaviour) did not load on either factor – this finding is consistent with what is generally found in samples of men (Hare, 1991).

It is also noteworthy that items 10 (poor behavioural controls) and 13 (lack of realistic long-term goals) cross-loaded on both factors, a finding which was later replicated by Salekin et al. (1997).

Perusal of Table 4.2 indicates that item 16 (failure to accept responsibility) consistently fails to load on either factor in samples of female offenders. Notably, however, a recent study by Warren and colleagues (2003)[2] suggested that this item had a fairly strong loading (0.53) on Factor 1 for a sample of 138 women; this is commensurate with that found in male samples. Conflicting evidence suggests that more research is required to evaluate whether the item should be dropped, or scoring criteria amended to be more applicable to women. As shown in Table 4.2, two out of three studies suggest that item 19 (revocation of conditional release) should be removed or re-worked for the assessment of psychopathy in women. More recent research by Warren et al. (2003) supports those earlier studies, indicating a poor loading for this item (0.27) on Factor 2.

On the basis of their data, Salekin et al. (1997) suggest that, for female offenders, the two factors broadly resemble those for men, with Factor 1 describing interpersonal traits and Factor 2 reflecting socially deviant behaviours. However, they suggest that the current descriptive criteria do not precisely describe psychopathy in women. Specifically, for women, they argue that 'the following constellations more appropriately represent the two factors: F1 is characterized by lack of empathy or guilt, interpersonal deception, proneness to boredom and sensation seeking and F2 is characterized by early behavioural problems, promiscuity and adult antisocial behaviour' (p. 582).

Grann (2000) examined the response patterns of 36 female Swedish forensic psychiatric patients between 1988 and 1990. Participants were matched to 36 male forensic psychiatric patients by age, ethnicity, index offence, socio-economic status and number of previous violent crimes. The investigator performed a stepwise discriminant analysis, using gender as the grouping variable and the 20 PCL–R items as independent variables. Results suggested that two PCL–R items were prototypically 'male' items: callous/lack of empathy and juvenile delinquency. One item was found as prototypically 'female': promiscuous sexual behaviour. Grann suggested that, while these results might reflect actual gender differences in psychopathy, they might also reflect biases in interviewers' questions or in information reported in or derived from patient files. Recent research (Bolt et al., 2004) confirmed differential item functioning for female offenders, particularly for Factor 2 items.

Concurrent Validity

To investigate the concurrent validity of the PCL–R in samples of women, three studies have used a self-report version of the same construct. Similar to the PCL–R, the Self-Report Psychopathy Checklist (SRP–II; Hare, 1985) contains two

---

[2]Results by Warren et al. (2003) are not included in Table 4.2 because the authors only presented item loadings as per Hare's (1991) two-factor model. This precluded analysis of items that may have differentially loaded on the other factor.

factors (SRP–F1 and SRP–F2) which add to a total score. The PCL–R showed good concurrent validity with the SRP–II with both female methadone patients ($r = 0.38, p < 0.01$; Rutherford et al., 1996) and female offenders ($r = 0.64, p < 0.001$; Strachan, 1993). Also, Strachan (1993) demonstrated that PCL–R Factor 2 scores were significantly correlated with SRP–F2 scores ($r = 0.70, p < 0.001$) and with SRP–II total scores ($r = 0.68, p < 0.001$). However, Factor 1 did not fare as well; its association with SRP–F1 was non-significant ($r = 0.14$), as was its correlation with the SRP–II total score ($r = 0.09$).

More recently, Vitale et al. (2002) used the Self-Report Psychopathy Scale (SRPS; Levenson, Kiehl & Fitzpatrick, 1995; cited in Vitale et al., 2002) to examine the concurrent validity of the PCL–R for a large sample ($n = 528$) of adult female offenders. Based on the PCL–R, the SRPS is composed of two factors similar to F1 (affective) and F2 (behavioural) dimensions of the PCL–R. Correlational analyses suggested that both the primary and secondary factors of the SRPS showed significant concurrent validity with women's total PCL–R scores; while this held true for both Caucasian ($n = 236$) and African-American ($n = 262$) women, correlations were higher for the former.

Convergent Validity

The construct of psychopathy in women has been supported by research showing a significant correlation between women's PCL–R scores and number of previous arrests ($r = 0.42, p < 0.001$) and months incarcerated ($r = 0.37, p < 0.01$) (Rutherford et al., 1996). Moreover, Strachan (1993) reported that psychopathic women were more likely to: have engaged in prostitution ($p < 0.01$), have a prior criminal conviction ($p < 0.005$), or have been convicted of one or more violent offences ($p < 0.04$). Similarly, Loucks and Zamble (2000) reported highly significant correlations between women's total PCL–R scores and: number of criminal convictions ($r = 0.49, p < 0.001$), number of violent criminal convictions ($r = 0.46, p < 0.001$), number of institutional convictions ($r = 0.63, p < 0.001$), and number of violent institutional convictions ($r = 0.38, p < 0.001$). More recently, Vitale and colleagues (2002) provided strong support for the association between women's PCL–R scores and number of crimes, both non-violent and violent. Significant correlations were reported for both Causcasian and African-American women. Similar associations have been reported with samples of male offenders (Hare, 1991, 2003).

While these data offer some preliminary support for the validity of the PCL–R for women, it is also important to note a limitation to using such static criminal history variables in assessing the validity of the construct. Specifically, a number of these variables might be considered in scoring individual PCL–R items; this threatens their validity as criteria. These items include: poor behavioural controls (item 10), juvenile delinquency (item 18), revocation of conditional release (item 19) and criminal versatility (item 20). However, research has shown that even when items related to criminal activities are omitted from the calculation of total PCL/PCL–R scores, the measure still shows a significant association with both general and violent criminal offending. This has been noted in samples of male (Hart & Hare, 1989, cited in Strachan, 1993) and female offenders (Loucks & Zamble, 2000).

Another way to assess the validity of the PCL–R involves an examination of its convergence with theoretically related constructs using standardized measures. Five such studies, using samples of women, were located (Neary, 1990; Rutherford et al., 1996; Salekin et al., 1997; Strachan, 1993; Vitale et al., 2002); results are summarized in Table 4.3.[3] In aggregate, the results are contradictory and therefore somewhat difficult to interpret. However, examination of the data indicates one conclusive finding: with samples of women, the PCL–R demonstrates very good convergence with assessments of Antisocial Personality.

Rutherford and colleagues (1996) argued that low scores on the Socialization subscale of the California Psychological Inventory (CPI–So; Gough, 1969, cited in Rutherford et al., 1996) suggest psychopathy and therefore should be negatively correlated with the PCL–R. This reasoning is consistent with data reported for male offenders. Hare (1991) reported negative correlations across five studies using the original PCL (Hare, 1985), ranging from -0.27 to -0.43 ($M = -0.33$). Contrary to their expectations, results from Rutherford and colleagues indicated no significant relationship between CPI–So and PCL–R scores. Notably, however, three independent studies revealed significant negative correlations between women's PCL–R and CPI–So scores (Neary, 1990; Strachan, 1993; Vitale et al., 2002).

In their assessment of the PCL–R's convergent validity, Rutherford et al. (1996) also included the Machiavellianism-IV scale (MACH–IV; Christie & Geis, 1970, cited in Rutherford et al., 1996). The authors argued that, since the MACH–IV scale is a measure of egocentricity, it should be positively correlated with the total PCL–R score. Hare (1991) reported a moderate positive correlation ($r = 0.24$) between PCL–R and MACH–IV scores in a sample of male offenders. As shown in Table 4.3, no statistically significant correlation was found in Rutherford and colleagues' sample of adult female methadone patients. The authors also hypothesized that various subscales of the Eysenck Personality Questionnaire – Revised (EPQ; Eysenck et al., 1985, cited in Rutherford et al., 1996) would demonstrate significant associations with the PCL–R. Specifically, they argued that:

> [T]he extroversion scale is thought to assess social sophistication and awareness (Corulla, 1987), much like the CPI–So and therefore should correlate negatively with the PCL–R. The lie scale, a measure of response set and social conformity, should also correlate negatively with the PCL–R as should the neuroticism scale, a measure of the individual's vulnerability to stress (Lodhi & Thakur, 1993). The psychoticism scale is actually a measure of impulsiveness and sensation seeking (Corrula, 1987) and is, therefore, expected to be positively related to the PCL–R. (p. 46)

---

[3]Forth, Brown, Hart & Hare (1996) assessed the convergence between the PCL–R and both childhood and adult symptoms of Antisocial Personality Disorder. Their results are not tabled because data are based on the screening version of the PCL–R and because the sample comprised university students. Similarly, results by Zágon & Jackson (1994) are not tabled because the sample consisted of university students and a Self-Report version (SRP–II) of the PCL–R was used.

Table 4.3 Convergent validity of the PCL–R with samples of women

Construct/scale	Total score	Factor 1	Factor 2
Data source: Neary (1990)			
California Psychological Inventory – Socialization (Gough, 1969)	−0.34***	NR	NR
DSM–III–R APD (American Psychiatric Association, 1987)	0.54***	NR	NR
Data Source: Strachan (1993)			
California Psychological Inventory – Socialization (Gough, 1969)	−0.48***	−0.04	−0.60***
DSM–III–R APD (American Psychiatric Association, 1987)	0.41***	0.02	0.52***
DSM–III–R Narcissistic Personality	0.42**	0.40*	0.33*
Narcissism Personality Inventory (NPI; Raskin & Hall, 1979)	0.18	0.28*	0.08
Interpersonal Reactivity Index (IRI; Davis, Hall, Young & Warren, 1987)			
• Perspective taking	−0.31*	−0.11	−0.36*
• Empathetic concern	−0.22	−0.09	−0.24
Data source: Rutherford et al. (1996)			
California Psychological Inventory – Socialization (Gough, 1969)	−0.19	−0.21	−0.18
MCMI–II APD (Millon, 1987)	0.54***	0.40**	0.58***
DSM–III–R APD (American Psychiatric Association, 1987)	0.62***	0.46***	0.70***
DSM–III–R Narcissistic Personality	0.18	0.19	0.15
Machevellianism–IV (Christie & Geis, 1970)	0.17	0.00	0.26
EPQ–R (Eysenck, Eysenck & Barret, 1985)			
• Extroversion	−0.15	−0.13	−0.17
• Neuroticism	0.00	0.05	−0.05
• Psychoticism	0.48***	0.36**	0.54***
• Lie	−0.12	−0.14	−0.05
Interpersonal Reactivity Index (IRI; Davis, Hall, Young & Warren, 1987)			
• Perspective taking	−0.57***	−0.50**	−0.51***
• Empathetic concern	−0.57***	−0.46**	−0.52***
Data source: Salekin et al. (1997)			
Personality Assessment Inventory – Antisocial (PAI; Morey, 1991)	0.53***	0.39***	0.56***
Personality Disorder Examination – Antisocial (PDE; Loranger, 1988)	0.72***	0.52***	0.77***
Correctional officer ratings of:			
• Violence	0.20	0.21	0.17

Table 4.3   (*Continued*)

Construct/scale	Total score	Factor 1	Factor 2
• Verbal aggression	0.13	0.12	0.09
• Non-compliance	0.18	0.16	0.16
• Manipulation	0.20	0.20	0.17
• Remorse	0.15	0.15	0.14
• Danger	0.18	0.18	0.13
Data source: Vitale et al. (2002)			
California Psychological Inventory – Socialization (Gough, 1969)	−0.46**	NR	NR
DSM–IV APD (American Psychiatric Association, 1994)	0.20**	NR	NR
EPQ–R Psychoticism (Eysenck, Eysenck & Barret, 1985)	0.20**	NR	NR
Data source: Warren et al. (2003) N = 138 female offenders			
SCID–II Diagnosis (First, Gibbon, Spitzer, Williams & Benjamin, 1995)			
• Antisocial	0.59**	0.27	0.63**
• Narcissistic	0.21**	0.12	0.23**

Note: NR = Not Reported; $^*p < 0.05$; $^{**}p < 0.01$; $^{***}p < 0.001$. References for measures cited in the table are each derived from their respective sources (shaded grey). Data from Vitale et al. (2002) represent the Caucasian subsample only.

As shown in Table 4.3, the extroversion, neuroticism and lie scales of the EPQ were unrelated to women's PCL–R scores. These results were consistent with those reported by Hare (1991), using the PCL with samples of male offenders. As expected, the psychoticism scale was positively and significantly correlated with PCL–R scores. This finding was later replicated by Vitale et al. (2002), though for Caucasian women only. For the African-American women ($n = 199$), there was no association.

Both Strachan (1993) and Rutherford et al. (1996) hypothesized that the 'perspective-taking' and 'empathetic concern' dimensions of the Interpersonal Reactivity Index (IRI; Davis et al., 1987; cited in Strachan, 1993) would correlate negatively with women's PCL–R scores. While both constructs are theoretically linked to psychopathy, research with male offenders has yielded only modest correlations between 'perspective-taking' ($r = -0.13$) and 'empathetic concern' ($r = -0.33$) with the PCL–R (Hare, 1991). As shown in Table 4.3, data presented by Rutherford and colleagues strongly supported convergence, though Strachan's (1993) results were less convincing.

The self-focused, self-aggrandizing personality of the narcissist, in theory, should be reflected in higher scores on the PCL–R, particularly on Factor 1. Previous research with male offenders demonstrated a fairly strong association, at $r = 0.34$ (Hare, 1991) between PCL–R total score and narcissism, as assessed by the Narcissism Personality Inventory (NPI; Raskin & Hall, 1979, cited in Hare, 1991). Strachan's sample of women showed less convergence between these two measures, though there was a significant positive correlation between NPI total scores and Factor 1 of the PCL–R. When narcissism was assessed with DSM–IIIR criteria, Strachan (1993) noted a more significant association. As expected, the correlation was stronger with Factor 1 than with Factor 2. In contrast, Warren and colleagues (2003) reported significant correlations between SCID–II diagnosis of Narcissistic Personality Disorder and PCL–R Factor 2 scores for women. Finally, Rutherford et al. (1996) showed no significant association between DSM–IIIR symptoms of Narcissistic Personality and women's PCL–R scores.

To assess convergent validity of the PCL–R in female offenders, Salekin et al. (1997) used correctional officers' ratings of the offenders on several dimensions including: violence, verbal aggression, non-compliance, manipulation, remorse and danger. Although correlations with PCL–R total score were all positive, ranging from 0.13 to 0.20, all failed to reach statistical significance (see Table 4.3). Further analyses to test associations between correctional officers' ratings and each PCL–R factor separately were also unreliable. Notably, all subjective ratings *were* significantly correlated with the 'Antisocial' subscale of the Personality Disorder Examination (PDE; Loranger, 1988, cited in Salekin et al., 1997). These data suggest poor convergence between PCL–R scores and independent subjective assessments of theoretically related behaviours.

While the aggregated data on the convergent validity of the PCL–R for women is equivocal, it is important to highlight the consistent finding that the PCL–R is very closely associated with measures of Antisocial Personality. Correlations across five distinct measures of Antisocial Personality, in six independent studies, revealed statistically significant findings well beyond chance levels. These data are consistent with what is typically found in male samples (Hare, 2003) and implies that diagnostic criteria for APD and psychopathy have considerable overlap.

Hare (2003) has suggested that a fundamental difference between psychopathy and APD is the fact that the former is a two-factor construct. Research with male offenders revealed an asymmetric relationship between APD and psychopathy, where the majority of those who meet criteria for psychopathy (about 90%) also meet the diagnostic (DSM–III, DSM–IIIR or DSM–IV; American Psychiatric Association, 1994) criteria for APD. However, only about 20 to 30% of offenders with APD also meet the PCL/PCL–R criteria for psychopathy (Hare, 1991). Strachan (1993) demonstrated a similar pattern for female offenders. Within her sample of 75 female offenders, the probability of a PCL–R rated 'psychopath' receiving a diagnosis of APD was 0.71. However, the probability of a woman diagnosed with APD receiving a PCL–R diagnosis of psychopathy was only 0.42. These data indicate that, as with samples of men, the concepts of APD and psychopathy are similar but asymmetrically related, with psychopathy being the more exclusive diagnosis. Hare (2003) argued that the PCL–R predicts APD well because:

> most criminal psychopaths engage in the sort of antisocial behavior (high scores on Factor 2) that also defines APD, whereas APD does not predict psychopathy very

well because the majority of prisoners and forensic patients with APD do not show evidence of the personality characteristics defined by Factor 1. Research that uses either DSM diagnosis of APD taps the social deviance component of psychopathy but misses much of the personality component. (p. 92)

Hare's position is supported by data from studies with male offenders, as well as that presented in Table 4.3. Specifically, the data for women consistently indicate a stronger relationship between APD and Factor 2, relative to Factor 1. Together, the results presented offer excellent evidence of convergent validity of the PCL–R, at least with respect to the construct of Antisocial Personality.

Discriminant Validity

There is also emerging support for the discriminant validity of the PCL–R with female offenders. For instance, there is evidence to suggest that psychopathy, as assessed by the PCL–R, is clearly discriminated from DSM Axis 1 disorders in women. For instance, when Rutherford et al. (1996) analysed their data for female methadone patients, they found no significant relationship between total PCL–R scores and either diagnosis of alcohol dependence ($r = -0.17$) or the variety of substance use disorders ($r = 0.24$) the women had experienced. Moreover, results showed that total PCL–R scores were independent of women's scores on the Beck Depression Inventory (Beck, 1987; as cited in Rutherford et al., 1996) at $r = 0.12$. This confirmed earlier findings reported by Strachan (1993; $r = 0.05$) and was later replicated by Vitale et al. (2002). Hare (2003) noted a similar lack of relationship ($r = -0.14$) between Beck Depression and PCL–R scores for male offenders.

Theoretically, psychopaths' shallow affect and lack of remorse suggests that they would experience less anxiety than their non-psychopathic counterparts. However, results of studies, especially those that have applied self-report anxiety inventories, have been inconsistent. In general, correlations between men's PCL–R scores and anxiety tend to be negative though not significant, and stronger for Factor 1 than Factor 2 (Hare, 2003). Strachan (1993) used the State-Trait Anxiety scale (Spielberger, Gorsuch & Lushene, 1970, cited in Strachan, 1993) to examine the discriminant validity of the PCL–R for women. Similar to research findings with male offenders, the author noted no association between anxiety and total or Factor 1 scores. Unlike the findings for male offenders, however, there was a significant *positive* correlation between Factor 2 and anxiety within Strachan's sample of female offenders ($r = 0.27$). Similarly, Vitale and colleagues (2002) reported significant positive correlations between total PCL–R scores and anxiety, as measured by the Welsh Anxiety Scale (Welsh, 1956; as cited in Vitale et al., 2002). The significant positive correlations reported by Vitale and colleagues were evidenced in both Caucasian ($r = 0.16$) and African-American ($r = 0.21$) subsamples of women. Taken together, these results suggest that self-reported anxiety is not independent of PCL–R scores for women.

Research results on the PCL–R's ability to discriminate psychopathy from DSM Axis II Personality Disorders were mixed. In general, results of studies using male samples suggest that PCL–R total scores are independent of most Axis II personality disorders, including Dependent, Avoidant, Compulsive and Schizoid. However, there is significant comorbidity with diagnoses of Schizotypal, Histrionic, Paranoid, Borderline and Passive Aggressive Personalities. Notably, the association is typically between the diagnostic category and PCL–R total scores and Factor 2 scores. Factor 1 appears relatively independent of Axis II personality disorders (Hare, 2003).

The pattern of results appears largely similar for female samples. Table 4.4 provides discriminant validity data for four independent samples of women.

Table 4.4 Discriminant validity of the PCL–R: female samples

Construct/scale	Total score	Factor 1	Factor 2
Data source: Strachan (1993) n = 75			
DSM–III–R Personality Disorders:			
Histrionic	0.45**	0.37*	0.38*
Borderline	0.47**	0.17	0.47**
Data source: Rutherford et al. (1996) n = 57			
DSM–III–R Personality Disorders:			
Histrionic	0.47***	0.49***	0.43***
Borderline	0.36***	0.32*	0.42***
Paranoid	0.11	0.15	0.05
Schizotypal	0.18	0.07	0.21
Dependent	0.02	0.03	−0.01
Avoidant	−0.11	−0.14	0.06
Obsessive–Compulsive	−0.11	−0.14	0.06
Passive Aggressive	0.27*	0.27*	0.24
Data source: Salekin et al. (1997) n = 103			
Personality Assessment Inventory (Morey, 1991)			
Borderline	0.22	0.08	0.28**
Paranoid	0.18	0.07	0.21
Personality Disorder Examination (Loranger, 1988)			
Borderline	0.38**	0.25	0.43**
Paranoid	0.24	0.22	0.23
Data source: Warren et al. (2003) n = 138			
SCID–II Diagnosis:			
Histrionic	0.20*	0.06	0.23**
Borderline	0.17	−0.04	0.23**
Avoidant	−0.13	−0.23	−0.02**
Schizoid	0.14	0.14	0.13
Paranoid	0.19*	0.00	0.32**
Schizotypal	0.17*	0.07	0.18*
Obsessive–compulsive	0.08	0.17*	0.00
Dependent	0.04	0.00	0.07

Note: $^*p < 0.05$; $^{**}p < 0.01$; $^{***}p < 0.001$. References for measures cited in the table are derived from their respective sources (shaded grey).

Both Rutherford et al. (1996) and Strachan (1993) examined the relationship between women's PCL–R scores and diagnostic criteria for Histrionic Personality Disorder (HPD) and results suggested significant overlap between the two. Several characteristics of HPD, such as self-dramatization, attention-seeking and emotional lability, are unrelated to the concept of psychopathy. However, close scrutiny of the diagnostic criteria also suggests some common features, such as self-centredness, shallow affect and sexual provocativeness (American Psychiatric Association, 1994). Notably, however, a study by Hart, Forth and Hare (1991) indicated no significant association between PCL–R scores and HPD criteria for male offenders. Researchers have confirmed these findings with data showing that the relation between psychopathy and HPD traits is stronger among women than men (Hamburger, Lilienfeld & Hogben, 1996). The authors also noted that the association between psychopathy and Antisocial Personality Disorder was stronger among men and suggested that gender was a moderator variable. They specifically argued that "similarities between ASPD and HPD are consistent with the hypothesis that they are manifestations of the same underlying syndrome, namely psychopathy" (p. 42).

The second outstanding feature of Table 4.4 is the consistently high correlation between Borderline Personality Disorder (BPD) and PCL–R scores. Unlike the PCL–R's biased association with HPD, the strong correlations between psychopathy and borderline features are consistent across both genders. Notably, correlations are particularly strong with Factor 2 of the PCL–R. BPD is characterized by a pattern of behavioural, emotional and cognitive instability and disregulation. The most marked behavioural manifestation of BPD is intentional self-harm. It is interesting to note that the association between the PCL–R and BPD criteria is particularly evident in Factor 2; the behavioural component of psychopathy. Although items 10 (poor behavioural controls) and 14 (impulsivity) could be broadly linked to BPD, the convergence between BPD and PCL–R remains largely theoretically unsupported. As such, the data presented in Table 4.4 (for HPD and BPD in particular) threaten the discriminant validity of the PCL–R.

Notwithstanding that, there is also evidence, presented in Table 4.4, to support the PCL–R's ability to discriminate other disorders in samples of women. Consistent with what has been noted for male subjects, Rutherford and colleagues (1996) found no significant associations between PCL–R scores and diagnostic criteria for a wide range of personality disorders, including: Paranoid, Schizotypal, Dependent, Avoidant and Obsessive–Compulsive. The PCL–R's ability to discriminate psychopathy from Paranoid Personality criteria was replicated with a larger sample of women, using two separate assessment measures (Salekin et al., 1997), although more recently Warren and colleagues (2003) reported conflicting results.

Predictive Validity

Predictive validity is extremely important in correctional psychology, particularly with respect to predicting criminal recidivism. While neither the PCL–R nor its predecessor were specifically designed to predict criminal behaviour, there is now a substantial body of literature to suggest that the PCL–R is a robust predictor of criminal behaviour, including violence (Hare, 2003). Accordingly, an important feature of the PCL–R is its ability to correctly identify recidivists (Hare, 1991, 2003).

To date, only three published studies have examined the predictive utility of the PCL–R with female offenders (Loucks & Zamble, 2000; Richards, Casey & Lucente, 2003; Salekin, Rogers, Ustad & Sewell, 1998). Salekin and colleagues (1998) used a 14-month follow-up to examine the psychopathy–recidivism relation in a sample of 78 female offenders. Using the standard cutoff score of 30, ten women were identified as 'psychopaths' with the PCL–R. Within the follow-up period, 50% of the women classified as 'psychopath' were re-arrested for a new criminal offence. The authors suggested that this rate is about 13% lower than the average rate of recidivism for male psychopaths over a comparable follow-up.

With respect to predicting re-arrest, the results of Salekin et al.'s (1998) study suggested that the PCL–R is a 'moderate to poor' predictor of recidivism for women. The correlation between PCL–R total scores and recidivism was not significant, at $r = 0.20$. While Factor 1 showed a significant association at $r = 0.26$ ($p < 0.05$), the relationship between Factor 2 and recidivism was negligible ($r = 0.14$). This finding is notable because two studies with male offender samples have shown that, relative to Factor 1 items, Factor 2 items are more closely related to general recidivism (Barbaree, Seto, Serin, Amos & Preston, 1994; Harpur, Hare & Hakstian, 1989; both cited in Salekin et al., 1998). With this sample of female offenders, use of the PCL–R to predict recidivism resulted in a high rate of false-negatives: about 90% of the women who recidivated had *not* been classified as psychopathic and about 9% of the women who did not recidivate were classified as psychopathic. The Receiver Operating Characteristic (ROC) area under the curve was 0.64 and odds ratios showed that the PCL–R did not provide much information beyond chance in predicting re-arrest. Thus, with respect to predictive validity, the data suggested that the PCL–R does not perform as well with women as it does with men.

Results of a study by Loucks and Zamble (2000) were somewhat more favourable. The investigation followed 80 released Canadian federally sentenced women for an average of 38 months. The recidivism rate, broadly defined to include revocation of release for any reason, was 47%. The authors examined several variables within four general classes of predictors: (1) social, personal and criminal history, (2) maladaptation history, (3) abuse history and (4) personality, ability and emotional functioning. While the authors reported that psychopathy was among the best predictors of recidivism, no substantiating data are presented in the report. Rather, through variable reduction techniques, the resultant linear prediction model, which included PCL–R rated psychopathy, had a correlation of 0.32 with recidivism. In their discussion, the authors suggest that "psychopathy is as important in predicting general offending in female serious offenders as it is in male serious offenders" (p. 31). However, as results are not disaggregated by predictor variable, the relative contribution of psychopathy remains unknown. This limits confidence in the authors' conclusions.

Richards et al. (2003) examined the predictive validity of the PCL–R for an initial sample of 404 incarcerated women in substance abuse treatment. Women's scores on the PCL–R were significantly associated with treatment response in terms of: attendance, programme retention, removal for non-compliance, disruptive and violent rule violations, avoidance of urinalysis testing and therapist ratings.

Richards and colleagues also examined the relationship between PCL–R scores and post-release outcome among 239 women who had completed at least 90 days of treatment. The women were followed up in the community for an average of 13.9 months, during which almost one-third (30%) were charged with a new offence. Results indicated a significant correlation between number of charge-free days and the total psychopathy score ($r = -0.24, p < 0.01$). The authors also performed Cox regression analyses to control for variability in time at risk. The results indicated that women's PCL–R scores, particularly Factor 1 scores, were significant in the prediction of new charges. Specifically, the exponential beta for Factor 1 indicated that, for each one-point increase in Factor 1 score above the group mean, there was an associated 11% increase in the likelihood of being arrested (Richards et al., 2003). To date, this comprises the most promising evidence in terms of using the PCL–R to predict treatment success and post-release outcome for women.

In sum, the PCL–R has been relatively well researched on samples of female offenders with respect to its factor structure and psychometric properties. However, the results are still equivocal in many areas. The greater part of the evidence suggests that there are some gender differences in the factor structure of the PCL–R and that particular items vary in salience by gender. In particular, the relationship of sexual promiscuity, numerous marital relationships and criminal versatility to the construct of psychopathy in women remains unclear. Recent research also suggests that a three-factor model might be a more appropriate reflection of the construct for women (Warren et al., 2003).

Overall, reliability estimates for samples of women are quite strong, though test–retest reliability will require further examination. With various female samples, the PCL–R has demonstrated robust concurrent and convergent validity. Notwithstanding, PCL–R assessed psychopathy in women is highly comorbid with other (theoretically dissimilar) personality disorders, such as Paranoid, Histrionic and Borderline. Warren and colleagues (2003) have therefore suggested that these results support the view of psychopathy as a constellation of personality traits (for women) rather than a distinct clinical entity. To date, results of predictive validity studies support Factor 1 as a strong predictor for women, though the predictive power of full-scale and Factor 2 scores is less promising.

In their review of the applicability of the PCL–R to female offenders, Vitale and Newman (2001) suggested that clinicians consider their reasons for choosing to use the PCL–R for assessment. They noted several potential uses, including predicting criminal recidivism, predicting institutional violence and planning and implementing correctional interventions. Based on their review, they concluded that "if clinicians were using the PCL–R for the sole purpose of predicting specific outcomes for any particular woman in these areas, they would be doing so without empirical evidence of the predictive power of the PCL–R [for women] in such domains" (p. 31).

It has been a few years since Vitale and Newman made that statement. While research supporting the PCL–R in terms of its psychometric properties is quickly accumulating, its application to female samples would undoubtedly result in considerable controversy. Its application has great potential for human rights abuses (Zinger & Forth, 1998). While the problem has more to do with the professional integrity of those employing the scale than the measure itself, we underscore this here because girls and women in the criminal justice system represent a particularly vulnerable population. It is therefore paramount that assessors weigh the advantages of using such a tool with the potential ramifications of its application. Further, psychopathy is believed to be a relatively stable, enduring trait; thus, PCL–R assessments are subject to the same criticism as the SIR–R1 – there is little provision for intervention and iterative assessments to track treatment-related change. Finally, we recommend that pertinent research results are based on the specific population of interest, consistent in terms of support for the tool and current because correctional populations are susceptible to change.

LEVEL OF SERVICE/CASE MANAGEMENT INVENTORY

Another standard risk assessment instrument used with both male and female correctional populations is the Level of Service/Case Management Inventory (LS/CMI; Andrews et al., 2004). Expanded from its predecessors, the LSI (Andrews, 1982b) and LSI–R (Andrews & Bonta, 1995), the LS/CMI is based on the social learning theory of criminal behaviour. It consists of 11 sections in addition to accommodation for supplementary information. These sections include: (1) general risk/need factors, (2) specific risk/need factors, (3) prison experience – institutional factors, (4) other client issues (social, health, mental health), (5) special responsivity considerations (includes gender-specific issues), (6) risk/need summary and override, (7) risk/need profile, (8) programme/ placement decision, (9) case management plan, (10) progress record and (11) discharge summary.

The general risk/needs section of the LS/CMI contains 43 items that are clustered into eight factors: criminal history (8 items), education/employment (9 items), family/marital (4 items), leisure/recreation (2 items), companions (4 items), alcohol/drug problems (8 items), procriminal attitude/orientation (4 items) and antisocial pattern (4 items). Scoring for the LS/CMI is based on a paper and pencil questionnaire, information retrieved from institutional file records and a semi-structured interview with the offender. Each of the 43 items in section 1 is scored either in a dichotomous fashion (yes/no), or a four-point rating format, ranging from 0 (suggesting a very unsatisfactory situation with a very clear and strong need for improvement) to 3 (a satisfactory situation with no need for improvement). Four-point ratings are collapsed to create dichotomous (0,1) scores and individual item scores (either 0 or 1) are then added to provide a composite scale score, which can range from 0 to 43. Higher overall scores suggest higher risk of recidivism and need for correctional intervention.

The original LSI (Andrews, 1982b) was constructed with a development sample of mostly male offenders in one Canadian province (Ontario). Importantly, however, norms were later established based on a large sample of both male and female ($n = 1414$ women) offenders (Andrews & Bonta, 1995). The most recent technical manual (Andrews et al., 2004) incorporates data from several US studies ($n = 11\,002$ women) and most results are disaggregated by gender. In addition, there are some normative data for two samples of offenders in the United Kingdom ($n = 1019$, including 131 females) and one release cohort from Singapore ($n = 1294$, including 262 females).

Like the SIR scale and the PCL–R, the LS/CMI[4] tends to assess female offenders as lower risk than their male counterparts. Similarly, samples of offenders under community supervision tend to score lower than those who are incarcerated (Andrews et al., 2004). Pooled North American data indicate that the mean score for incarcerated adult male offenders is 22.4, while that for incarcerated adult females is 21.8. The gender difference is more notable in the community samples, with men scoring an average of 14.2 and women having a mean score of 11.3. The Singaporean samples showed similar gender differences, although no between-gender differences were noted in the UK (Andrews et al., 2004).

Although only a few studies have analysed reliability and validity data for the LS/CMI with female offenders, the results are promising. With data from samples of women, full-scale internal consistency estimates have consistently been reported at about $\alpha = 0.90$, suggesting that LS/CMI items are converging on a single underlying dimension (Andrews et al., 2004). Rettinger (1998) reported very high inter-rater reliability ($r = 0.92$) for a subsample ($n = 136$) of female offenders in her study, which is slightly higher than that reported for (pooled) samples of male offenders (0.88; Andrews et al., 2004). Currently, there are no reports available examining the convergent or divergent validity of the LS/CMI with samples of women. However, five studies reporting on predictive validity were located (Coulson, Ilacqua, Nutbrown, Giulekas & Cudjoe, 1996; Holtfreter et al., 2004; Lowenkamp, Holsinger & Latessa, 2001; McConnell, 1996; Rettinger, 1998).

Rettinger (1998) followed up a sample of 441 Canadian provincially[5] sentenced female offenders for about five years. Over that period, almost half (46.5%) re-offended and 14.3% re-offended violently. Results revealed a strong positive relationship between women's LSI scores and their likelihood of re-offending ($r = 0.58, p < 0.0001$) within the follow-up. As expected, the recidivists had significantly higher total scores than the non-recidivists

$$(M_{\text{recidivists}} = 25.5, SD = 7.2; \quad M_{\text{non-recidivists}} = 13.6, SD = 7.0).$$

---

[4]Hereafter, the LS/CMI will refer to the current tool, as well as its predecessors, the LSI and LSI–R.

[5]In Canada, those offenders sentenced to terms of imprisonment of less than two years fall under provincial jurisdiction; those sentenced to two years or more fall under federal jurisdiction.

These results were supported by data presented by Gendreau, Goggin and Smith (1999). Using meta-analysis, the authors reported an average weighted effect size ($k = 9$) of $r = 0.50$ between LSI score and recidivism in studies on female offenders.

When Rettinger (1998) used cutoff scores to form risk groupings according to the LSI manual, a clear linear relationship was noted between risk category and post-release convictions. Specifically, while 3.6% of those in the lowest risk category re-offended, this was true for 84.2% of those in the highest risk category. Parallel findings were noted for analyses pertaining to violent recidivism. The correlation between LSI total score and violent recidivism was significant at $r = 0.34 (p < 0.0001)$. Women who recidivated violently had higher LSI scores than those who did not recidivate with violence

$$(M_{\text{violent recidivism}} = 28.8, SD = 6.4; \quad M_{\text{no violent recidivism}} = 17.4, SD = 8.5).$$

As with general re-offending, those in the lowest risk category were least likely to recidivate while those in the highest risk category were most likely to recidivate. For simplicity, Rettinger's (1998) results by risk category are presented in Table 4.5.

Coulson and colleagues (1996) also reported encouraging results, based on their sample of 526 Canadian provincially sentenced women. The authors collected data on three outcome measures, over a follow-up period of 39 months: (1) new charges or convictions (recidivism), (2) parole failure and (3) halfway house failure. Again, strong positive correlations were noted between LSI total scores and all three outcome measures. The point-biserial correlations were: $r = 0.51$ for new charges/convictions, $r = 0.53$ for parole failure and $r = 0.45$ for halfway house failure. All correlations between LSI total scores and outcome measures were statistically significant at $p < 0.01$. Analyses further revealed that LSI total scores accounted for 26.3% of the variance in recidivism, 27.9% of the variance in parole failure and 20.2% of the variance in halfway house failure.

Coulson et al. argued that, because women's LSI scores are lower than the average scores for males, lower cutoffs were warranted. Based on this argument, the authors created five risk categories, with an approximately equal number of women classified within each group. Results showed a consistent increase in the probability of failure as the LSI risk level increased; this finding held across all three measures of outcome. For a new set of comparisons, the authors collapsed the five risk categories into two, such that women with scores of 12 or less were designated as 'low risk' and those scoring 12 or above were designated as

Table 4.5 Recidivism and violent recidivism by LSI risk category (Rettinger, 1998)

LSI risk level	LSI score	N	% Recidivists	(n)	% Violent recidivists	(n)
Low	0–7	55	3.6	(2)	0.0	(0)
Medium	8–11	48	6.3	(3)	0.0	(0)
High	12–23	186	38.7	(72)	6.5	(12)
Very high	≥24	152	84.2	(128)	33.6	(51)

'high risk'. Chi-square analyses revealed a significant difference in recidivism between the low-risk and high-risk groups ($p < 0.001$). Predictive accuracy statistics, using recidivism as the outcome measure, demonstrated a Relative Improvement Over Chance (RIOC) of 60% in the first year post-release and 55% in the second year. The authors concluded, "the concepts underlying the LSI appear robust enough to bridge the boundaries of gender . . . the current findings show that risk assessment by the LSI can be incorporated in a systematic way into criminal justice decision-making for female offenders" (p. 437).

To date, there are no published reports exploring the reliability and validity of the LSI/LSI–R with federally sentenced Canadian women. In an unpublished Honour's thesis, McConnell (1996) tested the predictive ability of the LSI with a small sample ($n = 50$) of federal female offenders. The LSI was scored retrospectively based on file information and recidivism was defined as conviction for a new offence within three years of release. Not surprisingly, the mean LSI score ($M = 21.8, SD = 9.7$) for this sample of federally sentenced women was higher than those reported in provincial samples. Similar to findings presented by Coulson and colleagues (1996) and by Rettinger (1998), a significant positive correlation was found between LSI total scores and new convictions ($r = 0.60, p < 0.01$). While the LSI total score accounted for an impressive proportion (36%) of the variance in outcome, subsequent analyses revealed that only two (criminal history, companions) of the 10 LSI subscales contributed significantly to the prediction of recidivism.

Lowenkamp and colleagues (2001) tested the predictive validity of the LSI–R with a large sample of male ($n = 317$) and female ($n = 125$) felony offenders who had been sentenced to a US state prison. Results revealed very significant relationships between total scores and three measures of outcome for both males and females. In fact, across all criterion measures, the correlations were higher for the female sample. For the sample of women, the authors noted a strong relationship between total LSI–R score and reincarceration ($r = 0.37$, $p < 0.01$), programme completion ($r = -0.25, p < 0.01$) and absconding ($r = 0.18$, $p < 0.01$). Further analyses were completed collapsing the LSI–R scores into three discrete categories of risk: low (scores 0–20), medium (scores 21–30) and high (scores above 30). Chi-square statistics revealed highly significant between-group differences in reincarceration rates by group, particularly for the female sample. While about 17% of those in the lowest risk group were reincarcerated, this was true for 31% of those in the medium risk group and 56% of women in the highest risk group. Finally, multivariate logistic regression analyses confirmed the validity of the LSI–R. When LSI–R risk score, race, age, child abuse and time at risk were entered into the model for the total sample, only LSI–R risk score and time at risk emerged as significant predictors. Moreover LSI–R risk score accounted for over twice the variance than time at risk. When the analysis was run for the female sample only, the LSI–R risk score was the only significant predictor of reincarceration.

Holtfreter and colleagues (2004) tested the LSI–R with a sample of 134 female felony offenders under correctional supervision in one US state. A series of logistic regression analyses were performed. Dependent variables included self-reported re-arrest and self-reported violation (probation or parole). Independent variables included (slightly modified) LSI–R risk score, minority status, years of education and poverty. Results revealed that the LSI-R score was a significant predictor of self-reported re-arrest and violation for women. Specifically, for each unit increase in the LSI–R, there was a corresponding 7% increase in the odds of re-arrest and a 9% increase in the odds of violating conditions of supervision. However, follow-up analyses revealed a significant effect of poverty, which accounted for far more variance in outcome than the measure of risk. In fact, the effect of LSI–R risk scores was weak and not statistically significant after adjusting for poverty. The authors concluded that the LSI–R does not adequately take into account the economic marginality of adult female offenders.

More research will be required to support or refute these findings, although Farrington and Painter (2004) recently noted that low social class and low family income predicted offending more strongly in girls than in boys. Holtfreter et al. (2004) chose to use a self-report measure of outcome. It would be interesting to verify whether the same findings are sustained using official police data. As well, modifications to the instrument may have impacted upon the results. Finally, it would be worthwhile to test whether these findings hold true with samples in other jurisdictions such as Canada and the UK.

Taken together, the literature regarding the validity and practical utility of the LS/CMI for female offenders offers some promising results. In fact, the studies reviewed suggest that the LSI–R is even more accurate in predicting recidivism in female samples. Using meta-analysis, Gendreau et al. (1999) reported an average weighted effect size ($k = 9$) of $r = 0.50$ between the LSI score and recidivism in studies on female offenders. The same research, using data based entirely on males, showed an average weighted effect size ($k = 25$) of 0.34. While these results are promising, data are still required to test the concurrent, convergent and discriminant validity of the LS/CMI for women. Moreover, the impact of poverty on the variance accounted for in outcome warrants further investigation. Unlike the PCL–R and the SIR scale, the LS/CMI holds considerable promise in terms of directing treatment targets the provision of iterative assessments to evaluate change over time.

HISTORICAL CLINICAL RISK SCHEME

The Historical Clinical Risk Scheme (HCR–20; Webster, Douglas, Eaves & Hart, 1997; Webster, Eaves, Douglas & Wintrup, 1995) is a 20-item violence risk assessment instrument that conceptually aligns risk markers into past, present and future. The 10 historic (H) variables consider past behaviour and functioning; they are static or unchangeable. The five clinical (C) items reflect current, dynamic correlates of violence. Finally, the five risk management (R) items concern the future, focusing attention on situational post-assessment factors that may either aggravate or mitigate risk (Douglas, 1999). The scoring system, borrowed from the PCL–R, rates each item on a continuum from 0 (not present) to 2 (definitely present).

The HCR–20 has demonstrated robust psychometric properties and research results have been favourable in terms of its utility as a risk prediction measure for both men and women, particularly with respect to violent behaviour. However, the vast majority of these studies have drawn samples from civil psychiatric (Douglas, Ogloff & Nicholls, 1997; Douglas, Ogloff, Nicholls & Grant, 1999; Klassen, 1996; Nicholls, Ogloff & Douglas, 1997; Ross, Hart & Webster, 1998, cited in Douglas, 1999) or forensic psychiatric (Belfrage, 1998; Dernevik, 1998; Douglas et al., 1998; Grann, Belfrage & Tengström, 2000; Strand & Belfrage, 2001) settings.

To date, we could locate only two published studies using the HCR–20 risk assessment scheme with regular offender samples (Belfrage, Fransson & Strand, 2000; Douglas & Webster, 1999). Belfrage and colleagues (2000) documented the HCR–20's ability to predict institutional violence in a sample of 41 male inmates in two Swedish maximum security prisons. With a Canadian sample, Douglas and Webster (1999) coded the H and C scales of the HCR–20 for 75 male maximum security inmates. Results revealed that inter-rater reliability on the combined H and C scales was high, at $r = 0.80$. Convergent validity of the HCR–20 was evident in its moderate to strong correlations with other offender risk classification measures[6] (PCL–R and the Violence Risk Appraisal Guide; VRAG). Moreover, data from their postdictive research offered support for the use of the HCR–20 in classifying offenders into general and violent risk categories. The correlation between total scores and number of past charges was significant ($r = 0.33, p < 0.01$), as was the association between total score and number of past violent charges[7] ($r = 0.44, p < 0.001$). Offenders scoring above the median on the HCR–20 were almost five times more likely to have previous charges for violence ($p = 0.002$) and almost seven times more likely to have previous escape attempts ($p = 0.0006$). Similarly, those scoring above the median on the H and C scales were, on average, four times more likely to be scored positively on a variety of other indices of past violence and antisocial behaviour. Specifically, the mean odds ratios for the HCR–20 total scale, H scale and C scale were 4.01, 4.56 and 2.94, respectively.

Collectively, these findings offer important information in the validation of the HCR–20 on offender samples. However, the nature of the design precludes any conclusions regarding the predictive validity of the measure. Moreover, the aforementioned study results can only be generalized to other male maximum security inmates. There is currently not enough evidence to suggest that the HCR–20 would be as valuable in measuring risk in general female offender populations.

SUMMARY

In summary, some of the most well-researched and commonly used risk assessment instruments for offender populations include: the SIR–R1 scale (Nuffield, 1982), PCL–R (Hare, 1991, 2003), LSI–R (Andrews & Bonta, 1995), LS/CMI

---

[6]To control for confound, item H7 (psychopathy) was removed from all analyses between the HCR–20 and the PCL–R.
[7]To control for confound, item H1 (previous violence) was removed from all analyses between the HCR–20 and past violence.

(Andrews et al., 2004) and the HCR–20 (Webster et al., 1995). Unfortunately, relative to the data available for male offenders, there is currently less evidence to support the clinical use of these measures for female offenders. Thus, concerns with the method by which Dowden and Andrews (1999) classified their sample according to risk cannot be easily addressed. To date, there is no widely known, well-validated post-release risk assessment tool that has been developed specifically for women. In the absence of a gender-specific measure, we suggest that correctional practitioners consider the purpose of the assessment and be well informed regarding the viability of using their preferred mathematical tool with women. It is essential that those using such measures be trained accordingly and that they keep abreast of current gender-specific research regarding its use.

Risk classification in corrections can serve several purposes, including treatment planning, population management and predicting release risk. The research literature, including the present review, is focused primarily on the latter; the prediction of recidivism. This review has highlighted the need to test the reliability and validity of existing risk assessment instruments for women. However, it would be even more judicious to develop and validate a *gender-informed* model of risk assessment for women. Some authors argue that risk factors for females differ substantially from those for males (Funk, 1999), though there are still not a lot of data to substantiate this claim. As this review has demonstrated, some measures, initially developed for male offenders, appear to be performing well for samples of women. Nonetheless, there is also some evidence that tools developed specifically for women *from the outset* fare even better in terms of predictive accuracy (Blanchette, 2005).

The use of mathematical prediction measures, such as those reviewed, is advocated because there is substantial empirical evidence to suggest that they are superior to clinical prediction in assessing human behaviour (Grove & Meehl, 1996; Grove et al., 2000). It can be argued, however, that their utility diminishes with lower base rates of the outcome measure. Since most studies use predictive accuracy statistics which are base rate dependent, the estimated usefulness of the prediction tool is contingent on the prevalence of the criterion, the selection ratio, or both (Rice & Harris, 1995; Wormith & Goldstone, 1984). This may partially explain why some mechanical risk assessment measures do not perform as well with female offenders.

In keeping with the lower risk for re-offending posed by women, they are more likely to be granted discretionary release than their male counterparts (Motiuk, 1998) and are more likely to be successful upon release (Andrews & Bonta, 1998). Violent recidivism by women is an infrequent occurrence. While the discrepant general recidivism rates preclude any conclusions about the risk that released women present to society, it is clear that they, as a group, represent relatively less risk in comparison to men (Langan & Levin, 2002). This is particularly true given their small numbers and may partially explain why risk classification measures do not perform as well with this group. Although supporting evidence is beginning to accumulate, there is still a lack of conclusive reliability and validity data supporting mechanical risk assessment measures for women. As such, the first tenet of the *risk principle*, which asserts that recidivism can be predicted, is more tenuous when applied to women.

Few would argue that female offenders are a diverse group with respect to risk. Clearly, some women are at higher risk to recidivate than others. However, as the current review has demonstrated, more research is needed to garner confidence in the applicability of existing risk assessment technologies to female offenders. Alternatively, new measures will incorporate empirically derived, gender-specific criteria for women. This is an important point; Shaw and Hannah-Moffat (2000) have argued that "if a classification system, with all its diverse objectives, is based on expectations about the majority population, this may be inappropriate for minority populations with diverse backgrounds and experiences and much greater heterogeneity" (p. 165).

The first step in the development process is to ascertain which particular variables are salient in risk prediction for women. There is reliable evidence that static variables, such as criminal history, early family factors and age are appropriate for consideration in risk prediction paradigms for women (Blanchette, 1996; Loucks & Zamble, 2000; Simourd & Andrews, 1994). However, the evaluation of dynamic variables is also paramount because they drive correctional programming and add considerable predictive power to assessment technologies (Gendreau et al., 1996). As noted earlier, the incremental predictive power of dynamic factors has led to their inclusion in third-generation risk assessment paradigms. However, there is still little consensus regarding which dynamic factors should be incorporated into models of risk assessment for women. Continued research in this area is essential to the provision of appropriate assessment and effective intervention for female offenders.

CONCLUSIONS AND RECOMMENDATIONS

In conclusion, it is noted that this review has perhaps produced more questions than solutions. With respect to risk classification, the literature has demonstrated that mathematical/actuarial approaches are superior to clinical methods (Grove et al., 2000; Grove & Meehl, 1996). Notwithstanding that, the research has fallen somewhat short of identifying an empirically validated classification measure that could be applied reliably and validly for risk management purposes in adult female offender populations. However, the research base is growing and some measures are beginning to show positive results in terms of their psychometric properties.

All of the measures reviewed have been applied (in research and/or practice) to female offenders and they have consistently assessed women as lower risk than their male counterparts. This is notable because some authors have emphatically stressed that the application of 'gender-neutral' tools results in the relative over-classification of women (Bloom & Covington, 2000; Hannah-Moffat & Shaw, 2001). While there is some evidence to support the over-classification argument, it appears to be relegated to the application of *security classification* tools in some US states (Van Voorhis & Presser, 2001).

We must again acknowledge that some have expressed a strong reluctance to endorse the assessment of women for risk management purposes – i.e. the conventional notion of 'risk assessment' (e.g. Bloom, 2000; Hannah-Moffat, 1999). We do not want to be dismissive of the views of our colleagues. However, despite the gender differences noted, we suggest that the rates of institutional misconduct (Blanchette, 2005; Harer & Langan, 2001) and re-offence (Benda, 2005; Langan & Levin, 2002) for women are sufficiently large to warrant assessment for risk management purposes.

The ultimate solution is the development of actuarial measures that are informed by gender and built *from the ground up* for application to women. While some existing measures explicitly incorporate gender as a responsivity consideration (e.g. Andrews et al., 2004), or even a weighted covariate (Copas & Marshall, 1998), we suggest that the best option is one that steps beyond the existing risk technologies. In the absence of mathematical or actuarial tools that are gender-specific, we recommend that the assessment of girls and women be grounded in the best empirical evidence available. Assessors should first consider their reasons for providing the assessment (e.g. security classification, treatment planning, pre-release risk evaluation). If the assessor has opted to use a mechanical or actuarial tool to assist in the assessment process, he or she should be well aware of: (1) the population for which that measure was originally developed, (2) normative, reliability and validity data for the population for which the measure will be applied, (3) additional, gender-specific or other diversity considerations that might not be appropriately assessed within the protocol and (4) his or her ultimate authority to override the scale's recommendation in extraneous circumstances.

Chapter 5

ASSESSING WOMEN'S NEEDS

INTRODUCTION

In the mid-1980s, the term 'correctional afterthoughts' was coined in reference to female offenders (Ross & Fabiano, 1985a). The designation appropriately reflected the lack of research to guide strategies for intervention with this group. As a result, correctional services for both juvenile and adult female offenders were traditionally poorer in quality, variety and availability than those for their male counterparts (Ross & Fabiano, 1985a, 1986). Relative to what is known for male offenders, there is still a dearth of knowledge regarding what constitutes effective corrections for women. Accordingly, some still suggest that correctional interventions are male based and not appropriate for females (Beals, 2004).

As discussed in the previous chapter, assessment of offenders for risk manage-ment purposes routinely includes the application of mathematical or actuarial scales. Current measures, designed to reflect change through iterative assess-ments, have thus incorporated criminogenic needs as weighted scale items (e.g. Andrews et al., 2004). In doing so, the evaluative process provides an assessment of the offender for both treatment planning and predictive purposes (e.g. institutional adjustment, post-release outcome). The multi-purpose assessment thus provides direction in terms of individualized case management; it guides case-specific correctional programming, discretionary release decisions and post-release supervision strategies. This practice is consistent with the need principle which posits that correctional treatment should target those dynamic attributes of the offender that are related to criminal behaviour (i.e. criminogenic needs; Andrews & Bonta, 2003).

However, as with the risk principle, the need principle has been largely empirically validated with samples of male offenders. While few would disagree that correctional intervention should address those (changeable) areas most closely linked to the individual's offending, there is still a lack of consensus regarding whether the same domains should be targeted for intervention for women. Rather, some argue that female offenders have distinct criminogenic needs. Although these are sometimes hailed as 'gender specific', we suggest that a more appropriate nomenclature is 'gender informed'. While we concur that some dynamic factors may be more important treatment targets for females, we suggest that it is simply the base rate or degree of association with outcome that might differ between males and females.

This chapter will review the literature on 'criminogenic needs' as they pertain to female offenders. More specifically, it will examine the prediction of women's recidivism through dynamic risk (needs) assessment. We have opted to review seven broad need areas that correspond with psychological theory (Andrews & Bonta, 2003) and with routine correctional assessment in some jurisdictions (e.g. Motiuk, 1997). Each of these seven broad areas comprises several subcomponents. While we have made an attempt to be as comprehensive as possible, we recognize that there are additional potential criminogenic domains that are not discussed herein. In the absence of methodologically rigorous empirical treatment studies explicitly examining the need principle for females, we have included postdictive research and correlational analyses in this review. We suggest that this is an appropriate first step in discerning whether correctional intervention should target the same areas for women as men, or whether there are additional areas of concern for women.

NEED PRINCIPLE

As discussed, dynamic risk factors are attributes of the offender (or his or her situation) that are changeable, with changes associated with changes in the likelihood of recidivism. As such, dynamic risk factors (also called 'criminogenic needs') are promising targets for correctional intervention (Andrews & Bonta, 1998, 2003). In turn, those areas identified as promising targets for correctional intervention also tend to serve as good predictors of criminal recidivism.

Promising targets for intervention have been identified as: (1) antisocial attitudes and feelings, (2) antisocial associates, (3) poor self-control, self-management and/or problem-solving skills, (4) substance abuse problems, (5) lack of education and/or vocation, (6) lack of familial ties or dysfunctional family relationships and (7) poor use of recreational/leisure time. The general acceptance of these dynamic factors as *criminogenic* is based on a considerable body of research (Andrews et al., 1990, 1995; Andrews & Bonta, 1998; Gendreau et al., 1996; Lösel, 1995; Motiuk, 1997). However, the need principle's applicability to women has been disputed in the correctional literature. Again, the scepticism derives from the fact that the supporting research is based on samples of male offenders (Bloom & Covington, 2000; Hannah-Moffat, 2000; Kempf-Leonard & Sample, 2000; Shaw & Hannah-Moffat, 2000).

In general, it is not the need principle *per se* that has been subject to scrutiny. Rather, the debate is focused on *which* particular needs are 'criminogenic' in nature for women. There is some empirical evidence to suggest that the criminogenic factors associated with male offenders are also relevant to female offenders but their level of importance and the nature of association may differ (Brown & Motiuk, 2005; Dowden & Andrews, 1999; Howden-Windell & Clark, 1999; Simourd & Andrews, 1994). Several authors have suggested that female offenders have additional criminogenic needs, though more research is required to confirm the relationship of these variables to recidivism (Chesney-Lind, 2000; Federally Sentenced Women Program, 1994, cited in Hannah-Moffat, 1997; Jackson & Stearns, 1995; Koons et al., 1997; Leschied, Cummings, VanBrunschot, Cunningham & Saunders, 2000). Dynamic factors that are commonly cited as 'women-specific' criminogenic needs can be generally subsumed in the 'personal/emotional' domain and include low self-esteem, childhood and adulthood personal victimization and self-injury/attempted suicide. The remainder of this chapter will comprise a review of the applicability of the *need principle* for women, focusing explicitly on the aforementioned dynamic factors that have been identified as 'promising treatment targets', plus those areas suggested as 'female-specific' criminogenic needs.

A recent study conducted at the Correctional Service of Canada (Brown & Motiuk, 2005) demonstrated that a variety of dynamic factors, assessed at intake, could reliably predict recidivism in released adult female offenders. All federally sentenced women evaluated through the Offender Intake Assessment (OIA; Motiuk, 1997) process and released before September 2000 were included in the representative sample ($n = 765$). The authors used a three-year fixed follow-up to examine the predictive validity of several dynamic factors assessed through the OIA process: employment/education, marital/family situation, associates, substance abuse, attitudes, community functioning, personal/emotional orientation. Analyses revealed a consistent relationship between overall need level ratings and recidivism rate. As expected, women with higher need level ratings were more likely to recidivate than those with lower need level ratings: this was true for all seven dynamic domains. These findings suggest that the seven dynamic factors assessed at intake can be classified as *criminogenic* needs for women offenders. However, corroborative research in many of these need domains is either conflicting or non-existent.

Employment/Education

It is well established that offender populations have, on average, less education and fewer marketable skills than the general population (Andrews & Bonta, 2003; Harlow, 2003). Almost half of the inmates in Canadian federal facilities (53% of men, 42% of women) have less than grade 10 education (Brown & Motiuk, 2005). While the problem is not as pronounced for provincial inmates, data indicate that still over one-third (34% of men, 35% of women) have less than grade 10 education. This is true for only 19% of adults in the general population in Canada (Finn, Trevethan, Carrière & Kowalski, 1999). Similar data are reported for the US, where about 41% of state and federal prison inmates have only some high school education, compared to about 18% of adults in the general US population.

Employment problems are also prevalent in offender populations and they are more pronounced among women than men. This gender difference remains stable across various offender populations, including newly admitted prisoners (Finn et al., 1999; Motiuk & Blanchette, 2000), and those at various phases of

Table 5.1 Predictor categories created by Gendreau et al. (2000) for meta-analysis of the education/employment domain

1. Employment history: Frequently unemployed, ever fired, unstable work history

2. Employment needs at discharge: No employment plans after release, poor job motivation, employment need

3. Employment status at intake: Unemployed prior to incarceration

4. Financial: Poor financial management, major financial problems, low income

5. Education/employment: LSI–R education/employment domain, academic/vocational

6. School achievement: Fewer years of education, less than grade 12, poor school achievement

7. School maladjustment: Ever suspended/expelled, school discipline problems

conditional release (Dowden & Blanchette, 1998; Motiuk, 1998). Between 64 and 80% of women in Canada are unemployed at the time of admission to a correctional facility.[1] In comparison, only 10% of adults, both male and female, in the general population are unemployed (Finn et al., 1999). As such, treatment programmes targeting education, vocation and work programmes are considered fundamental to correctional rehabilitation.

A meta-analysis[2] of the general adult offender literature suggests that 'social achievement' (comprised mostly of education/employment predictors) is a strong predictor of recidivism (Gendreau et al., 1996). Similarly, a more recent meta-analysis of corrections-based education, vocation and work programmes revealed that programme participants recidivate at lower rates than non-partici-pants (Wilson, Gallagher & MacKenzie, 2000). Additional support comes from an independent study by Gendreau et al. (2000). The authors conducted a meta-analysis with 67 studies, generating 200 effect sizes[3] with recidivism. The overall weighted mean effect was statistically significant, though modest at $Mz+ = 0.13$. However, when the authors reclassified their studies into more specific categories (see Table 5.1), weighted effect sizes for employment history ($Mz+ = 0.18$, $k = 34$ effect sizes) and employment needs at discharge ($Mz+ = 0.19$, $k = 16$) were more impressive.

The link between the employment/education domain and criminal recidivism has led to its inclusion in many mathematical risk assessment paradigms. However, results of the above studies were not disaggregated by gender and the authors acknowledged that the vast majority of the data were derived from samples of male offenders.

---

[1]Data from Finn et al. (1999) indicate that between 43 and 54% of males are unemployed at the time of admission to custody.

[2]A meta-analysis is the statistical aggregation of results derived from many independent studies in order to integrate findings.

[3]The effect size reflects the degree to which the comparison and treatment groups differ on a particular outcome measure. It can range from 0 to 1, with greater effect size suggesting greater treatment effect.

Although there are a few studies examining the relationship between employment/education needs and female offender recidivism, findings from these are inconsistent. Results of studies that provided correlational statistics (Pearson r or Point biserial) for female offenders are provided in Table 5.2.

With a large sample ($n = 441$) of provincially sentenced Canadian women, Rettinger (1998) identified LSI-rated education/employment as an important contributor to the prediction of both general and violent recidivism. Statistically significant results have also been reported for federally sentenced women and adolescent girls (Blanchette & Motiuk, 1995; Simourd & Andrews, 1994). Recent results by Brown and Motiuk (2005) also support Rettinger's findings. As described earlier, the authors included a large sample of federally sentenced women ($n = 765$), assessed at intake and followed up for a fixed period of three years post-release. As shown in Table 5.2, correlational analyses revealed significant associations between women's education level and likelihood of return to prison. Similarly, those assessed as having an unstable employment history were more likely to recidivate. Although statistically significant, the strength of the associations are moderate. However, it is also important to highlight that they represent correlations between recidivism and women's needs *assessed at intake*. Presumably, correctional interventions offered during the course of women's incarceration (e.g. educational, vocational programming) could have mitigated the observed effects.

In contrast, Dowden and Andrews' (1999) meta-analysis of treatment effects revealed that programmes targeting school/work showed a non-significant *negative* correlation with reductions in recidivism. However, these results were based on seven studies and those included in the analysis may have comprised up to 49% males. Notwithstanding that, results reported by Dowden and Andrews (1999) lend support to earlier research, which suggests that the relationship between education/employment factors and recidivism for women warrants further investigation (Bonta et al., 1995).

Using a large representative sample ($n = 136$) of released federal female offenders, Bonta et al. (1995) suggested that employment status was not significantly related to recidivism. However, a chi-square analysis revealed that those women who had 'non-employment sources of income' were significantly more likely to recidivate. Moreover, women who depended on welfare were at higher risk for re-offending than those who did not. An independent study using a small sample of federal female offenders ($n = 66$) showed that women's overall level of employment problems, as rated by the Force Field Analysis (FFA)[4] was strongly associated with a likelihood of returning to custody. However, data from the same sample showed no significant relationship between either level of education or employment status at intake and recidivism (Blanchette, 1996).

Perusal of Table 5.2 suggests that there are no definite answers with respect to whether education/employment is a worthwhile treatment target for female offenders. Perhaps some of the ambiguity comes from the various ways in which researchers define this domain. However, notwithstanding the variety of

---

[4]The FFA assesses and prioritizes offenders' needs through analysis of 15 possible criminogenic factors. Factors are subsequently rank-ordered for correctional intervention.

Table 5.2 Correlations between education/employment predictors and recidivism: female offenders

Source	Sample	Predictor	Follow-up (M years)	Any return (r)	New offence (r)	New violent offence (r)
Rettinger (1998)	441 adult	LSI education/employment	5	—	0.39[***]	0.27[***]
Blanchette and Motiuk (1995)	81 adult	Poor employment history	5	—	0.35[**]	0.37[**]
Brown and Motiuk (2005)	765 adult	Less than grade 10 education	3	0.19[***]	—	—
		Unstable job history		0.25[***]	—	—
Blanchette (1996)	66 adult	Force Field Analysis: employment	2	0.43[***]	0.22	−0.02
		Level of education		−0.22	0.00	0.11
		Employment status at intake		−0.10	−0.12	−0.06
Dowden and Andrews (1999)	7 studies	School/work	Variable	−0.08		
Simourd and Andrews (1994)	34 effect sizes, adolescent girls	Educational difficulties (poor grades, dropout)	Variable	0.24[a]		

Note: [*] $p < 0.05$, [**] $p < 0.01$, [***] $p < 0.001$. Data from Dowden and Andrews (1999) and Simourd and Andrews (1994) are based on meta-analyses; definitions of recidivism vary across studies.
[a]Simourd and Andrews (1994) did not provide statistical probability levels. To avoid duplication, none of the primary studies cited is included in the meta-analyses.

definitions, there is conclusive evidence to indicate that education/employment variables predict recidivism in samples of male offenders (Gendreau et al., 2000). Accordingly, results of Benda's (2005) recent survival analysis study, comparing male ($n = 300$) to female ($n = 300$) boot camp graduates, suggested that job satisfaction and higher education lengthen the time in the community for men more than for women. Taken together, the study results are still equivocal in regards to whether this domain is truly criminogenic for women; more research is warranted.

FAMILY

The family is every individual's first experience with socialization. Not surprisingly, it has been documented that criminal offenders are over-represented among those with a history of significant familial disruption. About one-third of female prisoners are assessed as having considerable problems in this area (Finn et al., 1999; Motiuk, 1997). Studies examining the link between family factors and crime can generally be subsumed into any of five broad categories: family psychopathology, marital relationship, parent–child relations, family structure and birth order, and experiences of interfamilial childhood abuse (Oddone Paolucci, Violato & Schofield, 1998). However, again most of the research is based on samples of male offenders and is therefore not generalizable to women. Moreover, the small number of studies examining the role of family factors in women's recidivism precludes investigation of separate categories such as those listed above.

Even considering the more abundant literature based on male offenders, researchers are 'far from elucidating the causal relationship between family life and adult criminality' (Oddone Paolucci et al., 1998, p. 20). Meta-analyses have suggested that static variables such as family structure and family criminality are relatively weak predictors of recidivism, whereas variables reflecting family process/family rearing practices show more promise (Andrews et al., 1999; Gendreau et al., 1996).

Some authors have suggested that family issues are important treatment targets for female offenders in particular (Austin et al., 1992; Bloom, 2000; Federally Sentenced Women Program, 1994, cited in Hannah-Moffat, 1997). Empirical research has begun to offer some support for this contention, but there are also a few studies challenging it. Results of studies that provided correlational statistics for the marital/family recidivism link for female offenders are provided in Table 5.3.

Based on a review of the literature, Leischied et al. (2000) reported that dysfunctional family processes and family dynamics are instrumental in promoting and maintaining aggressive behaviour in adolescent girls. In their meta-analysis, Dowden and Andrews (1999) found that programmes treating family process issues ($n = 9$ studies) yielded the strongest reductions in re-offending for samples of women. More recent results, including a few more studies ($n = 12$), confirmed that programmes targeting family relationships for female offenders yielded the greatest treatment effects (Dowden, 2005). Similarly, Simourd and

Table 5.3 Correlations between marital/family predictors and recidivism: female offenders

Source	Sample	Predictor	Follow-up (M years)	Any return (r)	New offence (r)	New violent offence (r)
Rettinger (1998)	441 adult	LSI marital/family	5	—	0.22***	0.18***
Blanchette and Motiuk (1995)	81 adult	Feelings towards mother	5	—	0.31*	—
		Feelings towards father		—	—	0.27*
		Dissatisfied with childhood		—	0.39**	—
Brown and Motiuk (2005)	765 adult	Childhood lacked family ties	3	0.12**	—	—
		Parents' relationship dysfunctional (childhood)		0.11**	—	—
		Family unable to get along as a unit		0.18**	—	—
Blanchette (1996)	66 adult	Force Field Analysis: marital/family	2	0.15	0.11	0.07
		Married at time of offence		0.10	−0.10	−0.04
Dowden (2005)	12 studies	Family relationships	Variable	0.33*		
Dowden and Andrews (1999)	9 studies	Family process (affection, supervision)	Variable	0.51***		
Simourd and Andrews (1994)	41 effect sizes, adolescent girls	Poor parent/child relationship (attachment, supervision)	Variable	0.20[a]		
	17 effect sizes, adolescent girls	Family structure/parental problems (broken home, marital problems)		0.07[a]		

Note: * $p < 0.05$, ** $p < 0.01$, *** $p < 0.001$. Data from Dowden (2005), Dowden and Andrews (1999), and Simourd and Andrews (1994) are based on meta-analyses; definitions of recidivism vary across studies.
[a]Simourd and Andrews (1994) and Dowden (2005) did not provide statistical probability levels. To avoid duplication, none of the primary studies cited is included in the meta-analyses.

Andrews (1994) reported that a poor parent–child relationship (attachment and supervision) was a moderate correlate of offending behaviour among female youths. However, the same authors noted no significant association between family structure or parental problems and criminality.

Farrington and Painter (2004) conducted a prospective longitudinal survey of boys from age 8 to 48 and analysed crime data for their brothers ($n = 494$) and sisters ($n = 519$) to compare risk factors for offending in boys versus girls. The authors argued that the comparison between family members helps to control the potential differential impact of extraneous variables (e.g. neighbourhood, community) because they are held constant. Although results suggested that some family variables (large family size, convicted mother, convicted father, delinquent sibling, parental conflict) were very important risk factors for both genders, others were particularly salient for girls. These included: low parental interest in child, low praise, poor parental supervision, and harsh or erratic parental discipline.

In one of the few studies looking at parenting variables as criminogenic needs for adult women, Bonta et al. (1995) reported that while having dependents was not associated with post-release outcome, single parents showed significantly higher recidivism rates than those with partners. Rettinger's (1998) research results confirmed that parenthood was not predictive of recidivism and, although contrary to findings by Bonta et al., the data also showed no association between single parenthood and post-release outcome. Results of Rettinger's study did suggest, however, that family or marital conflict was predictive of violent recidivism. In contrast, Loucks and Zamble (2000) reported that family cohesiveness did not contribute to the prediction of recidivism in their sample of federal female offenders. Perhaps the magnitude of the relationship depends upon the nature of the family conflict. For instance, Blanchette and Motiuk (1995) found that both dissatisfaction with childhood and negative feelings towards mother were predictive of re-convictions. Interestingly, it was the women's feelings towards their father that predicted violent recidivism.

Data from a large sample ($n = 765$) of federally sentenced women suggest that their overall level of need in the marital/family domain is predictive of re-admission to federal custody within the three-year post-release follow-up (Brown & Motiuk, 2005). Meta-analytic research with both adult women and adolescent girls has demonstrated that family process variables, such as attachment, affection and supervision, are robust predictors of recidivism (Dowden & Andrews, 1999; Simourd & Andrews, 1994). These findings were confirmed in later work by Farrington and Painter (2004; reviewed above) and again recently by Benda (2005). Specifically, Benda found that while job satisfaction and higher education lengthen the time in the community for male offenders, for women it is the number of children and supportive family relationships that are more important for post-release community tenure. Similar results were found by Blanchette (2005) in her examination of the predictors of institutional security level and institutional misconduct. While family factors were not strong predictors for adult male offenders, prosocial family support was among the best predictors of positive institutional adjustment for women.

In sum, while there is some disagreement between research findings, the greater evidence suggests that family issues present a valuable treatment target for girls and women. These findings support theories of criminal behaviour that emphasize gender differences in the life course trajectories of offending (Sampson & Laub, 1993), as well as those that suggest that relationships (e.g. with parents, children, marital partner) are especially important for girls and women (Bloom et al., 2003, 2005; Covington, 1998).

ASSOCIATES

The dynamic factor of antisocial associates is routinely hailed as among the most potent predictors of recidivism, and is therefore recommended as a priority treatment target (Andrews & Bonta, 2003; Andrews et al., 1990b, 1999; Gendreau et al., 1996, 1998). The well-established criminogenic nature of 'antisocial associates' has led to its inclusion in most third-generation risk classification paradigms.

Research findings suggest that approximately 27% of men and about 20% of women inmates are assessed as having significant treatment needs in this area (Boe, Nafekh, Vuong, Sinclair & Cousineau, 2003; Finn et al., 1999). Although the majority of the evidence is based on samples of male offenders, research with female offenders has also offered consistent results: antisocial/procriminal associates represents an important criminogenic need domain for women. Results of studies that have provided correlational statistics for the relationship between antisocial associates and recidivism for female offenders are provided in Table 5.4.

Based on a sample of 81 released federally sentenced women, Blanchette and Motiuk (1995) demonstrated that 'criminal associates' was a powerful predictor of both new convictions and new violent convictions. Rettinger (1998) replicated those results with a larger sample ($n = 441$) of provincially sentenced women. Similarly, data from a three-year fixed follow-up of 765 female offenders revealed that global assessments of women's needs in the 'associates' domain (assessed at intake) were reliably correlated with re-admission to federal custody (Brown & Motiuk, 2005). Moreover, it merits highlighting, once again, that correlations between needs assessed at intake and post-release outcome might be mitigated by intervention offered during the course of incarceration. Earlier research with a small independent sample ($n = 66$) of adult women offenders produced similar findings. Specifically, the 'companions' component of FFA was highly predictive of new offences (Blanchette, 1996). While the relationship between FFA 'companions' and a broader definition of recidivism (any return) was not reliable, the magnitude of the association ($r = 0.27$) suggests that a larger sample may have yielded statistically significant results.

Meta-analytic research has confirmed the results of independent primary studies. Dowden and Andrews (1999) reported a strong positive association between correctional programming in the area of 'associates' and reduced reoffending for studies with 'predominantly' or entirely female samples. Similarly, Simourd and Andrews (1994) noted that a composite of antisocial peers/attitudes

Table 5.4 Correlations between associates predictors and recidivism: female offenders

Source	Sample	Predictor	Follow-up (M years)	Any return (r)	New offence (r)	New violent offence (r)
Rettinger (1998)	441 adult	LSI companions	5	—	0.43***	0.30***
Blanchette and Motiuk (1995)	81 adult	Criminal associates	5	—	0.37**	0.35**
Brown and Motiuk (2005)	765 adult	Has many criminal acquaintances	3	0.23**	—	—
		Has mostly criminal friends		0.28**	—	—
Blanchette (1996)	66 adult	Force Field Analysis: Companions	2	0.27	0.41**	0.11
Dowden and Andrews (1999)	9 studies	Antisocial associates	Variable	0.45**		
Simourd and Andrews (1994)	53 effect sizes, adolescent girls	Antisocial peers or attitudes	Variable	0.39[a]		

Note: * $p < 0.05$, ** $p < 0.01$, *** $p < 0.001$. Data from Dowden and Andrews (1999) and Simourd and Andrews (1994) are based on meta-analyses; definitions of recidivism vary across studies.
[a]Simourd and Andrews (1994) did not provide statistical probability levels. To avoid duplication, none of the primary studies cited is included in the meta-analyses.

comprised the greatest risk factor for adolescent girls. Benda's (2005) longitudinal study of boot camp graduates also suggested that 'criminal peers' was a strong predictor of recidivism for both men and women. Of note, however, was the finding that the 'criminal peer' variable was more predictive of recidivism for men and that (positive) friendships and partner relations were both more predictive of desistence for women. This suggests that these variables might also serve as protective factors for women in particular.

ATTITUDES

In general, antisocial attitudes encompass such things as endorsement of criminally oriented norms, identification with criminal others, tolerance, justification and/or rationalization of law violations and pride in the commission of criminal acts. Like antisocial associates, antisocial attitudes are considered among the most valuable treatment targets to reduce recidivism in offender populations (Andrews & Bonta, 2003; Andrews et al., 1990b, 1999).

Relative to their male counterparts, significantly fewer women are assessed as having considerable attitude problems requiring intervention (Boe et al., 2003). More specifically, while over 30% of male inmates are assessed as having significant attitude problems, this is true for only about 14% of female inmates (Boe et al., 2003; Finn et al., 1999). Although prevalence rates are low, there is preliminary evidence to suggest that the evaluation of antisocial attitudes is an important component for assessment of dynamic risk for women. For instance, research evidence has demonstrated a clear linear relationship between women inmates' antisocial attitudes and their security level (Blanchette, 1997a), as well as their involvement in institutional misconduct (Blanchette, 2005; Walters & Elliott, 1999). Similarly, one retrospective study showed that women with higher scores on assessments of criminal thinking styles had more prior arrests (Walters, Elliott & Miscoll, 1998).

Despite being recognized as one of the most promising treatment targets in correctional populations, there is relatively little research examining the relationship between antisocial attitudes and recidivism in female offenders. Results of prediction studies that provided correlational statistics for the association between antisocial attitudes and recidivism for female offenders are located in Table 5.5.

Rettinger's (1998) research revealed a strong positive correlation between the LSI 'Attitudes/Orientation' subscale and new criminal convictions for her sample of provincially-sentenced women. Moreover, women's antisocial attitudes were also predictive of violent recidivism. Similarly, Blanchette (1996) noted a moderately strong association between women's values/attitudes and their likelihood of general re-offending, while Brown and Motiuk (2005) found that those assessed as having negative attitudes towards the law, police or corrections at intake were more likely to be re-admitted to custody in the three-year follow-up.

Walters and Elliott (1999) also published moderate correlations between women's thinking styles (a good proximal measure for attitudes) and release outcome. The authors used the Psychological Inventory of Criminal Thinking

Table 5.5 Correlations between attitude predictors and recidivism: female offenders

Source	Sample	Predictor	Follow-up (M years)	Any return (r)	New offence (r)	New violent offence (r)
Rettinger (1998)	441 adult	LSI attitudes/orientation	5	—	0.45***	0.38***
Blanchette (1996)	66 adult	Force Field Analysis: Values/Attitudes	2	0.21	0.30*	0.12
Brown and Motiuk (2005)	765 adult	Negative attitude towards the law	3	0.18**	—	—
		Negative attitude towards police		0.12**	—	—
		Negative attitude towards courts		0.07	—	—
		Negative attitude towards corrections		0.11**	—	—
Walters and Elliott (1999)	118 adult	PICTS: Mollification scale	3	0.17*	—	—
		Cutoff scale		0.16*	—	—
		Entitlement scale		0.20*	—	—
		Power orientation scale		0.13	—	—
		Sentimentality subscale		0.38***	—	—
		Superoptimism scale		0.10	—	—
		Cognitive indolence scale		0.19*	—	—
		Discontinuity scale		0.20*	—	—
Dowden and Andrews (1999)	5 studies	Antisocial cognition	Variable	0.36*		
Simourd and Andrews (1994)	53 effect sizes, adolescent girls	Antisocial peers or attitudes	Variable	0.39[a]		

Note: * $p < 0.05$, ** $p < 0.01$, *** $p < 0.001$. Data from Dowden and Andrews (1999) and Simourd and Andrews (1994) are based on meta-analyses; definitions of recidivism vary across studies.
[a] Simourd and Andrews (1994) did not provide statistical probability levels. To avoid duplication, none of the primary studies cited is included in the meta-analyses.

Styles (PICTS; Walters, 1995) to assess antisocial cognitions in 118 female state prison inmates. In brief, the PICTS contains eight scales to assess cognitions which are theorized to contribute to the formation and continuation of criminal behaviour (Walters, 1995).[5] The author describes the eight PICTS scales as follows:

> The first thinking pattern, *mollification*, is observed when a person justifies and rationalizes his or her norm-violating behaviour by focusing on social injustice, minimizes the seriousness of specific antisocial acts, or projects blame onto the victims of his or her crimes. The *cutoff* style entails a rapid elimination of fear, anxiety and other psychological deterrents to criminal action, whereas the *entitlement* style exudes an attitude of ownership, privilege and misidentification of wants as needs. The criminal lifestyle also gives rise to a *power orientation*, wherein the subject engages in outward displays of aggression designed to control and manipulate others. Self-centred attempts to atone for one's past criminal violations by performing various good deeds come under the heading of the *sentimentality* styles, whereas overestimating one's chances of avoiding the negative consequences of a criminal lifestyle represents the *superoptimism* pattern. The *cognitive indolence* style reflects an inclination toward lazy thinking, short-cut problem solving and uncritical acceptance of personal ideas and plans. The *discontinuity* style, although related to cognitive indolence, presumes less premeditation and greater disruption of thought processes, the consequence of which is a person who has trouble following through on initially good intentions because of inadequate self-discipline. (p. 309)

Results of Walters and Elliott's (1999) study indicated that six of the eight PICTS thinking styles were predictive of recidivism for their sample of 118 female offenders (see Table 5.5). The average correlation, across the eight scales, was $r = 0.19$. The Sentimentality scale was a particularly robust predictor, remaining statistically significant even after the authors used the Bonferroni correction for multiple comparisons ($\alpha = 0.05/8 = 0.0062$). These results suggest that sentimentality, as assessed by the PICTS, is a poor prognostic sign for women released from prison. Walters and Elliott assert that, since sentimentality represents efforts to deny the reality of one's criminal behaviour, it may reflect a general unwillingness or inability to honestly evaluate one's actions, goals and beliefs. In turn, the authors argue that insight and self-evaluation skills are essential preconditions for long-term change (Ross & Fabiano, 1985b, cited in Walters & Elliott, 1999).

For their meta-analytic assessment of treatment effectiveness, Dowden and Andrews (1999) created a composite dynamic category labelled 'antisocial cognition'. The composite comprised treatments targeting: antisocial attitudes, values, beliefs and rationalizations, anger and resentment (see Andrews et al., 1999). Still, due to the lack of primary studies with female (or predominantly female) samples, the 'antisocial cognition' category included only five effect sizes. While results can only be considered preliminary, they suggest that antisocial

---

[5]Research has demonstrated that, when used with female offenders, the PICTS shows good internal consistency, test–retest reliability, and concurrent validity. Moreover, the PICTS maintains a comparable factor structure for men and women (Walters et al., 1998).

attitudes comprise a valuable treatment target for female offenders. Simourd and Andrews (1994) reported similar results in their meta-analysis of the predictors of recidivism for adolescent girls. Based on the results of their study, the authors suggested that their composite category of antisocial attitudes and peers as the most important risk factor for female youths.

It is apparent from this review that the dynamic factor of 'antisocial attitudes' holds considerable promise for practitioners working with female offenders, both in terms of prediction and treatment. Prospective research will more conclusively establish the utility of this factor with respect to treatment for female offenders; it will be important to establish a firmer causal link between treatment and decreased risk in this area.

SUBSTANCE ABUSE

The relationship between substance abuse and criminal activity is well documented: about two-thirds of offenders experience substance abuse problems to some extent (Boland, Henderson & Baker, 1998). Between 40 and 60% of adult female offenders are assessed as having significant substance abuse problems (Boe et al., 2003; Finn et al., 1999). Moreover, substance abuse appears to play an integral role in criminal offending for many women in the criminal justice system. A study by Lightfoot and Lambert (1992) revealed that about 60% of their sample of women said that they had used alcohol or drugs on the day of their offence and the majority of those said that their substance use had seriously impaired their judgment.

A review by Weekes, Moser and Langevin (1998; cited in Dowden & Brown, 2002) concluded that there is a consistent positive association between substance abuse and various forms of general and violent criminal activity. This conclusion supports results of other studies and theoretical arguments which maintain that substance abuse is a criminogenic need (Andrews & Bonta, 2003; Andrews et al., 1990b; Gendreau et al., 1996). Again, most of this research is based on samples of male offenders. While there is mounting evidence to suggest that substance abuse is also a valuable treatment target for female offenders, there is still some discrepancy in the literature.

Based on results of a large sample retrospective study with adult inmates (1030 male and 500 female), McClellan, Farabee and Crouch (1997) reported that substance abuse problems were more strongly associated with criminal activity for females than for males. Severity of substance abuse, as assessed by a number of DSM-III-R criteria for dependence, was very highly correlated with self-reported property crime for both women ($r = 0.39$, $p < 0.0001$) and men ($r = 0.28$, $p < 0.0001$), though its association with the criterion was stronger for women. With respect to recidivism, Dowden and Blanchette (1998) noted that female parolees with a history of substance abuse are at greater risk for returning to custody than those with no substance abuse problems.

Results of predictive investigations examining the relationship between substance abuse and recidivism for female offenders have demonstrated, for the most part, a significant positive relationship between various measures of substance abuse and recidivism. Data from research studies that provided correlational statistics are provided in Table 5.6.

Using the LSI to rate alcohol/drug problems in provincially sentenced female offenders, Rettinger (1998) found that substance abuse was highly predictive of both general and violent recidivism. Similar results have been noted for federally sentenced women. As shown in Table 5.6, results of the recent study by Brown and Motiuk (2005) suggest that women's assessed level of substance abuse problem is predictive of returning to custody within the three-years fixed follow-up. Moreover, their results suggest that drug abuse is a better predictor for women than alcohol abuse. Independent studies of treatment effectiveness support these results, indicating that treated female substance abusers are less likely to re-offend than their untreated counterparts (Dowden & Blanchette, 1999; Prendergast, Wellisch & Wong, 1996; Wexler, Falkin & Lipton, 1990).

Although most of the relevant research identifies substance abuse as a criminogenic need for women, there are still studies to negate that position. For instance, Bonta and colleagues (1995) found that substance abuse was not predictive of post-release outcome for their sample of federal female offenders. Similarly, data presented by Loucks and Zamble (2000) suggested that, although drug abuse was highly correlated with criminal history, neither alcohol nor drug abuse was an important predictor of re-offending for women. Notably, however, neither of these studies controlled for treatment effects or supervision on reducing recidivism for substance abusers. This is an important consideration because, as mentioned, researchers have demonstrated that untreated female substance abusers recidivate at a significantly higher rate than their treated counterparts. With post-hoc analyses, Dowden and Blanchette (1999) showed that these results could not be attributed to group differences in overall risk level, as groups were equivalent with respect to pre-release risk. Moreover, recidivism rates for women who were treated for substance abuse problems approximated those of women who were assessed as having no treatment needs in this area.

Results of Dowden and Andrews' (1999) research are contradictory. Their meta-analytic review of five treatment studies produced an average effect size of −0.01, which suggests that substance abuse is not a valuable treatment target for female offenders. However, the research methodology integrated studies comparing treated female substance abusers to other female offenders who did not receive substance abuse treatment. Importantly, this latter group most probably comprised primarily women with no substance abuse problems. Study results have shown that female substance abusers are markedly higher risk than non-abusers ($p < 0.001$; Dowden & Blanchette, 1999). As such, it is suggested that a more meaningful analysis would compare treated substance abusers to their untreated counterparts on measures of post-release outcome.

Dowden and Brown (2002) recently produced a comprehensive meta-analysis examining the role of substance abuse in predicting criminal recidivism. In their review of the literature, the authors noted five common predictor categories in the 'substance abuse' domain and classified their data accordingly. Categories included: (1) alcohol abuse problem, (2) drug abuse problem, (3) alcohol/drug problem, (4) past or present substance abuse charge and (5) parental substance abuse.

Table 5.6 Correlations between substance abuse predictors and recidivism: female offenders

Source	Sample	Predictor	Follow-up (M years)	Any return (r)	New offence (r)	New violent offence (r)
Rettinger (1998)	441 adult	LSI alcohol/drug problem	5	—	0.44***	0.30***
Brown and Motiuk (2005)	765 adult	Alcohol abuse	5	0.21**	—	—
		Drug abuse		0.34**	—	—
Dowden and Brown (2002)	6 effect sizes	Alcohol abuse problem	Variable	0.07		
	7 effect sizes	Drug abuse problem		0.19*		
	4 effect sizes	Past or present substance abuse charge		−0.13*		
	6 effect sizes	Parental substance abuse		0.20*		
	23 effect sizes	Total (composite of above categories)		0.14*		
Dowden and Andrews (1999)	5 studies	Substance Abuse	Variable	−0.01		

Note: * $p < 0.05$, ** $p < 0.01$, *** $p < 0.001$. Data from Dowden and Brown (2002) are based on a meta-analysis; definitions of recidivism vary across studies. Data from Dowden and Brown (2002) represent *weighted* effect sizes. To avoid duplication, none of the primary studies cited is included in the meta-analysis. Some primary studies included in Dowden and Andrews (1999) were also included in Dowden and Brown (2002). Both are tabled because the former is a treatment study, the latter a prediction study.

For inclusion in Dowden and Brown's meta-analysis, studies met the following criteria: (1) substance abuse factors were assessed prior to recidivism, (2) sufficient statistical information was available such that the reported statistic could be converted into an effect size estimate and (3) recidivism was defined in a dichotomous manner (i.e. studies providing only 'more' versus 'less' dispositions were excluded). Using these criteria, 45 studies were included, producing 116 individual effect sizes with general recidivism. While the majority of the effect sizes were based on studies of male offenders, 20% were derived exclusively from female offender samples ($n = 23$ effect sizes).

With the exception of the combined alcohol/drug category, the authors disaggregated the results by gender.[6] As shown in Table 5.6, the average weighted effect sizes varied considerably by category. The results revealed a significant negative correlation between substance-related charges and general recidivism. Consistent with the findings by Brown and Motiuk (2005), relative to alcohol abuse, drug abuse problems were more highly associated with recidivism. Overall, Dowden and Brown noted that the findings for studies with female offenders paralleled those found for males. Interestingly, the one predictor category to yield a significant between-group difference was 'parental substance abuser'. Specifically, the weighted mean effect size for men ($Mz+ = 0.09$) was significantly smaller than that for women ($Mz+ = 0.20$). This suggests that the impact of parental alcohol and drug use may be more profound for females than for males, which is consistent with research findings cited earlier with respect to the influence of dysfunctional family dynamics on criminality/recidivism for girls and women.

Dowden and Brown reported an overall weighted mean effect size, across all four categories, of $Mz+ = 0.14$. This suggests that substance abuse is a moderate predictor of recidivism for female offenders and is still somewhat conservative given that 'past or present substance abuse charge', yielding a significant negative effect, was included in the composite. Notably, this is somewhat higher than the overall effect found for male offenders ($Mz+ = 0.10$) and supports earlier research by McClellan et al. (1997).

Taken together, the research suggests that substance abuse is a meaningful treatment target for female offenders, particularly for those with drug abuse problems. It is important to highlight, however, that substance abuse is a complex need area. As suggested by the results of Dowden and Brown's meta-analysis, researchers should be very specific with respect to their operational definitions in this area. Moreover, classification and programming efforts should be similarly precise.

Blanchette (1996) found that varying the definition/method of measurement for 'substance abuse problem' affected the study results accordingly. Specifically, with a sample of 66 adult female offenders, analyses revealed that DSM–III diagnostic criteria for substance abuse disorder was not predictive of recidivism. However, when the variable was redefined according to whether or not the offender had consumed alcohol/drugs prior to the commission of her original

---

[6]Results for the combined alcohol/drug abuse category were not disaggregated by gender because there were not enough effect sizes (<3) for meaningful analysis for women.

offence, 'substance abuse' *was* predictive of recidivism. This suggests that, of female offenders who could be classified as 'substance abusers', there is a subset for whom the need is criminogenic. For other female offenders, their substance abuse problems do not necessarily represent a need that is *criminogenic* in nature.

In general, substance abusers present with a multitude of collateral problems. As noted earlier, a study by Dowden and Blanchette (1999) revealed that, at least among federally sentenced women, substance abusers are significantly higher in static risk than non-abusers. Moreover, their study results showed that women with substance abuse problems tend to have more difficulties in several other areas as well. Specifically, women with substance abuse problems were also more likely to be assessed as requiring intervention in the domains of employment, marital/family relations, associates and attitudes. This highlights the fact that women's substance abuse problems are not one-dimensional and interact with a number of other need areas to produce varying recidivism rates. While some authors have suggested that substance abuse serves to exacerbate problems in other areas of women's lives (Lightfoot & Lambert, 1992; Shaw et al., 1991), there is also a good possibility that women with multiple needs resort to substance abuse as a means of coping.

It is apparent from this review that substance abuse is a multi-faceted problem for female offenders. While the prediction literature generally suggests that substance abuse is an effective predictor of post-release outcome for women, results of treatment outcome studies are less clear. It seems likely that the complex interplay between substance abuse and several other need areas produces increased recidivism rates for female substance abusers. This highlights the importance of controlling for static and dynamic risk in treatment outcome research.

Currently, it is clear that substance abuse problems are prominent in the female offender population. Additionally, women who are substance abusers are rated as higher in static risk compared to non-abusers. Finally, female substance abusers tend to have more needs than non-abusers in seemingly unrelated areas as well. Collectively, these findings provide direction for appropriate treatment for women, as will be discussed in the following chapter.

COMMUNITY FUNCTIONING

The assessment of an offender's 'community functioning' is a composite of constructs that are used to evaluate his or her living situation outside of prison. Measures of community functioning include components such as leisure (e.g. hobbies, community activities), accommodation, finance, support (e.g. use of social services), self-care (e.g. hygiene, self-presentation), and health. Less than 15% of female inmates are assessed as having significant problems in this area (Boe et al., 2003; Finn et al., 1999).

According to the results of a meta-analysis by Gates et al. (1998), the research support for 'community functioning' as a predictor of recidivism is only weak to moderate. The authors identified 20 predictive studies that yielded 79 effect sizes pertaining to community functioning variables. An overall weighted mean effect size of $Mz+ = 0.10$ was obtained. While the majority of the effects were based on studies of males, the second author disaggregated the data by gender and found 12 effect sizes in studies of exclusively female offenders. The weighted mean effect size of 'community functioning' variables for women was $Mz+ = 0.09$, suggesting that 'community functioning', at least in a broad sense, is not a promising treatment target for women (C. Dowden, 15 August 2000, personal communication).

Only one published study has examined the association between the composite 'community functioning' category (including all elements listed previously) and recidivism for female offenders (Brown & Motiuk, 2005). Upon admission to a Canadian federal correctional facility, each of the women included in the study ($n = 765$) was assessed in the broad 'community functioning' domain along a four-point rating scale (ranging from 'asset to community adjustment' to 'considerable need for intervention'). Upon release, all women were followed up for a fixed three-year period. Results indicated that those women assessed as requiring considerable intervention were significantly more likely to return to custody (54%) than those assessed positively in this domain (17% re-admission).

A number of additional studies have examined particular components of the broad community functioning domain in relation to female offender recidivism. Results of these are provided in Table 5.7.

While there is little conclusive evidence that the composite category of 'community functioning' holds predictive value for women, there is a some evidence that particular subcomponents of this domain might be valuable predictors. Examination of Table 5.7 demonstrates that the predictive value of subcomponents varies considerably, as correlations with new offences range from −0.03 (health) to +0.41 (financial problems prior to offence).

Results of analyses looking at the 'financial' subcomponent have been somewhat mixed, though examination of the collective evidence in this area yields a very interesting picture that signals a call to action: this area might be particularly important for women. Rettinger's (1998) data suggested that LSI-rated financial problems were predictive of new offending, but not new violent offences. Recently, Brown and Motiuk (2005) reported a significant association between women's financial problems (no bank account(s), reliance on social assistance, unemployment/employment instability) and their likelihood of returning to custody after release from prison. These results support earlier research reporting that pre-admission financial problems were predictive of returning to custody and of new offences for women (Blanchette, 1996). Similarly, one study showed that a poor history of self-support was highly predictive of both recidivism (new offences) and violent recidivism (Blanchette & Motiuk, 1995).

Farrington and Painter's (2004) longitudinal study of almost 400 families revealed that socio-economic risk factors such as low social class, low family income, poor housing and large family size were among the best predictors of criminal offending for girls. Moreover, these variables predicted offending more strongly for girls than for boys. Recent Canadian research yielded similar results, suggesting that parental economic dependence (poverty) has a significantly greater impact on the incidence of female delinquency in mid-adolescence,

Table 5.7 Correlations between community functioning predictors and recidivism: female offenders

Source	Sample	Predictor	Follow-up (M years)	Any return (r)	New offence (r)	New violent offence (r)
Gates et al. (1998)	12 effect sizes	Community functioning (composite)	Variable	0.09	—	—
Brown and Motiuk (2005)	765 adult	Unstable accommodation	3	0.19**	—	—
		No bank account(s)		0.17**	—	—
		Has used social assistance		0.15**	—	—
Rettinger (1998)	441 adult	LSI accommodation	5	—	—	0.22***
		LSI financial		—	0.13**	0.02
Blanchette (1996)	66 adult	Force Field Analysis: Financial management	2	0.18	0.25	0.21
		Force Field Analysis: Health		0.16	-0.03	0.23
		Financial problems in year prior to offence		0.34*	0.41*	0.00
		Relied on social assistance in year prior to offence		0.12	-0.02	0.05
Blanchette and Motiuk (1995)	81 adult	Poor history of self-support	5	—	0.28*	0.40**

Note: * $p < 0.05$, ** $p < 0.01$, *** $p < 0.001$. Data from Gates et al. (1998) are based on a meta-analysis; definitions of recidivism vary across studies. The second author provided data for women from the dataset of Gates et al. (1998). To avoid duplication, none of the primary studies cited is included in the meta-analysis.

relative to that of males. This was particularly true for violent delinquent acts (Bélanger, Lanctôt & Leblanc, 2005; Lanctôt & Leblanc, 2005). Finally, Holtfreter et al. (2004) provided very compelling evidence to suggest that poverty is particularly salient in the prediction of recidivism for women. Using a community corrections sample of 134 female felony offenders from one US state, the authors examined factors associated with self-reported re-arrest and probation or parole violations over a six-month period. Results revealed that poverty status increased the odds of re-arrest by a factor of 4.6 and that of supervision violation by a factor of 12.7. Examination of the bivariate distributions indicated that 27 of the 30 women (90%) who were re-arrested were living in poverty (as per Census Bureau guidelines).

Collectively, these findings lend support to theories of women's crime that emphasize resource scarcity and survival strategies as central tenets. Notably, and perhaps surprisingly, comprised therein are both evolutionary (Campbell, 2002) and feminist pathways perspectives (Bloom et al., 2004).

Overall, the results indicate that some components of the 'community functioning' dimension are good potential predictors of recidivism for female offenders. However, replication studies are warranted before firm conclusions can be drawn. Importantly, published studies examining the effects of treatment programmes targeting 'community functioning' (or any of its components) for female offenders are currently non-existent. While programmes targeting vocational skills might help to address the poverty issue, we note a weaker association between women's employment histories and recidivism. This suggests that there are broader social factors at play.

PERSONAL/EMOTIONAL

The personal/emotional domain of offender assessment protocols represents an aggregate of needs that cover a broad range of personal attributes that could be targeted for correctional intervention. Need areas that are commonly assessed in this domain include: self-concept, cognitive problems (e.g. impulsivity, poor problem-solving, lack of empathy), behavioural problems (e.g. hostility, assertion, neuroticism), mental ability and mental health. A significant proportion (over 60%) of adult female offenders is assessed as having considerable needs in this area (Boe et al., 2003).

Similar to the variety of constructs assessed under the auspice of 'community functioning', the research indicates varying levels of support for the 'personal/ emotional' domain as a promising treatment target for offender populations, dependent on the specific need(s) assessed. For example, Andrews and colleagues (1986) demonstrated that 8 out of 10 specific 'emotional/personal' variables predicted recidivism among provincial probationers at statistically significant levels (range $r = 0.15$ to $r = 0.31$). Similarly, Motiuk and Brown (1993) reported that about half (6 of 11) of the items within the Community Risk Needs Management Scale (CRNMS) 'personal/emotional' domain predicted suspension within six months for their sample of ($n = 573$) male offenders. Gendreau and colleagues (1996) found that a composite category called 'personal distress' was a relatively weak predictor of recidivism in their meta-analysis $(Mz+ = 0.05)$. Notably, 24 of the 66 effect sizes within the composite category tapped psychiatric symptomatology such as psychosis and/or prior psychiatric history. Separate analyses with this subset revealed no correlation $(r = 0.00)$ with recidivism (Gendreau et al., 1996).

With their large sample of 765 released federal female offenders, Brown and Motiuk (2005) demonstrated good predictive accuracy for a global measure of personal/emotional problems assessed at intake. Within the three-year post-release follow-up, about 20% of those women assessed as having 'no difficulty' in this domain returned to custody, compared to 31% of women assessed as having 'some' difficulty and 41% of women assessed as having 'considerable' difficulty. There was thus a clear linear relationship between degree of assessed need and likelihood or recidivism; chi-square analyses revealed that between-group differences were statistically significant $(p < 0.001)$.

Although studies looking at the personal/emotional domain as a composite risk predictor are generally positive, research looking at individual variables within the aggregate is less consistent. As with other need areas, there is limited research examining the predictive accuracy of variables within the 'personal/emotional' composite using female offender samples. Moreover, relevant studies on the impact of treatment-related change for females are even scarcer. Research results from pertinent female offender studies providing correlational outcome data are presented in Table 5.8.

Based on their meta-analysis, Dowden and Andrews (1999) argued that programmes targeting antisocial cognition and skill deficits in women $(n = 8$ studies) reduced recidivism, on average, by 32%. Similarly, as noted earlier, a measure of antisocial thinking – the Psychological Inventory of Criminal Thinking Styles (PICTS) – was found to be moderately successful in predicting institutional adjustment and post-release outcome for female offenders (Walters & Elliott, 1999). As indicated in Table 5.8, correlations between diverse predictors under the 'personal/emotional' rubric and recidivism were quite strong. Moreover, it appears that the best predictors in this area include such factors as thrill-seeking, impulsivity, low frustration tolerance and disregard for others/lack of empathy. Notably, these areas are also highly valued treatment targets within male offender populations (Andrews & Bonta, 2003).

A comprehensive review of the literature pertaining to the predictive utility of the 'personal/emotional' domain (and its components) further suggests that the predictive subcomponents for females are similar to those for males (Robinson et al. 1998). In particular, the review by Robinson and colleagues supported particular variables (such as lack of self-control, problem-solving deficits) as predictive and did not support others (e.g. mental ability, mental health problems). Similarly, the female-specific data in Table 5.8 also suggest that personal distress, mental ability and mental health variables are not strongly associated with women's likelihood of recidivism. In particular, Motiuk and Brown (1993) reported an insignificant association $(r = 0.08)$ between 'low mental functioning' and parole suspensions within six months for male offenders. The meta-analysis by Gendreau and colleagues (1996) similarly showed only a weak weighted effect $(Mz+ = 0.07)$ for the predictor domain labelled 'intellectual functioning' $(n = 32$

Table 5.8 Correlations between personal/emotional predictors and recidivism: female offenders

Source	Sample	Predictor	Follow-up (M years)	Any return (r)	New offence (r)	New violent offence (r)
Brown and Motiuk (2005)	765 adults	Difficulty solving interpersonal problems	3	0.13***	—	—
		Disregard for others		0.15***	—	—
		Impulsive		0.18***	—	—
		Lacks empathy		0.10	—	—
		Aggressive		0.16***	—	—
		Copes poorly with stress		0.22***	—	—
		Low frustration tolerance		0.24***	—	—
		Thrill seeking		0.19***	—	—
		Manipulative		0.21***	—	—
		Current diagnosis mental disorder		0.01	—	—
		Mentally deficient		0.06	—	—
Blanchette and Motiuk (1995)	81 adult	Major problem area is personal	5	—	0.34***	—
		Has attempted suicide		—	—	0.47***
Rettinger (1998)	441 adult	LSI emotional/personal	5	—	0.13**	0.07
Blanchette (1996)	66 adult	Any DSM–III major mental disorder	2	0.13	0.02	−0.08
		Force Field Analysis: Emotional stability		−0.13	−0.07	−0.02
		Force Field Analysis: Mental ability		0.07	0.03	−0.02
		Victim of abuse in childhood		−0.01	−0.16	0.00
		Victim of abuse in adulthood		0.00	−0.24	0.04
Larivière (1999)	12 effect sizes	Self-esteem	Variable	−0.38***		
Dowden and Andrews	8 studies	Antisocial cognition and skill deficits	Variable	0.32*		
Simourd and Andrews (1994)	14 effect sizes, adolescent girls	Personal distress	Variable	0.10[a]		

Note: * $p < 0.05$, ** $p < 0.01$, *** $p < 0.001$. Larivière's outcome measures include general delinquency, aggression and violence; data include postdictive studies. Data from Dowden and Andrews (1999) are based on a meta-analysis; definitions of recidivism vary across studies.
[a]Simourd and Andrews (1994) did not provide statistical probability levels. To avoid duplication, none of the primary studies cited is included in the meta-analyses.

effect sizes). Finally, meta-analytic research by Bonta, Law and Hanson (1997) actually revealed a *negative* association between clinical (mental disorder) variables and recidivism. While mental health problems are arguably more prevalent within female offender populations (Boe et al., 2003; Byrne & Howells, 2002), their assessment does not appear to offer any more predictive value relative to that for male offenders.

SELF-ESTEEM

Based on research evidence with male samples, most empiricists believe that self-esteem is not criminogenic (Andrews & Bonta, 2003; Andrews et al., 1999; Gendreau et al., 1996). Dowden's recent meta-analysis of treatment studies ($n = 3$) suggested no effect (-0.06) of self-esteem interventions for female offenders. However, qualitative research by others has suggested that self-esteem is a promising treatment target for female offenders (Koons et al., 1997). Although relevant gender-specific empirical data are scarce, there is some evidence to support results by Koons and her colleagues. For example, Simourd and Andrews' (1994) meta-analysis of the correlates of delinquency found a fair effect size of 0.10 for females and 0.09 for males (14 studies each) for a predictor domain labelled 'personal distress'. The applicability of these findings to self-esteem research, however, is limited; 'personal distress' also included effect sizes relating to anxiety and psychopathology. However, researchers must recognize that low self-esteem is likely to have originated with other personal problems such as victimization, rejection by family, or mental illness. Consequently, some researchers suggest that low self-esteem is an appropriate rehabilitative target for women in particular (Morash et al., 1998).

Larivière (1999) referenced several studies correlating low self-esteem to acts of violence against weaker, vulnerable victims (as in spousal abuse and child abuse). Moreover, he cited six studies linking low self-esteem *in women* to acts of child abuse (5 studies) and neglect (1 study). Larivière's own research (1999) also supports this position. Using meta-analytic techniques, he reviewed 39 studies containing 80 effect sizes pertinent to self-esteem. Results revealed a significant overall effect ($r = -0.17$), suggesting a moderately strong association between self-esteem and antisocial behaviour (general delinquency, aggression and violence). Notably, the magnitude of the effect more than doubled ($r = -0.38$) when the focus was narrowed to female offenders ($n = 12$ effect sizes). Larivière argued that this finding is not surprising since, relative to men, women tend to express more guilt about criminal and aggressive behaviours, experience more anxiety about the harm they have caused and demonstrate less support for the use of violence (Campbell, 1995, cited in Larivière, 1999). The author cautioned, however, that female samples included in the meta-analysis were over-represented by subjects who had engaged in child abuse, possibly resulting in an increased effect size. It is also important to highlight that the studies included in Larivière's meta-analysis were both postdictive and predictive in nature. Future prediction and treatment outcome will further elucidate our understanding of the feasibility of low self-esteem as a criminogenic need for women.

PERSONAL VICTIMIZATION

Compared to male inmates, female inmates report significantly more victimization experiences (McClellan et al., 1997). It is now incontestable that there is a strong correlation between experiences of abuse and criminal behaviour (Howden-Windell & Clark, 1999; Kelly & Caputo, 1998), with the majority of female offenders having been victimized at some point in their lives (Blanchette, 1996; Belknap & Holsinger, 2006; Shaw, 1991a, 1991b). One study revealed self-reported victimization rates as high as 82% among Canadian female offenders (Task Force on Federally Sentenced Women, 1990), a rate comparable to that reported in other countries (Byrne & Howells, 2002). Moreover, in comparison to both the general population of women and to male offenders, female offenders are more likely to have experienced victimization that is violent, sexual, incestuous, committed by numerous perpetrators and extended over a long period of time (Task Force on Federally Sentenced Women, 1990).

The appallingly high incidence of abuse reported by the Task Force has been supported by independent Canadian research. Tien, Lamb, Bond, Gillstrom and Paris (1993) noted that 81% of their sample of adult female offenders reported experiencing some form of abuse (sexual, physical or psychological) in their current relationship. More recently, these findings were supported by Bonta et al. (1995), where 61% of their adult female offender sample reported past physical abuse and 54% reported past sexual abuse. Similarly, in Blanchette's (1996) sample of federally sentenced women, 61% were identified as victims of childhood abuse and 59% were identified as victims of abuse in adulthood. Data from US female inmate samples is comparable, with about 60% reporting childhood victimization, and about 75% reporting experiencing abuse as an adult (McClellan et al., 1997). Thus, there is a well-documented link between victimization experiences, both in childhood and adulthood, and criminal behaviour in women. The exact nature of this relationship, however, remains nebulous.

Loucks (1995) examined the nature of the association between victimization experiences and antisocial behaviour in a sample of adult female inmates ($n = 100$). Results of his study revealed that pre-adolescent abuse (sexual and physical) correlated positively with criminal violence ($r = 0.25, p < 0.01$). Abuse in adulthood was also associated with criminal violence ($r = 0.23, p < 0.01$). However, when the victimization variables were entered into a prediction equation with other variables, their value was negligible. Notably, Loucks' (1995) study was retrospective in nature and therefore simply re-affirms the correlational link between personal victimization and criminal behaviour.

In an investigation into the predictors of recidivism among Canadian federally sentenced women, Bonta et al. (1995) reported that victimization experiences were not statistically predictive, with the exception of physical abuse as an adult. Importantly, those who had experienced physical abuse as an adult were actually *less* likely to re-offend than their counterparts. These findings were supported by Blanchette (1996), who, controlling for time at risk in the community, noted no relationship between victimization experiences and recidivism. Moreover, as shown in Table 5.8, these results were sustained regardless of how recidivism was defined.[7] Similar to findings reported by Bonta et al., a negative association ($r = -0.24$) was reported between abuse in adulthood and criminal (new conviction) recidivism; the correlation approached statistical significance. Finally, results presented by Rettinger (1998) also suggest that abuse experiences are not statistically predictive of recidivism or of violent recidivism in adult female offenders. Finally, Dowden (2005) reported a non-significant *negative* effect of treatment for victimization (-0.10) for female offenders.

Collectively, the research to date suggests that victimization, although very common among female offenders, is not a criminogenic need. These findings do not necessarily lie in contrast to the position of some authors (e.g. Widom, 2003) that early childhood maltreatment does in fact predict delinquency. Overall, study results suggest that, while victimization experiences quite possibly play a role in the onset of criminal offending, they are not associated with recidivism. Despite this, the astonishingly high prevalence of survivors of abuse in the correctional system signals a requirement for service providers to address this issue. Although some authors argue that past victimization represents an important treatment target for female offenders, this does not necessarily infer that 'victimization' represents a need that is criminogenic (Gray et al., 1995; Koons et al., 1997). Rather, it has been suggested that it is the psychological sequelae to victimization experiences that contribute to behaviours such as substance abuse, criminal offending, maladjustment while incarcerated and recidivism (McLean, 1998; Messina & Grella, 2005). Many women suffer from post-traumatic symptoms that can potentially impede progress in addressing other (criminogenic) need areas. According to Byrne and Howells (2002), post-traumatic stress may elicit coping behaviour that includes the use of alcohol and/or other drugs. The offending behaviour that follows could be a product of the original or subsequent victimization experience(s), the post-traumatic stress that follows, or the resultant substance abuse.

It is therefore suggested that female offenders' victimization histories are an important part of a holistic approach to case-based classification for effective correctional intervention. Its predominance within female offender populations in particular, often comorbid with multiple psychological/psychiatric problems and compounded by ineffectual coping, underscores the importance of offering intervention in this area. Accordingly, Byrne and Howells (2002) aptly noted that establishing whether personal victimization is a cause, or merely a correlate, of criminal behaviour is not useful. Even in the absence of a direct causal connection, there is a requirement on the part of the correctional system to offer treatment for past abuse as requisite in the *duty of care*.

---

[7]Various definitions of 'recidivism' were used, including: return to custody for any reason, revocation for technical violation, new criminal conviction and new violent criminal conviction.

SELF-HARM/PARASUICIDE

Women in prison show much more frequent mental health problems than women in general, men in general and incarcerated men; they also portray higher levels of depression, and suicidal or self-injurious behaviour (Blanchette, 1996, 1997b; Loucks & Zamble, 1994). Studies of Canadian federal female offenders report that about 54–59% have engaged in some form of self-injurious behaviour such as head-banging, cutting, burning or slashing (Heney, 1990; Loucks, 1995). Rates of attempted suicide among Canadian federal female offenders are reported at 48% (Loucks & Zamble, 1994), with a range of 20–71%, depending on security level (Blanchette, 1997b). Rates are slightly lower for provincially sentenced women, with about 34% having attempted suicide at some point (Rettinger, 1998).

With a sample of 100 female offenders, Loucks (1995) examined the relationship between self-harm and criminal behaviour. The researcher used a broad definition of self-harm, including any intentional action that resulted in physical harm to the self; he did not distinguish between actions that were intended to commit suicide and those that were for other reasons (e.g. attention-seeking). Results revealed that 54% of the sample reported engaging in at least one incident of self-harm at some point in their life. Moreover, self-harm was found to be positively correlated with both criminal convictions ($r = 0.25$) and criminal violence ($r = 0.24$).

While the prediction research in this area is not copious, those studies that do exist suggest that self-injury/attempted suicide is criminogenic in nature. Bonta et al. (1995) found that self-injury was predictive of general recidivism (new convictions or parole revocations) in a sample of federal female offenders; 78% of those with a history of self-injurious behaviour recidivated, versus 25% of those with no such history. Blanchette and Motiuk (1995) reported that a history of attempted suicide was a potent predictor of violent recidivism ($r = 47$; $p < 0.001$) in a sample of 81 federally sentenced women. Statistical analyses further revealed that, together with two other variables (expectations about incarceration, associates), a history of attempted suicide accounted for 45% of the variance in violent recidivism. These findings were supported by a larger sample of provincially sentenced women ($n = 441$), where a history of self-injury was predictive of violent recidivism (Rettinger, 1998).

SUMMARY AND CONCLUSIONS

The most obvious conclusion to be drawn from this review is that more research is needed with respect to female offender needs. It is apparent from this review of the literature that, as suggested by Dowden and Andrews (1999), the need principle is applicable to female offenders. What is more contentious is whether the traditional[8] criminogenic needs are also applicable to women, or whether

---

[8]Traditional criminogenic needs are those based largely on research with male offenders, including: employment/ education, marital/family, associates, substance abuse, attitudes, community functioning and personal/emotional orientation.

women have unique criminogenic needs. The extant research suggests that both are true: while some of the traditional dynamic factors, such as antisocial attitudes, antisocial associates and substance abuse are promising treatment targets for women, there is also mounting evidence that some criminogenic needs are more relevant to women, such as poverty, family factors and propensity to self-injure or attempt suicide.

It is important here to differentiate among three levels of evidence with respect to the examination of the need principle: (1) correlational, (2) predictive or (3) causal. Within each of the dynamic factors reviewed here, there is good correlational evidence with female offender samples. Specifically, female offenders generally exhibit more problems in these various areas than non-offenders. In most of the need areas reviewed, there is at least some predictive evidence using female offender samples. Although there is much variability in the amount of predictive evidence available, prediction studies have generally set the stage for case-based classification and correctional intervention. The field is most lacking in research establishing causality for various offender needs. While this is true in general, nowhere is it more apparent than in the female offender domain.

Despite the lack of causal evidence, our review indicates that women offenders are disproportionately disadvantaged in a number of areas. They are entitled to intervention to assist them in addressing these areas, irrespective of whether they are identified as 'criminogenic needs' (Andrews & Bonta, 2003), 'obstacles' to 'good lives' (Ward & Brown, 2004), or treatment entitlements (Hannah-Moffat, 2004). Moreover, as noted, many of these needs coexist and may even covary, including: poverty, personal victimization, poor coping, mental health difficulties, substance abuse and self-injurious behaviour. The overlapping nature of these areas of concern, particularly among women, suggests a need for a holistic intervention approach. While some domains such as victimization might not be criminogenic in and of themselves, the ramifications might impact upon a woman's ability to successfully engage in correctional treatment. As such, consideration of, and intervention for, past victimization should be treated as a responsivity issue under the broad rubric of 'holistic' intervention.

There is good empirical support for poverty as a predictor of both initial involvement in crime and recidivism for girls and women. This is consistent with both evolutionary and feminist pathways theoretical perspectives. To assist in the determination of whether poverty is a criminogenic need as defined by Andrews and Bonta (2003), sound treatment studies would be required. This raises an important question: how does correctional intervention address women's poverty? We suggest that the answer is twofold. First, we argue that women's poverty is a broader political and social issue that obviously requires revisiting. Public policy reform is essential to mitigate the effects of poverty on women in the criminal justice system (Bloom et al., 2004). Second, we suggest that the best course of action that correctional services can take in this domain is to equip women with practical skills that can assist them to earn a 'living wage' upon release. We are not so naïve as to suggest that the provision of job skills to female offenders will eradicate poverty. However, it is not the purview of correctional services to treat the wider society – the central mandate is offender rehabilitation, which begins with assessment and intervention at the individual level.

Consideration of the demographics and history of the female offender population is vital in the development of gender-informed classification and programming. Some authors have suggested that an understanding of the unique life experiences of women, the context in which they live, and their pathways to crime, are essential for female-specific programme planning and delivery (Bloom, 2000; Chesney-Lind, 2000, Covington, 2000). This position is not inconsistent with the general psychological principles (risk, need and responsivity) put forth by Andrews and colleagues. Clearly, a reconciliation of the two points of view is possible.

Having said that, however, it has been noted that "there is no uniform procedure or instrument for identifying women's needs, nor is there a commonly accepted theory-based method for matching clients to programmes and services" (Prendergast et al., 1995, p. 252). Results of the current comprehensive review certainly support those sentiments. While few would argue that gender-specific issues should be reflected in the development of women-centred assessment paradigms, more empirical work is needed to determine *how* best to assess womens' needs and *which* needs are the most viable treatment targets for women.

It has been suggested that programmes for female offenders are sorely lacking in solid outcome evaluation data. This is true in both Canada (Kendall, 1998) and the United States (Austin et al., 1992; Koons et al., 1997). New programme development strategies should 'build in' assessment into their treatment paradigms. This means that the collection of data related to treatment effectiveness would be an integrated component of the programme. Evaluation of new approaches and programmes for female offenders is especially important to gauge their success against the more traditional programmes, which have been developed primarily for men.

Evaluation is particularly challenging for women's programmes, as a number of unique issues are presented. Sound, gender-specific programme theory is non-existent, and researchers continue to debate the most appropriate methodology to use in evaluative studies. The relatively small, heterogeneous and geographically dispersed population of women inmates in most jurisdictions further impedes the collection of both qualitative and quantitative data for evaluative purposes.

The importance of recognizing the distinctive qualities of female offenders is inestimable. While there are many similarities in the social characteristics of male and female offenders, there are also considerable gender differences that should be reflected in correctional assessment and intervention. Here, it is paramount to highlight, once again, that the assessment of offender needs does not necessarily preclude the assessment of her strengths as well. In fact, some authors have pervasively argued for the implementation of strengths-based assessment models for female offenders in particular (Sorbello et al., 2002; Van Wormer, 2001; Ward & Brown, 2004). In brief, these approaches, variously referred to as 'strengths-based', 'enhancement' or 'good lives', recommend a shift in focus from criminogenic needs/harm avoidance to enhancing offender capabilities. Proponents of the strengths-based approach argue that the best way to lower offenders' likelihood of recidivism is to equip them with the necessary resources to live more fulfilling lives.

Our review suggests that some variables (e.g. family) can serve as either risk factors (e.g. dysfunctional family) or as protective factors (e.g. supportive prosocial family). Moreover, it is clear that, relative to male offenders, females are both less likely to engage in crime and more likely to desist after initial engagement. These facts suggest that gender moderates risk. Those endorsing relational theory would argue that women's relationships with others serve as insulating or protective factors. More research is required before conclusive statements can be made in this regard. Nonetheless, we suggest that the assessment of women's needs and strengths offers the most comprehensive picture of the offender. We further suggest that the next generation of actuarial risk assessment tools incorporate strength/protective factors into the model. In this way, correctional practitioners can capitalize on both needs-based and strengths-based approaches.

Chapter 6

RESPONSIVITY, TREATMENT AND WOMEN OFFENDERS

INTRODUCTION

As noted, Andrews and colleagues published one of the first detailed articulations of the risk, need and responsivity principles in 1990. To reiterate, the risk and need principles indicate 'who' should be treated and 'what' needs should be targeted, respectively. In contrast, the responsivity principle focuses on 'how' treatment should be delivered. It delineates empirically based factors that help to promote optimal treatment response, which in turn, maximizes recidivism reduction.

This chapter describes the responsivity principle as originally conceptualized by Andrews and colleagues (Andrews, 1980, 1989, 2001; Andrews et al., 1990a; Andrews & Bonta, 2003; Andrews, Kiessling, Robinson & Mickus, 1986; Bonta, 1995; Gendreau, 1996; Gendreau et al., 2004). Moreover, recent elaborations of the principle offered by other criminal justice researchers (i.e. Kennedy, 2001; 2004; Ogloff & Davis, 2004; Serin, 2001; Serin & Kennedy, 1997) are also discussed. Next, theoretical and empirical research pertaining to women and responsivity is reviewed. In response, we propose a tentative reformulation of the responsivity principle that explicitly incorporates women-centred principles. Contemporary criticisms levied against the responsivity principle are also described along with our appraisal of their validity. Specifically, concerns raised by Ward and colleagues (e.g. Sorbello et al., 2002; Ward & Brown, 2004; Ward & Eccleston, 2004; Ward & Stewart, 2003a, 2003b) and some feminist scholars (e.g. Hannah-Moffat & Shaw, 2000a; Kendall, 2002, 2004) are outlined. Lastly, a brief overview of women-centred approaches from three different correctional jurisdictions is provided. We conclude with our recommendations for future research and practice.

DEFINING THE RESPONSIVITY PRINCIPLE

In 1990, Andrews et al. defined responsivity as a classification principle for offender rehabilitation that promotes effective service delivery, namely, recidivism reduction. The responsivity principle is described as follows:

Styles and modes of service are matched to the learning styles and abilities of offenders. A professional offers a type of service that is matched not only to criminogenic need but to those attributes and circumstances of cases that render cases likely to profit from that particular type of service.

(Andrews et al., 1990a, p. 20)

There are two types of responsivity: general and specific. The general responsivity principle dictates that, in general, optimal treatment response will be achieved when treatment providers deliver structured behavioural interventions in a warm and empathic manner while simultaneously adopting a firm but fair approach (Andrews et al., 1990a; Gendreau et al., 2004). Three classes of structured behavioural interventions fall under the rubric of general responsivity: operant conditioning, social learning and cognitive behavioural. In brief, these approaches utilize the following techniques in some combination or another: positive reinforcement, prosocial modelling, prosocial skills acquisition, extinction and cognitive restructuring (Andrews & Bonta, 2003; Gendreau et al., 2004). Each technique is briefly described.

- *Positive reinforcement* is the process of reacting to desirable behaviours with reinforcers or rewards that are tangible (e.g. money, material goods), social (e.g. attention, approval, verbal praise), or activity-oriented in nature (e.g. television, sports and music).
- *Prosocial modelling* is a strategy whereby a change agent (e.g. therapist, parole officer, family member) demonstrates his or her own anticriminal/prosocial attitudes/behaviours to the offender in concrete and vivid ways, for example, through words and actions.
- *Prosocial skills acquisition* is a specific technique that teaches prosocial skills such as effective parenting or successful job interviewing. There are many ways to teach offenders how to acquire prosocial skills; however, one specific method involves the use of role plays coupled with positive reinforcement. The objective of this approach is to promote a sense of personal mastery and enhanced self-efficacy (i.e. the belief that one is able to successfully execute a specific task). Strong self-efficacy increases the probability that the newly acquired skill will generalize to the real world (Bandura, 1997).
- *Extinction* is a social learning strategy that involves ignoring undesirable behaviour until it eventually dissipates.
- *Cognitive restructuring* is the final social learning technique. It seeks to alter thinking styles conducive to crime (e.g. teaching violent offenders how to re-interpret ambiguous social situations in a non-hostile rather than hostile manner).

Thus, the responsivity principle encompasses a wide range of programmes including those that are grounded in radical behaviourism (e.g. token economies), those labelled cognitive-behavioural, as well as those that rely primarily on prosocial modelling to bring about behaviour change (e.g. Andrews, 1980). In brief, general responsivity was originally conceptualized and continues to be conceptualized as a multi-dimensional construct that addresses the characteristics of the intervention itself, therapist characteristics and, lastly, the therapeutic environment.

While the general responsivity principle specifies what is most likely to work in most cases with most offenders, the specific responsivity principle focuses on case-specific factors that may impede or facilitate treatment effectiveness. Extrapolating from the collective works of Andrews (2001), Bonta (1995), Kennedy (2004), Ogloff and Davis (2004), Serin (2001) and Serin and Kennedy (1997), specific responsivity factors can be categorized along two dimensions: internal and external. Internal factors are client-specific and include:

- personality (e.g. psychopathy, interpersonal anxiety)
- emotional/mental health (e.g. mental illness, post-traumatic stress disorder)
- cognitive/intellectual ability (e.g. low intelligence, poor verbal skills, learning disability)
- motivation
- demographic factors (age, gender, ethnicity/race, language) and
- strengths.

In contrast, external responsivity factors include elements associated with the therapist and the treatment milieu. Specifically, therapists who evidence strong relational skills – respectful, open, warm, caring, non-blaming, flexible, reflective, mature and enthusiastic, who endorse positive rehabilitative sentiments and who possess the prerequisite competencies for programme delivery facilitate rather than impede positive treatment outcomes. Similarly, optimal treatment outcomes occur when community-based, as opposed to institutional-based, treatment is provided and when correctional workers differentially associate with individuals who support rehabilitative efforts as opposed to punishment or deterrence models (Andrews, 2001; Kennedy, 2004). The specific responsivity principle also recognizes the need to match case-specific factors with (1) treatment modality (e.g. don't put a highly anxious individual in group therapy) and (2) therapist personality (Bonta, 1995; Kennedy, 2004; Serin & Kennedy, 1997).

To summarize, both the general and specific responsivity principles underscore the importance of matching treatment style to offender learning styles. While the general responsivity principle asserts that most offenders will respond optimally to structured behavioural interventions, the specific responsivity principle specifies that case-specific factors must also be addressed. We now explore both general and specific responsivity germane to women offenders.

GENERAL RESPONSIVITY AND WOMEN

This portion of the chapter reviews what is currently known about women-specific factors that are best conceptualized as general responsivity factors – general in the sense that they should apply to most adult female offenders, most of the time. In order to facilitate our ultimate objective – to propose a tentative reformulated responsivity principle that is gender-informed – we discuss the findings of two comprehensive reviews (one quantitative, one qualitative) that address women offender treatment. Additionally, we explore two areas that hold considerable promise in regard to effecting change with women offenders: feminist therapy and relational theory. Lastly, research findings pertaining to womens learning and communication styles, holistic treatment targets, therapist characteristics and client strengths are also discussed.

Koons et al. (1997) published one of the first detailed narrative reviews that attempted to identify programme elements linked to successful treatment outcome in women. Utilizing a strong qualitative design, the researchers solicited information from correctional administrators, programme deliverers and programme participants from each of the fifty states comprising the United States. In sum, study participants identified various programme elements perceived to produce successful treatment outcomes with women. According to those surveyed, the most successful programme elements for women offenders were as follows:

- positive programme staff characteristics (e.g. dedicated, qualified, caring, ex-addicts/ex-offenders, female role models)
- specific and multiple treatment targets
- positive programme participation (e.g. high participant satisfaction, participants help run the programme)
- prosocial peer influence (e.g. peer pressure to be a good mom)
- structured and individualized programmes
- adequate technical support and resources
- acquisition of 'real' skills
- positive treatment environment (e.g. 'homey', small size)
- victimization issues (e.g. self-esteem, domestic violence, empowerment, self-sufficiency) and
- assistance from outside the facility (e.g. interagency communication).

Notably, a number of the programme elements identified by Koons et al. are entirely consistent with the responsivity principle and with the 'What Works' literature (see Andrews, 2001; Gendreau et al., 2004; McGuire, 1995).

Using a quantitative approach, Dowden and Andrews (1999) examined the extent to which programmes adhering to the general responsivity principle generated reductions in criminal recidivism in adult and youthful female offenders. Dowden and Andrews used a meta-analytic approach to test the empirical validity of the general responsivity principle with female offenders. The authors identified 26 unique treatment outcome studies comprised entirely (sixteen studies) or predominantly (ten studies) of female offenders. In sum, the results demonstrated that programmes adhering to the general responsivity principle generated a 25% (solely female) to 27% (predominantly female) reduction in criminal recidivism. Noteworthy is the reporting of comparable results with male offenders (Andrews et al., 1990b). Moreover, Dowden (2005) recently expanded the 1999 meta-analysis. The expanded analysis included 38 studies with 55 treatment comparisons. In brief, the preliminary results indicated that counselling programmes classified as 'general', 'family' 'individual' or 'group' generated mild reductions in recidivism ranging from 7 to 10%.

The results of Dowden and Andrews (1999) are encouraging. However, they should be interpreted judiciously for a number of reasons. First, as the authors note, the meta-analysis was based on a smaller number of studies relative to comparable research with male offenders (i.e. 500+). Second, most of the studies comprised youthful female offenders. The extent to which the results generalize to adult female offender samples is therefore largely unknown. As the majority of studies were published prior to 1990, the meta-analysis does not permit a 'fair test' of contemporary approaches. However, Dowden's (2005) recent meta-analysis partially addressed this issue. Lastly, the statistical rigour of the meta-analysis is relatively weak in comparison to similar quantitative reviews. For example, confidence intervals and the fail-safe N procedure are not reported, nor is there reference to weighted versus unweighted effect size estimates. Despite these limitations, the meta-analysis coupled with Koons et al.'s (1997) qualitative review provides an excellent starting point for the creation of a gender-informed responsivity principle.

FEMINIST THERAPY

Feminist therapy has existed for almost 40 years (Enns, 1997) and is now incorporated regularly in counselling textbooks (e.g. Corey, 2001; Sharf, 2003). Contemporary feminist therapy accepts therapists and clients of both genders and aims to provide non-gendered and culturally fair therapeutic approaches. Evans, Kincade, Marbley and Seem (2005) state:

> The basic premise of feminist therapy [is] that the political is the personal. In feminist therapy, there is no lasting individual change without social change. Clients are enmeshed in their sociopolitical and cultural contexts and true and lasting psychological change must address the issues within these contexts as well as individual issues (p. 269).

Additionally, the following elements are interwoven within feminist therapy: (1) identification of client strengths and resiliencies; (2) emphasis on collaboration and egalitarianism between therapist and client (e.g. client is considered to be his or her best expert); (3) application of diagnostic labels with caution (consider the social meaning, consequences and context of labels); and lastly (4) open and honest dialogue between therapist and client. Furthermore, feminist therapists use a variety of techniques ranging from bibliotherapy to cognitive-behavioural approaches (Evans et al., 2005; Worell & Remmer, 2003). Notably, Katherine van

Wormer (2001) advocates using several of these strategies in the context of treating female victims as well as female offenders.

Although feminist scholars such as Worell (2001) recognize the need for empirical evaluations of feminist therapies, there remains a dearth of well-controlled evaluations of these approaches. This absence remains regardless of whether or not the outcome variables include traditional factors such as symptom reduction or feminist programme objectives such as increases in personal strength and empowerment. Nonetheless, we believe that the existence of widespread cultural support for feminist philosophies sufficiently justifies its inclusion in the (tentative) reformulated gender-informed responsivity principle, provided that we empower women to lead prosocial lives.

RELATIONAL THEORY

Relational theory posits that connecting to other human beings is necessary for healthy human development in both genders but is particularly important for women. Further, the theory posits that healthy relationships are characterized by empathy, empowerment and mutuality. Mutuality simply refers to relationships characterized by bi-directional influences. It is posited that these criteria promote zest and vitality, empowerment to act, knowledge of self and others, self-worth and a desire for increased connection (Bloom et al., 2003, 2005; Covington, 1998; Miller, 1986b). In brief, we concur with Bloom et al.'s (2005) assertion that "connection, not separation, [should be] ... the guiding principle of growth for girls and women" (p. 5). However, consistent with Andrews and Bonta, we also believe that treatment effectiveness will be maximized if the *connection principle* explicitly narrows its focus to include healthy yet *prosocial* relationships.

It is important to emphasize that relational theory complements the relational elements of the general responsivity principle. Recall that the general responsivity principle advocates employing therapists who engage in warm and empathic modes of service delivery. This position is clearly aligned with relational theory which asserts empathy, empowerment and mutuality define healthy relationships. Although the existing responsivity principle directly incorporates empathy, it does not explicitly address empowerment and mutuality factors.

Importantly, there is some evidence that empowerment is a valid responsivity factor in that it helps to develop competencies and enables women to achieve independence (Austin et al., 1992; Blanchette & Eldjupovic-Guzina, 1998). Although Dowden's (2005) updated meta-analytic review reported that targeting 'empowerment' did not reduce recidivism for women, it is important to highlight that this finding was based solely on one study. Thus, the 'empowerment' hypothesis has not been adequately tested. Further, we would argue that empowerment is best conceptualized as a potential moderator variable of treatment outcome rather than a criminogenic need factor. Thus, its usefulness in the risk–need–responsivity (RNR) model does not necessitate a demonstrated, direct relationship with criminal conduct. In brief, based on the existing, albeit limited, evidence as well as our belief that the intended 'spirit' of the responsivity principle can readily accommodate the concepts of empowerment and mutuality we advocate their inclusion in the reformulated, gender-informed responsivity principle.

LEARNING AND COMMUNICATION STYLES

There have been virtually no systematic attempts to understand the potential moderating effects of gender on learning and communication styles in correctional settings. However, research gleaned from the education literature may help to inform corrections-based interventions, or at the very least, help to guide prospective research avenues. Severiens and ten Dam (1994) conducted a narrative and meta-analytic review that examined gender and learning styles in students over the age of 18. In sum, a number of notable differences emerged. Specifically, males were more likely than females to be extrinsically motivated, achievement oriented and were more likely to hold negative attitudes towards studying. In contrast, females were more often interested in learning for learning's sake or, phrased differently, evidenced intrinsic motivation more frequently than their male counterparts. The extent to which these differences generalize to offender populations requires validation.

From a social learning perspective little is known about the extent to which gender may or may not moderate the effectiveness of positive reinforcers or self-efficacy enhancement techniques. While relational theory suggests that social reinforcers of an interpersonal nature (e.g. verbal praise, warm therapeutic relationships) may be particularly salient for women, evolutionary and feminist theorists would most likely assign central significance to monetary reinforcers. These hypotheses require empirical testing.

Self-efficacy research attending to gender has focused primarily on occupational self-efficacy. In brief, this body of literature has demonstrated that while women perform equally well in quantitative and scientific-related endeavours, women continually perceive themselves as less efficacious in these domains (Bandura, 1997). Bandura has concluded that "such findings suggest that gender-related efficacy impediments arise less from the discrete skills themselves than from their linkage to stereotypically male occupations" (p. 423). Thus, employment-related interventions must not only provide women with marketable skill sets, but they must also make women *believe* that they are capable of learning and performing these new skills. Future research in this area is vital given that two, seemingly divergent paradigms – (1) RNR framework and (2) feminist approaches (Bloom et al., 2003, 2005) – have identified *skill-specific* self-efficacy as a promising treatment target. Moreover, the potential role that enhanced occupational self-efficacy can play in combating female poverty cannot be overstated.

It is a commonly held belief that male and female communication styles are markedly different. Not only has popular culture perpetuated this belief as evidenced by mainstream best sellers – *Men are from Mars, Women are from Venus* – but the empirical evidence also suggests that men and women do in fact communicate differently. For example, DeLange (1995) has made the following observations. Men and women listen for different things. While men listen for the 'bottom line' in order to take action and 'resolve the problem' women listen for details. Similarly, women tend to use body language (e.g. eye contact, head nods, display more empathic behaviours) more frequently than men. As well, DeLange (1995) reported that contrary to popular belief, men talk more than women and interrupt more, particularly in group settings. Correctional researchers have also underscored the necessity of dealing with gender-related impediments to treatment delivery such as male-dominated groups (e.g. Kennedy, 2004).

While the exact manner in which gender-differentiated communication styles either facilitate or impede correctional-based treatment has not been empirically investigated, some pertinent findings have recently emerged within the context of substance abuse treatment. In particular, four studies have examined whether adult females participating in substance abuse programmes do better or worse in single-gender versus mixed-gender formats. In sum, three of the four studies revealed that women performed better in single- versus mixed-gender formats (Ashley, Marsden & Brady, 2003; Lex, 1995). Noteworthy, the sole study that employed a randomized design (Dahlgren & Willander, 1989, cited in Ashley et al., 2003) reported significant treatment gains (reduced alcohol consumption and employment retention) two years post-treatment.

WOMEN-SPECIFIC HOLISTIC TREATMENT TARGETS

The literature has identified a number of elements, many of which could be conceptualized as external, non-criminogenic responsivity factors that can either impede or facilitate correctional treatment outcome in women. The most commonly identified factors include childcare and antenatal services, protection from abusive partners, physical and mental health care, safe and affordable housing, access to reliable transportation and access to staff after hours (Ashley et al., 2003; Bloom et al., 2003; Richie, 2001; Wellisch, Anglin & Prendergast, 1993).

Most importantly, it must be emphasized that there is empirical support for including many of these elements. Specifically, Ashley et al. (2003) narratively reviewed 38 substance abuse treatment studies that examined one or more of the above noted factors. The authors concluded that substance abuse programming for women is most effective when it concurrently provides antenatal care, mental health care, women-specific comprehensive programming (e.g. children are integral to the treatment effort and live with their mothers in the therapeutic community) and women-specific supplemental services (e.g. targeting breast health, breast self-examination, sexual and reproductive anatomy, sexually transmitted diseases (STDs), HIV and AIDS prevention, assertiveness and communication skills). There is also some evidence to suggest that these effects apply to female offender populations as well. As per our review in the previous chapter, the current state of research evidence suggests that a holistic approach to classification and treatment of female substance abusers is most promising (Covington, 1998, 2000; Task Force on Federally Sentenced Women, 1990).

THERAPIST CHARACTERISTICS

Bloom et al. (2003) conducted a series of focus groups with American correctional stakeholders including front-line staff, correctional administrators, as well as female offenders themselves. In brief, the study revealed that correctional workers harbour negative attitudes towards female offenders. Examples of these negative attitudes included the belief that female offenders are more difficult to work with and that they constitute less prestigious work assignments. Noteworthy, Pollock (1986) has reported similar findings. In response, Bloom et al. (2003) recommended training for correctional workers who interact with women offenders. She suggested that training target multiple factors including sexual misconduct, understanding the impact of victimization, gender differences in communication style and gender-appropriate interactions.

CLIENT STRENGTHS

There is consensus in yet another area. Individual strengths, resiliencies and/or protective factors should be incorporated into any model of offender rehabilitation (Andrews, 2001; Andrews & Bonta, 2003; Bloom et al., 2003; Sorbello et al., 2002; Ward & Brown, 2004). While this area has received considerable theoretical attention it remains largely unchartered in an empirical sense. While our review suggests that women in the general population evidence specific strengths in the area of motivation (e.g. more likely to exhibit intrinsic motivation), the extent to which these strengths generalize to incarcerated populations merits investigation. Additionally, given that women commit substantially less crime than men (see Chapter 1), it logically follows that women possess naturally occurring protective factors that buffer or insulate them from crime-inducing factors. The extent to which future research will disentangle the mechanisms underlying these naturally occurring resiliencies will greatly impact female programming efforts.

SPECIFIC RESPONSIVITY AND WOMEN

As previously noted, Andrews and colleagues have conceptualized gender as a specific responsivity factor. However, apart from acknowledging a need for research that examines "differential effectiveness of rehabilitation programmes with women" (Andrews & Bonta, 2003, p. 264) along with the observation that therapist relational factors (e.g. being respectful, empathic, warm, caring, non-blaming) may be particularly salient to women, additional guidance is not offered. Consequently, the goal of this section is to review case-specific factors that may be relevant to women. The following six internal or client-specific factors are discussed: personality, mental health, physical health, cognitive ability, demographics and motivation. Moreover, the importance of matching therapist and client characteristics is briefly reviewed.

Personality

Psychopathy and borderline personality disorder are particularly germane to women offenders, albeit for different reasons. First, in regards to psychopathy, prevalence estimates are markedly lower among female offenders in comparison to their male counterparts. For example, Hare (2003) estimates that the base rate is only 7.5% in female offenders but is 15% in male offenders. Thus, the extent to which treatment progress may be impeded by psychopathy should be less of a concern when treating women. Notwithstanding low base rates, recent evidence does suggest that psychopathy can moderate treatment outcome in female offenders and, thus, should not be dismissed entirely. For example, Richards et al. (2003) illustrated that women's PCL–R scores were significantly (negatively) associated with treatment retention in a Therapeutic Community (TC) condition. Specifically, those with higher total, F1 and F2 PCL–R scores were more likely to be removed from TC substance abuse treatment than those with lower scores. Interestingly, the 'responsivity' effect of the PCL–R was not evidenced in the other non-TC treatment conditions.

In contrast, unlike psychopathy, women in general (specifically 75%) account for the vast majority of borderline personality disorder diagnoses (American Psychiatric Association, 2000). Australian (Howells, Heseltine, Sarre, Davey & Day, 2004) as well as Canadian correctional researchers (McDonagh, Noël & Wichmann, 2002) have also highlighted similar findings. Noteworthy, the Correctional Service of Canada recently implemented a comprehensive treatment approach, namely Dialectical Behaviour Therapy (DBT; Linehan, 1993) specifically designed to meet the needs of women exhibiting features of borderline personality disorder (McDonagh, Taylor & Blanchette, 2002).

Mental Health

There is consensus that the mental health needs of female offenders are quantitatively as well as qualitatively different from those of their male counterparts. Female offenders evidence higher levels of depression and anxiety disorders (Bloom et al., 2003; Her Majesty's Prison Service, 2004; Howells et al., 2004; Peters, Strozier, Murrin & Kearns, 1997) in comparison to male offenders. Similarly, there is evidence that female offenders score lower on measures of self-esteem relative to male offenders (McMurran et al., 1998). Lastly, women have multiple and co-occurring mental health needs (Howells et al., 2004). This last finding has led some individuals (e.g. Susan Kennedy, Her Majesty's Prison Service, personal communication 29 September 2005; Peters et al., 1997) to conclude that female offenders are most likely to benefit from holistic treatment approaches that utilize concurrent (e.g. target substance abuse and mental health issues simultaneously) rather than sequential treatment strategies. It is important to highlight that targeting multiple treatment areas concurrently in no way violates the responsivity principle.

Physical Health

Not only do women exhibit more physical health needs than men but these needs are qualitatively different. Women offenders are more likely to utilize health care services while incarcerated (Bloom et al., 2003; Her Majesty's Prison Service, 2004). For example, Her Majesty's Prison Service (2004) reported that 20% of the incarcerated female prison population seek medical attention daily, a figure that is twice as high in comparison to men. In Canada, federally incarcerated female offenders are more likely to be taking medication (87%) compared to the general female population (55%) (Langner, Barton, McDonagh, Noel & Bouchard, 2002). Noteworthy, Langner et al. also reported that the most commonly prescribed medication among federally incarcerated females was psychotropic in nature. Additionally, female inmates are 50% more likely than male inmates to be HIV positive. Lastly, it is estimated that 5–6% of women entering prison and/or jail in the United States are pregnant (Bloom et al., 2003).

Cognitive Ability

Little research has been done comparing the cognitive abilities of male and female offenders, although Brown and Motiuk (2005) recently reported that male and female offenders evidenced no differences in intellectual capacity. Moreover, the extent to which female offenders differ from females in the general population remains largely unknown. However, like men, it stands to reason that females with learning disabilities or below average IQ require specialized intervention strategies.

Demographics

Attending to cultural diversity in programme delivery is paramount for both men and women. Recall from Chapter 1 that, in some jurisdictions, minorities and indigenous peoples are over-represented among female offenders – in some cases to a greater extent relative to men. Thus, female programming initiatives must be particularly diligent in terms of addressing language and cultural barriers to treatment. While the need to respect cultural diversity in correctional programme delivery is not disputed, there remains a dearth of empirically evaluated programmes in this area.

Motivation

Lastly, like male offenders, the extent to which female offenders are motivated to change varies as a function of the individual. However, as noted, evidence gleaned from the general population suggests that females may be more advantaged. Specifically, research based on non-criminal populations indicates that women are more likely to be intrinsically motivated. The extent to which this pattern will generalize to incarcerated samples requires investigation.

MATCHING THERAPIST AND CLIENT

Bowman, Scogin, Floyd and McKendree-Smith (2001) conducted a meta-analytic review of 60 studies that examined the potential moderating effect of therapist gender on a variety of therapeutic outcomes. In brief, the authors concluded that there was no relationship between the gender of the therapist and therapeutic outcome. Notwithstanding, the extent to which treatment outcome will be influenced by therapist gender should be examined on a case by case basis, particularly in light of the high prevalence of male-perpetrated, abuse among incarcerated females (Task Force on Federally Sentenced Women, 1990). Lastly, the extent to which the personality of the therapist may facilitate or impede therapeutic progress should also be evaluated on a case by case basis.

A GENDER-INFORMED RESPONSIVITY PRINCIPLE: A TENTATIVE, PROPOSED REFORMULATION

Based on our review we would like to propose how the general responsivity principle could be reformulated in order to ensure it is truly gender-informed. Our tentative reformulation of the general responsivity principle is as follows:

> A gender-informed responsivity principle states that in general, optimal treatment response will be achieved when treatment providers deliver structured behavioural interventions [grounded in feminist philosophies as well as social learning theory] in an empathic and empowering manner [strength-based model] while simultaneously adopting a firm but fair approach.

Thus, in contrast to the contemporary RNR model, we have moved gender to the forefront of offender rehabilitation by positing that gender should be conceptualized as a *general* rather than specific responsivity factor. Moreover, we have assigned equal importance to both risk and strength factors in the rehabilitative process. Our definition of empowerment is commensurate with Worell who defines empowerment as a method of 'incorporating strategies that serve to strengthen and inoculate individuals against further environmental assault' (Worell, 2001, p. 337). Worell also underscores that empowerment incorporates both internal and external factors. While she argues that internal factors operate at the individual level (e.g. development of interpersonal and constructive life skills), external factors operate at the societal level (e.g. prevention, education, community change). Clearly, our reformulated responsivity principle focuses exclusively on the individual facet of Worell's empowerment construct. We believe that Worell's conceptualization of empowerment will yield the greatest dividends in terms of the field's ability to operationalize and implement intervention strategies that are truly informed by gender. Our tentatively reformulated responsivity principle requires empirical validation and, undoubtedly, will require subsequent revision in response to emerging research findings.

CRITICISMS OF THE RESPONSIVITY PRINCIPLE

Some feminist scholars (e.g. Covington & Bloom, 2003; Hannah-Moffat, 2004; Hannah-Moffat & Shaw, 2000a; Kendall, 2002, 2004; Pollack, 2005; Shaw & Hannah-Moffat, 2004) and correctional researchers (Sorbello et al., 2002; Ward & Brown, 2004; Ward & Eccleston, 2004) have criticized the RNR model. Our qualitative review of the extant literature identified five central criticisms levied directly against the responsivity principle. Each responsivity-focused criticism is described followed by our appraisal of its validity.

Criticism 1: Cognitive Behaviourism Individualizes and Decontextualizes Women

The first criticism asserts that the responsivity principle is problematic because it targets individual change while simultaneously ignoring an individual's ecology, both immediate (e.g. partner, family, friends) and distal (e.g. society, cultural, political, economic) (Covington & Bloom, 2003; Hannah-Moffat, 2004; Kendall, 2004; Pollack, 2005; Shaw & Hannah-Moffat, 2004). A woman's immediate ecology is concerned largely with relational aspects of her life focusing on connections and interdependence with others (Covington & Bloom, 2003). The societal, cultural and political factors that characterize a woman's distal ecology include oppression, racism, sexism, poverty and victimization (Pollack, 2005). It is further argued that cognitive-behavioural treatment approaches fail to recognize the unique nature of women's pathways into crime, specifically how individual trauma and abuse coupled with systemic racism, poverty and oppression catapult women into a life of crime as a means of survival (Bloom et al., 2005; Chesney-Lind, 1998; Pollack, 2005). Kendall (2002; 2004) has been particularly critical of the main premise of cognitive-behavioural programmes – that criminal conduct is the consequence of faulty and deficient thinking patterns, rather than the larger structural factors noted above. In sum, critics have argued that cognitive-behavioural approaches should not be used with women because they run counter to a fundamental principle of feminist philosophy; the need to adapt a holistic approach when attempting to understand and help women.

The first and most compelling response to this criticism is that cognitive-behavioural approaches and feminist philosophies can and do coexist. In a recent review article of feminist therapy, Evans et al. (2005) described how feminist therapy is a multi-disciplinary philosophy that incorporates the psychology of women (Miller, 1976), developmental research (Gilligan, 1982), cognitive-behavioural techniques (Worell & Remer, 1992, 2003), multi-cultural awareness

(Comas-Diaz & Greene, 1994) and social activism (Brown, 1994). Additionally, Judith Worell and Pamela Remer – two iconic feminist psychologists who have accumulated a wealth of knowledge and experience through teaching, researching and practising therapeutic interventions with women – have concluded that cognitive–behavioural therapy is entirely appropriate for women:

> We believe that CB theory [cognitive-behavioural] is a comfortable choice for feminist therapists because so many of its tenets are compatible with our view of effective treatment for women. CB constructs and interventions meet the criteria for a feminist format, ... in that they are gender-balanced (do not differentiate constructs by gender), flexible (can be applied to all clients regardless of their social or personal identities), interactionist (attend to the reciprocal interaction between individuals and their environments) and can be applied across the life span ... concepts such as reinforcement, generalization, expectancy and self-efficacy are not embedded in a developmental structure that defines females and males or dominant and subordinate groups in differing terms. Social Learning Theory in general has emphasized that a positively reinforcing environment encourages flexibility of behavioural repertoires and has discouraged the use of negative procedures because they inhibit prosocial behaviour ... CB interventions may thus be tailored for use with individuals from differing age, ability, or gender groups and from diverse ethnic and cultural populations.
>
> (Worell & Remer, 2003, p. 103)

Our second response is that a number of innovative, cognitive-behavioural approaches designed for youthful offenders (e.g. Henggeler, 1999; Patterson, 1992; Patterson et al., 1975) utilize a holistic model. In accordance with the responsivity principle, these programmes (e.g. Henggeler's *Multisystemic Therapy (MST)*; Patterson's *Social Learning Theory (SLT) Approach to Family Intervention*) are grounded in social learning principles and, consequently, employ cognitive-behavioural methods coupled with an array of other social learning techniques (e.g. role modelling) to promote prosocial behaviour. However, unlike traditional, corrections-based programmes for adult offenders, MST and SLT apply social learning techniques to both the offender *and* other individuals in his or her immediate environment (e.g. family members).

Third, proponents of the RNR model have always recognized the need to treat both the individual as well as the environment (Andrews & Bonta, 2003; Dowden & Andrews, 2004; Gendreau et al., 2004). As an example, RNR supporters fully endorse *advocacy brokerage* or *inter-agency communication*. Briefly, inter-agency communication is defined as "the agency aggressively makes referrals and advocates for its offenders so that they receive high quality services [employment, health care] in the community" (Gendreau et al., 2004, p. 27). While advocacy brokerage has not been formally incorporated into the RNR model *per se*, Andrews and Bonta (2003) fully endorse its application within the context of *The Dimensions of Effective Correctional Counseling: The 'What and How' of Effective Modelling and Reinforcement* (see page 311 of Andrews & Bonta, 2003; also see page 27 of Gendreau et al., 2004).

Fourth, general responsivity is a multi-dimensional construct that complements rather than opposes seemingly divergent theories (i.e. relational theory) or applications (i.e. enhance self-efficacy). Despite recent articulations of the principle equating general responsivity with cognitive-behavioural approaches (see Andrews & Bonta, 2003), cognitive-behavioural approaches comprise but one element, albeit an integral one, of the general responsivity principle. The true spirit of the responsivity principle is much broader, encompassing social learning principles as well as relational aspects of the therapeutic alliance (e.g. mutual respect, warmth, empathy, firm but fair use of authority). Moreover, these general responsivity elements dovetail seamlessly with relational theory (Covington, 1998). Recall that, consistent with feminist philosophies, relational theory posits that women in particular are significantly interested in feeling connected to other human beings. Additionally, the theory asserts that connectedness is best achieved via empathic, empowering and mutually contributing or respectful relationships. Thus, as stated, the responsivity principle and relational theory can and do coexist peacefully. We believe we have already taken the first step towards reconciliation by explicitly incorporating the concept of empowerment into the proposed, reformulated responsivity principle.

General responsivity and gender-responsive philosophies converge on another important dimension; the belief that correctional strategies should enhance skill-related self-efficacy (belief in oneself regarding one's abilities to perform a specific task). For example, Bloom et al. (2003, 2005) assert that enhancing women's sense of self-efficacy through skills enhancement is a central, defining feature for gender-responsive programming. Similarly, Gendreau et al. (2004) indicate that the primary goal of social learning techniques (e.g. successive approximation and positive reinforcement) is to enhance the client's sense of skill-specific mastery. Thus, the failure to recognize the similarities between the two approaches has once again resulted in a missed opportunity for reconciliation.

The fifth and final response to Criticism 1 addresses the assertion that the general responsivity principle or, more accurately, cognitive-behavioural programmes, are inappropriate for women because they do not directly address broad, structural factors (e.g. poverty, systemic oppression and racism). First, we concur with the observation that the responsivity principle targets individual rather than societal factors. However, we believe that targeting change at the individual level is the most viable and most empirically defensible option available to correctional agencies. This does not mean that policy reforms aimed at eradicating poverty, preventing family violence, improving employment or providing subsidized housing are unwarranted. They simply fall outside the purview of correctional jurisdictions, both fiscally and legally. Moreover, the ability of community-based initiatives to significantly impact criminal activity has been empirically questioned (Morris & Braukmann, 1987). Further, some voices within the feminist community have stated that "there is little evidence that therapists are able to combine feminist therapeutic practice with social activism to effect individual change ... the evidence that does exist is anecdotal and difficult to prove" (Evans et al., 2005, p. 274).

It is our contention that the most effective strategy currently available to correctional agencies for combating poverty, overcoming past trauma and preventing future victimization is to empower women, one by one. This includes providing women with the ability to live self-sustaining lives through the acquisition of viable employment skills. It also includes empowering women by provisioning them with the necessary skill set to parent effectively, to cope in prosocial and healthy ways with past trauma, to overcome substance abuse addiction and/or to think in more prosocial and constructive ways. Yes, we unabashedly proclaim that 'thinking style' plays a fundamental role in understanding the psychology of female criminal conduct. And yes, we believe in the existence of a psychology of female criminal conduct. Targeting the above noted factors will enhance self-efficacy and, consequently, self-esteem once mastery in skills acquisition and generalization is achieved. However, the onus is not only on the individual to change but we must treat that individual's immediate ecology, including intimate partners, parents and children.

Criticism 2: The Responsivity Principle is Empirically Derived

The second criticism in the extant literature proclaims that the RNR model is problematic because it was empirically informed by quantitative meta-analytic results. For example, Kendall (2002, 2004) argues that the reliance on meta-analytic results to inform women-specific treatment strategies is problematic because qualitative and small-scale studies are excluded. Additionally, she emphasizes that meta-analytic approaches cannot incorporate feminist pathways research that, by definition, necessitates reliance on qualitative approaches that include *women's voices*. Kendall (2004) also describes other methodological limitations associated with meta-analyses that have long been recognized within the meta-analytic community. Hannah-Moffat and Shaw (2000b) have also faulted meta-analyses for reaching conclusions that run counter to qualitative research. For example, they underscore how qualitative studies have indicated that women offenders prefer individual, client-centred counselling. This result runs counter to quantitative meta-analytic reviews that have concluded client-centred counselling is ineffective in reducing recidivism.

Correctional researchers have responded to this criticism at length (Andrews & Bonta, 1998, 2003; Andrews & Wormith, 1989; Gendreau, Goggin, Cullen & Paparozzi, 2002b). To summarize, they persuasively argue that anti-empirical sentiments exemplify knowledge destruction techniques; these are either methodological or philosophical in nature. Examples of methodological criticisms include statements such as 'the effect size is never big enough', 'the outcome measure only focused on official crime', or 'meta-analytic approaches are problematic for establishing a knowledge base'. In contrast, ideological criticisms dismiss research for reasons such as it is morally flawed or naïve, it contradicts basic common sense, the researcher is morally flawed or the techniques themselves were developed by men and consequently cannot be trusted.

Notwithstanding the conclusion that the anti-meta-analytic sentiments fall firmly within the realm of knowledge destruction techniques, meta-analyses are not beyond reproach. They cannot mitigate poor-quality primary research studies, they cannot account for the dearth of women-specific studies or the noticeable absence of ethnic diversity research. Additionally, as others have noted (e.g. Gendreau et al., 2004) meta-analytic approaches require subjective coding that, at times, may be problematic. For example, categorizing similar variables into one, all-encompassing predictor category may require grouping heterogeneous rather than homogeneous variables. Moreover, meta-analytic reviews can and do vary in terms of statistical rigour. Despite these limitations, we argue that gender-informed strategies for women must be empirically informed. However, our definition of empirically informed includes both quantitative as well as qualitative studies. If and when these approaches diverge, the methodological rigour associated with each respective approach must be carefully scrutinized before reaching firm conclusions.

Criticism 3: White, Middle-Class Men Developed Cognitive Behaviourism

The third criticism levied against cognitive behaviourism stems largely from Kendall's (2002, 2004) distrust of science, particularly psychology. Kendall argues that science and empiricism reflect the values of the dominant class in society, namely; white, middle-class men from the Western world. She posits that the realm of correctional psychology is no exception, pointing out that not only was one of the co-developers of the original, offender-based cognitive-behavioural programme, *Reasoning and Rehabilitation*, a white, middle-class male but the 'What Works' champions are also predominantly white, middle-class men. Consequently, Kendall strongly objects to the notion that such a programme or philosophy could benefit women, particularly culturally diverse women. Additionally, Kendall argues that cognitive-behavioural approaches have become so entrenched within the Western correctional ethos, not because they work, but because they are compatible with the manner in which a liberal democracy governs societal conduct.

We recognize that science has historically focused its lens on those issues most salient for the hegemonic standard. Thanks, this is now changing in large part thanks to (a) vocal feminist advocates who continuously challenge the status quo and (b) the rigorous work of feminist scientists. We also concede that there are biases in science and so-called 'objective' methods. Nonetheless, we reiterate our belief in the self-correcting nature of science. While Kendall's work is contributory in a philosophical sense, we suggest that girls and women in the criminal justice system are best served by the provision of evidence-based intervention strategies.

Criticism 4: Cognitive Behaviourism Dehumanizes Women

Kendall (2002) argues that cognitive-behavioural programmes are dehumanizing to women because they focus on 'otherness'; making the assumption that women offenders are somehow inherently different from law-abiding citizens in the way they think. The most straightforward response is that renowned *feminist foremothers* (i.e. Worell & Remer, 2003) recommend that cognitive-behavioural approaches be interwoven into the feminist therapeutic framework. Moreover, to our knowledge there is no quantitative or qualitative evidence to support the contention that women feel dehumanized after participation in a cognitive-behavioural intervention.

Criticism 5: The RNR Model Lacks Conceptual Resources

Ward and Eccleston (2004) argue that the RNR model lacks the necessary *conceptual resources* to effect offender rehabilitation. Specifically, they posit that the RNR model: (1) does not adopt a positive approach to treatment and consequently does not incorporate individual strengths; (2) does not address the relationship between risk management and good lives; (3) does not address the *causal preconditions* of therapy, namely treatment readiness and motivation; and, lastly, (4) does not address how therapists' attitudes toward offenders influence treatment outcome. In response, they provide an alternative model of offender rehabilitation, the 'good lives model'. As discussed in Chapter 3, the 'good lives model' is a strengths-based approach that argues that reductions in recidivism will result when interventions address offender strengths and target human needs (i.e. non-criminogenic). Given that the second criticism pertains to treatment targets rather than treatment modalities, it has been addressed in Chapter 5. However, the remaining criticisms are responsivity-focused and consequently are discussed in this chapter. Moreover, while Bonta and Andrews (2003) and Ogloff and Davis (2004) have eloquently responded to the 'good lives' criticisms we would like to make a few additional comments.

First, Ward and Brown (2004) and Sorbello et al. (2002) assert that the RNR model focuses too much attention on risk reduction (e.g. treat offender deficits, impediments to treatment) to the detriment of individual strengths and facilitative treatment factors. We concur that the RNR model focuses on offender deficits. However, it is important to underscore that the RNR model is not silent on strengths; in fact, Andrews (2001) recently outlined 18 principles for effective correctional programmes, the eleventh of which explicitly states, "Assess responsivity and strength factors" (Andrews, 2001, p. 11). Thus, there is room within the RNR framework for strength factors, as Serin and Kennedy (1997) have demonstrated. We fully support the incorporation of strength factors into the RNR model as evidenced by the proposed reformulated responsivity principle described earlier. However, it is necessary to highlight that while strength-based approaches are appealing, in practice they are challenging to implement. Definitional issues concerning the meaning of a protective factor abound. A protective factor should be more than an absence of a risk factor and it should do more than simply moderate the relationship between risk factors and outcome (Farrington & Painter, 2004). Regardless, we advocate a balanced approach that recognizes the importance of risk and strength factors in the rehabilitative process.

Second, Ward and Brown assert that the RNR model "is silent on questions of therapist factors and attitudes to offenders" (p. 246). This is a curious statement given that therapist factors comprise an integral component of the general responsivity principle as evidenced by the requirement for empathic therapists who utilize 'firm but fair' approaches. Ironically Andrews (1980) is perhaps the only correctional researcher to have empirically demonstrated using a methodologically rigorous research design – classical experimental design with random assignment – that empathic probation officers who actively challenge criminal sentiments while simultaneously rewarding prosocial thinking can reduce recidivism by almost 80%.

Moreover, Andrews and colleagues have been considerably vocal regarding the impact of staff attitudes on treatment outcomes. In fact, Andrews' (2001) recent treatise delineating 18 principles of effective correctional programming explicitly underscored the importance of staff attitudes. For example, Principle 16, labelled, 'Attend to Staff', describes six desirable attributes of a correctional worker:

1. a knowledge base favouring human service activity;
2. a belief that offenders can change;
3. a belief that core correctional practices work;
4. a belief that personally they have the skills to practice at high levels both in terms of relationship and structuring;
5. a belief that important others value core practice and value; and
6. a belief that reducing recidivism is a worthwhile pursuit.

Thus, it is clear that Andrews believes correctional workers to be deserving of a position in the rehabilitative equation.

In brief, there is no doubt that the responsivity principle will and should evolve in response to new theoretical paradigms and emerging empirical evidence – a position recognized by Bonta and Andrews (2003). Fortunately, researchers have already commenced this journey. For example, Drs Ralph Serin and Sharon Kennedy (1997) have made substantial theoretical advancements in fleshing out the responsivity construct by incorporating research from the therapeutic alliance and motivation to change literature. Similarly, Ogloff and Davis (2004) have made parallel advancements in their recent, eloquently crafted reconciliation of the 'good lives' and RNR model.

ADVANCES IN WOMEN-CENTRED CORRECTIONS: AN INTERNATIONAL PERSPECTIVE

The last section of the chapter briefly describes the philosophies that currently direct women-centred corrections in Canada, the United States and England and Wales.

Canada

In 1990, a Task Force on Federally Sentenced Women made several recommendations to the Correctional Service of Canada (CSC) aimed at improving the correctional experience of federally sentenced women.[1] In sum, the final Task Force Report, *Creating Choices: Report of the Task Force on Federally Sentenced Women*, recommended that five basic principles should drive correctional programming for women, specifically, empowerment, meaningful and responsible choices, respect and dignity, supportive environment and shared responsibility. Each principle is now briefly described.

- *Empowerment* refers to the process of enhancing women's self-esteem and internal locus of control (the belief that they have the power and control to direct their own lives) such that they gain insight into their personal situation and identify their strengths. In addition, they are supported and challenged to take positive action to gain greater control of their lives. This principle emerged from the recognition that women in society, particularly incarcerated women, have been disempowered as a consequence of several factors such as poverty, family violence and racism, particularly against Aboriginal women.
- *Meaningful and responsible choices* provide women with options that allow them to make responsible choices that relate to their needs, past experiences, culture, values, spirituality, abilities and skills. Unfortunately, a history of dependence (e.g. alcohol/drugs, men, financial assistance) has denied many women the opportunity and/or ability to make meaningful and responsible choices in their lives. It is further argued that it is only through the provision of meaningful and responsible choices that women will take control of their lives and consequently raise their self-esteem and become empowered.
- *Respect and dignity* refers to the reciprocal respect that is needed between offenders, between staff and, lastly, between staff and offenders. Moreover, the principle acknowledges that respectful treatment naturally addresses unique cultural, religious or spiritual needs of minority groups in a holistic manner.
- *Supportive environment* reflects the need to provide services within a positive milieu. Environmental aspects include both physical elements (e.g. clean air, access to fresh air, light, adequate nutrition) and broader interpersonal and spiritual aspects (e.g. positive social interactions characterized by mutual respect, opportunities to engage in spiritual and culturally relevant practices). Otherwise, the goals of empowerment, self-esteem enhancement, spiritual and personal development, physical and psychological well-being will not be realized.
- *Shared responsibility* refers to the suggestion that all levels of government, corrections, volunteer organizations, businesses, private sector services and the community have a role to play in the development of support systems and continuity of service for federally sentenced women.

Thus, it is evident that the Correctional Service of Canada (CSC) has adopted a set of guiding principles that are heavily grounded in feminist philosophies and relational theory. To the current day, these five principles direct how CSC manages and treats its female offender population.

---

[1]As noted in previous chapters, Canadian offenders sentenced to periods of imprisonment of two years or more fall under federal jurisdiction. Those sentenced to less than two years are the responsibility of the provinces.

The United States

Parallel principles have also emerged in the United States. A three-year study commissioned by the National Institute of Corrections (NIC) culminated in a proposed gender-responsive strategy for women (Bloom et al., 2003, 2005). The underlying premise of the strategy is that women are different from men and, consequently, require a distinctly different treatment approach. In brief, the authors provided the following six guiding principles that encapsulate gender-responsive programming.

- *Gender matters.* The first and foremost principle is the acknowledgement that men and women are different. Specifically, they diverge in terms of the pathways that brought them to prison, supervision and custody responses, the risk that they pose to society and the nature and extent of their needs.
- *Environment.* The second principle asserts that women must be cared for in an environment that embodies safety, respect and dignity. This type of environment is necessary to facilitate behavioural change and to prevent women from being revictimized.
- *Relationships.* The third principle specifically states, 'Develop policies, practices and programmes that are relational and promote healthy connections to children, family, significant others and the community' (Bloom et al., 2003, p. 79). This principle acknowledges the centrality of relationships in women's lives, in particular, the influence that important relationships (e.g. with a partner, children) can have on promoting prosocial change.
- *Services and supervision.* The fourth principle states, 'Address substance abuse, trauma and mental health issues through comprehensive, integrated and culturally relevant services and appropriate supervision' (Bloom et al., 2003; p. 80). Thus, this principle emphasizes holistic intervention approaches that focus on multiple needs that are particularly salient to women: trauma, mental health and substance abuse.
- *Socio-economic status.* This principle speaks to the necessity of affording women the opportunity to become educated and trained such that they will be able to support themselves as well as their children. Moreover, it stresses the need to remove road blocks that impede women's progress towards financial independence. For example, approximately half of the individual states do not allow convicted drug felons to access benefits, including public housing.
- *Community.* The final guiding principle states, 'Establish a system of community supervision and reentry with comprehensive, collaborative services' (Bloom et al., 2003, p. 82). Specifically, the authors describe a number of community partners that should play an integral role in the reintegration of women: mental health system, family service agencies, emergency shelter, health care, transportation, self-help groups.

Thus, it is highly evident that Bloom et al.'s (2003) guiding principles are not only commensurate with feminist philosophies and relational theory but that they also incorporate elements from the male-oriented rehabilitation model (e.g. community brokerage).

England and Wales

Lastly, Her Majesty's Prison Service is currently developing a female-centred programme that is heavily grounded in feminist and relational principles. For example, the programme is being designed to meet the multiple needs of violent female offenders simultaneously. The programme, *Choices, Actions, Relationships and Emotions* (CARE) has thus adopted a holistic framework in which co-occurring problems (e.g. substance abuse, violence, self-harm and mood disorders) can be addressed concurrently rather than sequentially. The programme is still in the development phase (Susan Kennedy, personal communication, September 26, 2005).

CONCLUSIONS AND RECOMMENDATIONS

To summarize, both the general and specific responsivity principles underscore the importance of matching treatment style to offender learning styles. While the general responsivity principle asserts that most offenders will respond optimally to structured behavioural interventions, the specific responsivity principle specifies that case-specific factors must also be addressed. This chapter also demonstrated how feminist philosophies and relational theory dovetail seamlessly with the responsivity principle. Moreover, the chapter also demonstrated that the vast majority of criticisms that have been levied against the responsivity principle can generally be remedied if the full breadth and intended spirit of the responsivity principle are considered. A number of women-specific responsivity factors were also discussed, including gender differences in learning and communication styles, holistic treatment elements (e.g. the need to provide viable transportation, protective from abusive partners, incorporate children). Notably, Ashley et al. (2003) demonstrated that substance abuse treatment effects were most robust when women-specific factors (e.g. health care, child care, mental health) were best conceptualized as responsivity factors and were treated concurrently with substance abuse.

Chapter 7
CONCLUSION

We can confidently conclude that girls and women no longer constitute *correctional afterthoughts* (Ross & Fabiano, 1985a, 1986) in the realm of criminological theory and correctional practice. However, this has not always been the case. The traditional failure to consider gender in the theoretical understanding, assessment, classification and rehabilitation of women offenders is deplorable. Fortunately, gender-based analysis is becoming considerably more prevalent in correctional theory and in research and policy development – a requisite in the attempt to develop 'best practices' for the provision of correctional services to girls and women.

In this final chapter, we summarize the main conclusions that have been garnered throughout the book and present a number of recommendations for future correctional research and practice. Most of the recommendations are firmly supported by empirical research findings. However, others are embedded in theory and/or derived from what are anecdotally hailed as 'best practices' for female offenders; this was a requisite in a field of research that is still in its formative years.

SUMMARY

This text opened with the statement that there is one universally accepted fact about crime – men commit more than women; a finding that persists regardless of time, culture, criterion measure, or scholarly orientation of the observer. On average, women comprise about 5% of incarcerated populations world wide. While this percentage is small it is necessary to underscore that, internationally, the female incarceration rate has grown at a faster pace relative to males, particularly during the last two decades. The rapid increase in the number and proportion of women under correctional supervision world wide signals an urgent call to action. Not surprisingly, profile analyses conducted across a diversity of correctional jurisdictions internationally concur that incarcerated female offenders are generally poor, young, uneducated and lack employment skills.

Despite the growing incarceration rate for females, it is still clear that the overwhelming majority of those arrested, convicted and incarcerated are male. Moreover, the gender disparity is greatest for crimes involving physical violence. The social psychological literature highlights the importance of considering relational or covert behaviours in the measurement of aggression. Briefly, unlike overt aggression which focuses on the threat or the actual damage to one's physical well-being, covert or relational aggression is the harming of others through damage or threat of damage to relationships (e.g. threatening to end a friendship unless a peer complies with a request). In essence, it represents the 'dark side' of Miller's (1986b) relational theory that emphasizes the positive side of women's relationships, specifically the need women have to feel connected to others through empathic and empowering relationships. In brief, the evidence that was reviewed, although derived exclusively from girls and pre-schoolers, suggested that gender differences in aggression are minimized when the form of aggression is covert. On rare occasions when women do engage in overt aggression, it tends to reflect the centrality of their relationships in their lives; it is most commonly directed against family members, particularly intimate partners.

Chapter 1 also highlighted research findings showing that the motivational factors that contribute to familial female violence appear to differ from those of their male counterparts. For example, while jealousy, infidelity, desertion and control appear to be the driving catalysts behind husbands who murder their partners, escaping domestic abuse is often what motivates wives who murder their partners. Collectively, the research also revealed similarities and differences in regards to extra-familial crime. Specifically, the violent crime perpetrated by both genders is often motivated by vindication or attempts to restore personal integrity. The literature pertaining to property crime, although relatively scant, suggests that males and females alike engage in property crime for economic reasons. However, women's economic motivations are more often described in noble terms (e.g. to feed their children) while men's economic motivations are described as hedonistic, driven by an insatiable thrill-seeking urge to accumulate flashy material goods for reputation building. While these observed gender differences are consistent with both evolutionary psychology and feminist perspectives, they are based on a few limited empirical studies and thus must be interpreted judiciously.

In Chapter 2 we reviewed a number of contemporary theories of female criminal conduct. Theories were classified as gender-neutral, female-centred or hybrid perspectives, though we acknowledge that the distinctions are not always clear. Gender-neutral theories included mainstream or general criminological models that either explicitly stated or implicitly assumed that the core assumptions and predictions delineated by the theory did not vary as a function of gender. Because they have been applied to both men and women, they have been acclaimed as 'gender-neutral'. However, while the 'gender-neutral' appellation implies impartiality, the normative standard is male. In brief, the following gender-neutral theories were considered: control theories (Gottfredson & Hirschi, 1990; Hirschi, 1969, 2002; Sampson & Law, 1993), social learning perspectives (Akers, 1998), the personal–interpersonal community reinforcement model (Andrews & Bonta, 2003), life-course theory (Moffitt, 1993) as well as evolutionary (Campbell, 2002) and biological (Caspi et al., 2002) explanations.

In contrast, female-centred paradigms assign a central role to gender. Our review of female-centred theories included: (1) women's liberation, also known as the emancipation hypothesis (Adler, 1975; Simon, 1975); (2) economic marginalization perspectives including an integrated liberation/marginalization model (Hunnicutt & Broidy, 2004); (3) socialization theories (Chesney-Lind, 1997; Covington, 1998); (4) relational theory (Miller, 1986b); (5) power-control theory (Hagan et al., 1990); and two feminist perspectives including (6) power-belief theory (Dougherty, 1998) and (7) feminist pathways research (Belknap, 2001; Chesney-Lind, 1998). In addition, two 'hybrid' perspectives were also reviewed: general strain theory (Agnew, 1992) and gendered theory (Steffensmeier & Allan, 1996). In brief, we can firmly conclude that feminist criticisms of mainstream criminological perspectives are unquestionably correct in one important regard. Traditionally, most 'gender-neutral' theories have either explicitly or implicitly disregarded half of the human experience in their failure to consider the female gender. Fortunately, our review illustrated that many contemporary scholars are now asking female-specific questions regarding the applicability of 'gender-neutral' theories to women.

A perennial question in this body of literature is whether mainstream or 'gender-neutral' theoretical perspectives provide sufficient explanations of female offending or, alternatively, whether female-specific theories are required. Some scholars have concluded that the answer lies with female-specific theories that emphasize the role of poverty, family violence and childhood trauma as causal determinants of female criminal conduct. However, our review suggests that the evidence is still not strong enough to unequivocally support this conclusion.

The empirical evidence to date clearly indicates that gender-neutral theories have a sizeable role to play in the explanation of female criminal conduct. Moreover, while a number of 'female-centred' paradigms have emerged, they are relatively more novel and have not been studied to the same extent as their gender-neutral counterparts. Nonetheless, the extant research suggests that our understanding of female criminal conduct may be enhanced by incorporating elements from 'gender-informed' as well as 'female-centred' perspectives. In fact, we observed that a number of seemingly divergent theoretical perspectives were actually complementary. This holds promise for prospective theoretical advancements that adopt conciliatory rather than adversarial approaches. A good example of evidence supporting a convergence of perspectives is the relative importance of poverty in the prediction of female recidivism. This finding is consistent with two apparently opposing theoretical perspectives; poverty plays a central role in both evolutionary and feminist 'pathways' explanations of girls' and women's involvement in the criminal justice system. As such, we suggest that this finding provides theoretical convergent validity, though it is still debatable whether poverty is best framed as a 'criminogenic need', suggesting treatment for the individual (e.g. vocational training), or whether public policy requires reform. While we as feminist researchers concede that women's poverty is at least partly reflective of broad systemic problems, we also recognize that it is not within the purview of correctional services to 'fix' society's fundamental problems. As such, the best alternative is to offer interventions to girls and women.

Chapter 3 addressed the role of assessment in the classification and treatment of female offenders. In a broad sense, it underscored the importance – or rather the absolute necessity – of classification for risk management purposes. We emphasized that individualized assessment is necessary to establish *risk* (to safely manage offender populations) and to match offenders' *needs* to treatment resources. A brief history of offender classification was provided, as well as a description of static and dynamic risk, followed by a discussion of actuarial versus clinical assessment processes. An example of a gender-informed classification method for women was also described. To date, there is no widely-known, well validated post-release risk assessment tool that has been developed specifically for women. In the absence of a gender-specific measure, we suggest that correctional practitioners consider the purpose of the assessment and be well-informed regarding the viability of using their preferred mathematical tool with women. It is essential that those using such measures be trained accordingly and that they keep abreast of current gender-specific research regarding its use.

Collectively, Chapters 4, 5 and 6 examined the applicability of the Risk–Need–Responsivity model to female rehabilitation. The risk principle suggests that: (1) with appropriate assessment, recidivism can be predicted and (2) level of risk should be matched with the level of service provided. Specifically Andrews and colleagues posit that higher levels of service should be provided to higher risk offenders, while those assessed as lower risk derive better outcomes from less intensive intervention. Our review of some of the most commonly-used mathematical risk assessment tools clearly demonstrated that the science of recidivism prediction for girls and women lags far behind that for males. There are fewer supportive reliability and validity data available and base rates of post-release violence by women has led some to question the utility of classifying women for risk management purposes. Without disregard for the views of our colleagues, we suggest that the rates of institutional misconduct (Blanchette, 2005; Harer & Langan, 2001) and re-offence (Benda, 2005; Langan & Levin, 2002) for women are sufficiently large to warrant assessment for risk management purposes. Of all the male-derived assessment measures reviewed, we suggest that the LS/CMI demonstrates the most promise in terms of utility for treatment planning and prediction of recidivism. Nonetheless, we maintain our position that the preferred strategy is to build gender-specific assessment tools from the 'ground up'.

The need principle contends that, to reduce criminal recidivism, intervention must focus on the 'criminogenic needs' of the offenders. Criminogenic needs are characteristics of the offender (or his or her social situation) that relate directly to his or her risk of re-offending. Accordingly, changes in levels of criminogenic needs are associated with changes in risk to re-offend. Our review of the literature suggested that the need principle is applicable to female offenders. The extant research suggests that many of the dynamic factors traditionally assessed for men are also promising treatment targets for girls and women. However, there is also mounting evidence that some criminogenic needs are *more* relevant to women, such as poverty, family factors and propensity to self-injure or attempt suicide.

Our review suggested that some variables (e.g. family) can serve as either risk factors (e.g. dysfunctional family) or protective (e.g. supportive prosocial family) factors for girls and women. Accordingly, we suggest that the consideration of both needs and strengths offers the most comprehensive assessment of the offender. We further suggest that 'fourth-generation' actuarial risk assessment tools incorporate strength/protective factors. In this way, correctional practitioners can capitalize on both needs-based and strengths-based approaches.

The responsivity principle posits that treatment services should be delivered in a style and mode that match the learning style and ability of the offender. The responsivity principle subsumes two general types of consideration. The first, commonly called 'broad' or 'general' responsivity, states that, for most offenders, optimal treatment response will be achieved when treatment providers deliver structured interventions (e.g. cognitive-behavioural strategies) in a warm and empathic manner while using a firm but fair approach. Thus, the general responsivity principle describes attributes of the intervention that are external to the offender (Ogloff & Davis, 2004). The second type of responsivity pertains to internal characteristics of the individual being assessed. These are referred to as 'specific' responsivity considerations and examples include: gender, ethnicity, motivation to change, literacy level and intelligence. The specific responsivity principle also recognizes the need to match individual therapist characteristics with those of the client in order to maximize treatment gain.

Interestingly, our review of the literature pertaining to responsivity suggested that both feminist philosophies and relational theory dovetail seamlessly with the responsivity principle. Accordingly, we also demonstrated that the vast majority of criticisms that have been levied against the responsivity principle are addressed if the full breadth and intended spirit of the responsivity principle are considered. Additionally, a number of female-specific responsivity factors were discussed, such as gender differences in learning and communication styles, as well as holistic treatment targets (e.g. the need to provide viable transportation, protective from abusive partners and incorporate children). Notably, Ashley et al. (2003) demonstrated that the effects of substance abuse treatment were most robust when women-specific factors (e.g. health care, child care and mental health) were treated concurrently alongside the primary treatment target, that being substance abuse. This finding is especially important given that it provides one of the first empirical validations of the popular belief that holistic approaches will enhance treatment outcome in women. The extent to which this finding will generalize to offender populations requires empirical validation. Lastly, our review of the responsivity literature inspired us to boldly propose a reformulated general responsivity principle. The reformulated principle not only propels gender to the forefront of offender rehabilitation by positioning it as a general rather than specific responsivity factor, but it also assigns equal importance to both risks and strengths in the rehabilitative process.

LIMITATIONS

This book is not a panacea. We do not purport to offer a definitive 'best practice' guide for girls and women in conflict with the law. While we hope and trust that readers will concur with our reconciliation of various valuable correctional approaches, several limitations to this text must be underscored. First, the sheer dearth of women-specific research precludes any ability to make bold proclamations regarding 'What Works' for this particular group. In contrast, the vast repository of knowledge pertinent to male offenders has resulted in correctional principles that have been so robustly empirically supported that they are embedded in everyday correctional practice in most Western jurisdictions. Recall the following statements from the Preface:

> In brief, the 'What Works' repository of knowledge has conclusively demonstrated that correctional intervention can reduce criminal recidivism (Andrews et al., 1990a, Andrews et al. 1999; Izzo & Ross, 1990; Lipsey, 1995; Lipton, Pearson, Cleland & Yee, 2002). Indeed, the 'average' correctional treatment results in a 10% reduction in recidivism (Andrews et al., 1990a; Lösel, 1995). Moreover, treatment approaches that follow empirically validated principles of effective intervention (Andrews et al., 1990b) yield substantially higher reductions in criminal recidivism, ranging from 26% to 40% (Andrews et al., 1990b, 1999; Lösel, 1996).

We enthusiastically look forward to the day when we will be able to make equally compelling statements regarding 'What Works' for girls and women in conflict with the law. Although female offenders no longer constitute 'correctional afterthoughts', the research supporting theory and interventions that are gender-informed is still in its infancy. As a result, even the most well-intentioned interventionists cannot confidently offer the same quality services to females, relative to that for males.

Second, we acknowledge that female offenders are a heterogeneous group and that this text has attended very little to other diversity (e.g. ethno-cultural) issues. We noted that some minority groups (e.g. indigenous/Aboriginal females) are over-represented within incarcerated populations. Sadly, in some jurisdictions, their rate of incarceration (i.e. Australia) almost approximates that of the male incarceration rate. Despite the noted disproportionate representation of minority females, we concede that this text focused very little on issues that might be particularly salient to these groups.

We conceded at the outset that gender was our primary focus; nonetheless, we hope that some of the recommendations proposed herein can be extrapolated to some extent to other diversity considerations. Regardless, we emphasize the heterogeneous nature of the female offender population and suggest that additional diversity concerns be afforded pre-eminence in future theoretical and empirical explorations.

Finally, we acknowledge our professional and ideological biases as feminist psychological researchers. Our review and recommendations were, wherever possible, grounded in empiricism. Nonetheless, empirical methods are not infallible and even aggregated research (e.g. meta-analyses) has limitations. We have attempted to use methodologically strong, interdisciplinary research and theory to guide our proposed solutions. As demonstrated, in some cases, seemingly disparate models yielded similar results or recommendations. Accordingly, we suggest that there are both strengths and weaknesses inherent in all models of thought and methods of research. It will be in the extraction of the most promising tenets of each and the reconciliation of various paradigms that the greatest dividends will result.

RECOMMENDATIONS

Based on a comprehensive review and synthesis of information provided in this book we make the following major recommendations:

1. Perform a paradigm shift in regards to theory development. Specifically, theories must steer away from 'gender-neutral' and become 'gender-informed'. This involves operationalizing theoretical constructs in concrete ways that fully reflect gender differences. For example, social control theories have focused primarily on the role of marital attachment and employment. In order to become a 'gender-informed' theory, social control must operationalize its core constructs in such a manner that readily accommodates women-specific bonding factors (e.g. attachment to children, the importance and centrality of positive healthy relationships).

In their efforts to develop gender-informed theories (or adapt existing theories), social science theorists must be exceptionally vigilant of stereotypes based on gender. As such, it will be an immense challenge for progressive theorists to develop and apply their work in a manner that is informed by gender, yet devoid of stereotypic schemas.

2. Develop models of assessment for girls and women that are informed by gender. A gender-informed model of assessment for women offenders should capitalize on the seminal work by Andrews and colleagues. This would be achieved through continued validation and refinement of the Risk–Need–Responsivity model, focusing explicitly on girls and women.

Importantly, this recommendation does not suppose that the *same* risk and need factors should be incorporated into routine assessments for rehabilitative services for girls and women. Rather, it posits that the operational principles of assessment for classification set out by Andrews and colleagues apply to women.

Recall that the risk principle directs resources to where they are most needed, suggesting that higher intensity intervention should be provided to those assessed as higher risk. Although we suggest that the risk principle could well apply to girls and women, we must add an important caveat. Our review has clearly demonstrated that women, on average, are much lower risk than their male counterparts. Adherence to the risk principle, in our view, must consider the relative risk an individual poses *within his or her peer group*. Succinctly, we are not suggesting that women be offered fewer or less intensive interventions than their male counterparts. On the contrary, we are suggesting that women's needs are manifold, though there is also evidence to suggest that some women are at higher risk to re-offend than others. While we argue that higher intensity services should be provided to higher risk cases, we also concur that this presents a challenge, given the lack of actuarial instrumentation developed specifically for girls and women.

While we also suggest that adherence to the needs principle holds promise for recidivism reduction for women, we must acknowledge that we do so with some trepidation. Assessment of criminogenic needs is requisite for the provision of appropriate case-based correctional intervention. The need principle suggests that, to reduce recidivism, intervention should target criminogenic needs. While we fundamentally support the application of the need principle itself to girls and women, some potential ethical issues are raised when the tenets of the needs principle are extrapolated to the assessment of offender risk. Hannah-Moffat (1997, 1999, 2004) has repetitively expressed concern over the reformulation of need factors into risk factors, thereby further marginalizing and penalizing women with the most needs. This is a valid concern. However, there is a very large body of research supporting the utility of criminogenic needs as predictors of recidivism. This presents an enormous ethical quandary for correctional policy-makers and administrators. For example, if past victimization or poverty is conclusively predictive of increased recidivism for females in particular, how should correctional administrators/policy-makers use that information? Would it be unethical to include such variables into an actuarial model of risk assessment for women? Would it be unethical not to include such information, because it might compromise the accuracy of the instrument and therefore jeopardize public safety?

There is often a fine distinction between criminogenic and non-criminogenic needs. We suggest that variables such as victimization and poverty do not reflect *true* criminogenic needs, as originally conceptualized by Andrews and colleagues. Although they may be associated with criminality or recidivism (be it correlationally or causally), they are not treatable dynamic factors. While the psychological or behavioural sequelae (e.g. post-traumatic stress, low self-esteem) to victimization might be appropriate treatment targets, the victimization itself is not. Similarly, poverty might be reflective of a lack of education, little employment history or lack of employable skills. While these correlates are viable treatment targets, the poverty itself is not. As such, we recommend the incorporation of those variables that are promising treatment targets into the evaluation paradigm for dual-purpose assessments (i.e. treatment and risk management).

3. Construct actuarial assessment tools that are gender-informed and built *from the ground up* for the specific populations to which they will be applied – in this case, girls and women. We trust that we have convincingly argued for the appropriateness of actuarial assessment approaches. Recall that actuarial approaches use statistically determined, weighted risk criteria to render a

score. Accordingly, there is good evidence that some static (e.g. criminal history) and dynamic (e.g. antisocial attitudes) variables are valid predictors of behaviour for girls and women.

While we concur that such criteria should be incorporated into actuarial approaches for girls and women, we also suggest that the 'fourth-generation' assessment protocol should incorporate offenders' strengths and protective factors into the scoring criteria. More precisely, we argue that gender-informed models of assessment for girls and women should profit from tenets of strength-based approaches and test the viability of capabilities/protective factors as (negative) predictors of risk outcome or, alternatively, (positive) predictors of desistence. Strength-based approaches might be optimally applicable to women, given their relatively lower risk in comparison to men.

To be clear, we must emphasize that we use the term 'protective factor' in a very specific manner. As others have noted (e.g. Farrington and Painter), to be classified as 'protective', the factor in question must be *more* than simply the *absence* of a risk factor (e.g. no substance abuse problem). Interestingly, Caspi et al. (2002) have identified one potential protective factor that is biological in nature. Recall from Chapter 1 that the authors demonstrated how childhood maltreatment predicted conduct disorder in girls, but only among girls who possessed a certain genetic predisposition (i.e. low activity MAOA gene present on both X chromosomes). In contrast, childhood maltreatment did not predict conduct disorder in the high activity MAOA group. The authors argued that as a result of having two as opposed to one X chromosome (thus two chances to inherit a normal functioning MAOA gene), females have been afforded extra protection or resiliency potential in comparison to males when exposed to hostile environments. Thus, in this case the MAOA gene may be a female-specific protective factor.

Even with the incorporation of strengths/protective factors into the model, critics of actuarial approaches will probably continue to suggest that they fail to consider the uniqueness of the individual being assessed. We acknowledge that there are exceptions to every rule and anomalous events/personal circumstances that could impact upon an individual's risk level. We have noted several times that the female offender population is heterogeneous and that we cannot address all diversity issues simultaneously. As such, this recommendation to develop actuarial risk-management tools for the *specific* populations of interest must be tempered with a note of caution. In particular, the population of interest must be sufficiently large to meet statistical requirements for the development of such a tool and the costs incurred must be balanced with the practical utility of the model. Finally, an important caveat is that all actuarial measures *must* include provisions for professional override considerations.

4. Empirically test the reformulated gender-informed responsivity principle. Once again, we emphasize the tentative nature of this proposal. Our reformulated version of the original responsivity principle is informed by theory and founded in what little empirical work was available to us. We concede that it is heavily based in the feminist therapeutic 'best practice' literature, which has not been rigorously evaluated.

5. Adopt a reconciliatory rather than adversarial approach to both research and operational practice concerning girls and women. Use a multi-method research strategy whenever possible to capitalize on the strengths of each. Avoid knowledge destruction based on value-laden philosophical criteria and challenge the status quo through the production of sound empirical work.

DIRECTIONS FOR FUTURE RESEARCH

Throughout this text several avenues for future research emerged. In summary, we propose five general areas for prospective research.

1. First and foremost, female-centred research must utilize research designs that boast high methodological rigour. As Moffitt and Caspi (2001) underscore, longitudinal research designs that study an entire cohort over a lengthy period of time is requisite in theory construction. Moreover, researchers who are predominantly interested in studying female crime must include comparison groups comprised of male offenders as well as at-risk females who do not engage in crime. In the absence of such comparison groups it is virtually impossible to make firm conclusions regarding the causal pathways to crime for women. Although a number of notable exceptions are emerging (e.g. Farrington & Painter, 2004; Giordano et al., 2002), more research of this nature is required.
2. Female-centred researchers should consider using multi-method research approaches, namely quantitative and qualitative analytic strategies. While certain research objectives lend themselves more readily to one approach over another, we are confident that the greatest contributions will be made when integrated strategies are adopted. Giordano et al.'s (2002) research is one noteworthy exemplar. The authors tested social control theory in a sample of male and female adjudicated youths utilizing a methodologically rigorous design that was not only longitudinal in nature but also incorporated data from multiple sources, including open-ended life history narratives, structured interviews, self-reported criminal activity and official arrest rates. Thus, the authors were successful in incorporating feminist (e.g. use of open-ended life history narratives that permit women's voices to be heard) as well as 'non-feminist' methodological approaches simultaneously.
3. Future research should also thoroughly investigate whether or not observed gender differences are real or simply statistical artifacts. Specifically, Farrington and Painter (2004) have convincingly postulated that the reliance on statistical approaches that fail to address the base rate differential between male and female criminality may have inadvertently led to erroneous conclusions. Accordingly, it is essential to examine more closely the observation that most offender risk classification schemas (originally developed on male samples) decline in predictive validity when applied to female samples. Specifically, it must be ascertained whether or not the reduction in predictive accuracy is the result of shrinkage – a phenomenon characteristic of all cross-validation procedures and statistical artifacts – or whether it reflects a true inability of male-based tools to perform equally well with women.

4. Cultural diversity research is also recommended. Clearly, theory and practice must not only be gender-informed but must also address unique cultural factors.

5. Lastly, and most importantly, collaborative, interdisciplinary research is recommended. Specifically, research teams comprised of biologists, sociologists and psychologists operating from a range of conceptual frameworks (e.g. feminism to evolution) should work in partnership to delineate the complex interactions between macro-level (racism, sexism) and micro-level (personality, biology) variables that contribute to the explanation of female criminality.

CONCLUDING REMARKS

In conclusion we would like to respond to Bloom's question (2000): "Does women's offending relate to criminogenic risks and needs, or is it a factor of the complex interconnection of race, class, gender, abuse, trauma, addiction, or a combination?" Our response is that women's criminal offending is the result of an exceedingly complex interplay of risk and need factors, both internal and external to the individual. Women's offending *is* indeed related to criminogenic risk and needs. However, we also acknowledge the role of broader societal issues (e.g. oppression/trauma, racism, poverty) in women's crime. Nonetheless, we maintain that the best way for correctional services to mitigate the effects of systemic marginalization is through the provision of gender-informed services that address the needs of girls and women. This will be accomplished most effectively through the reconciliation and application of various theoretical and empirical approaches that seek to improve the lives of girls and women in conflict with the law.

REFERENCES

Adler, F. (1975). *Sisters in crime*. New York: McGraw-Hill.

Agnew, R. (1992). Foundation for a general strain theory of crime and delinquency. *Criminology*, **30**, 47–87.

Aitken, G. & Logan, C. (2004). Dangerous women? A U.K. response. *Feminism and Psychology*, **14** (2), 262–267.

Akers, R.L. (1998). *Social learning and social structure: A general theory of crime and deviance*. Boston: Northern University Press.

Akers, R.L. (1999). Social learning and social structure: Reply to Sampson, Morash and Krohn (Symposium on social learning and social structure). *Theoretical Criminology*, **3** (4), 477–493.

Akers, R.L. & Jensen, G.F. (2003). Social learning theory and the explanation of crime: A guide for the new century. In R.L. Akers & G.F. Jensen (Eds), *Social learning theory and the explanation of crime* (pp. 339–361). New Brunswick, NJ: Transaction Publishers.

Alarid, L.F., Burton, V.S. Jr & Cullen, F.T. (2000). Gender and crime among felony offenders: Assessing the generality of social control and differential association theories. *Journal of Research in Crime and Delinquency*, **37** (2), 171–199.

Alexander, J. (1986). Classification objectives and practices. *Crime and Delinquency*, **32**, 323–338.

American Psychiatric Association (1994). *Diagnostic and statistical manual of mental disorders* (4th edn). Washington, DC: Author.

American Psychiatric Association (2000). *Diagnostic and statistical manual of mental disorders* (4th edn, text revision). Washington, DC: Author.

Andrews, D.A. (1980). Some experimental investigations of the principles of differential association through deliberate manipulations of the structure of service systems. *American Sociological Review*, **45**, 448–462.

Andrews, D.A. (1982a). *A personal, interpersonal, and community-reinforcement (PIC-R) perspective on deviant behaviour*. Toronto, Ontario: Ministry of Corrections Services.

Andrews, D.A. (1982b). *The level of supervision inventory (LSI): The first follow-up*. Toronto, Ontario: Ministry of Correctional Services.

Andrews, D.A. (1989). Recidivism is predictable and can be influenced. Using risk assessment to reduce recidivism. *Forum on Corrections Research*, **1** (2), 11–18.

Andrews, D.A. (2001). Principles of effective correctional programs. In L.L. Motiuk & R.C. Serin (Eds), *Compendium 2000 on effective correctional treatment* (pp. 9–17). Ottawa, Ontario: Research Branch, Correctional Service Canada.

Andrews, D.A. & Bonta, J. (1995). *LSI–R: The level of service inventory – revised*. Toronto, Ontario: Multi-Health Systems.

Andrews, D.A. & Bonta, J. (1998). *The psychology of criminal conduct* (2nd edn). Cincinnati, Ohio: Anderson Publishing Company.

Andrews, D.A. & Bonta, J. (2003). *The psychology of criminal conduct* (3rd edn). Cincinnati, Ohio: Anderson Publishing Company.

Andrews, D.A., Bonta, J. & Hoge, R.D. (1990a). Classification for effective rehabilitation: Rediscovering psychology. *Criminal Justice and Behaviour*, **17** (1), 19–52.

Andrews, D.A., Bonta, J. & Wormith, J.S. (2004). *Level of service/case management inventory: LS/ CMI manual*. Toronto, Ontario: Multi-Health Systems.

Andrews, D.A., Dowden, C. & Gendreau, P. (1999). *Clinically relevant and psychologically informed approaches to reduced re-offending: A meta-analytic study of human service, risk, need, responsivity and other concerns in justice contexts*. Unpublished manuscript, Carleton University, Ottawa, Ontario, Canada.

Andrews, D.A., Kiessling, J.J., Robinson, D. & Mickus, S. (1986). The risk principle of case classification: An outcome evaluation with young adult probationers. *Canadian Journal of Criminology*, **28**, 377–384.

Andrews, D.A. & Wormith, J.S. (1989). Personality and crime: Knowledge destruction and construction in criminology, *Justice Quarterly*, **6**, 289–309.

Andrews, D.A., Zinger, I., Hoge, R.D., Bonta, J., Gendreau, P. & Cullen, F.T. (1990b). Does correctional treatment work? A clinically relevant and psychologically informed meta-analysis. *Criminology*, **28**, 369–404.

Ashley, O.S., Marsden, M.E. & Brady, T.M. (2003). Effectiveness of substance abuse treatment programming for women: A review. *American Journal of Drug and Alcohol Abuse*, **29**, 19–53.

Austin, J. (1983). Assessing the new generation of prison classification models. *Crime and Delinquency*, **29** (4), 561–576.

Austin, J. (1986). Evaluating how well your classification system is operating: A practical approach. *Crime and Delinquency*, **32**, 302–322.

Austin, J., Bloom, B. & Donahue, T. (1992). *Female offenders in the community: An analysis of innovative strategies and programs*. Washington, DC: National Institute of Corrections.

Austin, J. & Hardyman, P.L. (2004). *Objective prison classification: A guide for correctional agencies*. Washington, DC: National Institute of Corrections (Accession Number 019319).

Baird, S.C. (1981). Probation and parole classification: The Wisconsin model. *Corrections Today*, **43**, 36–41.

Bandura, A. (1977). *Social learning theory*. Englewood Cliffs, NJ: Prentice Hall.

Bandura, A. (1997). *Self-efficacy: The exercise of control*. New York: W.H. Freeman and Company.

Beals, F. (2004). The invisibility of women in New Zealand's technology needs-based penal system. *Feminism & Psychology*, **14** (2), 237–242.

Beattie, J. (1975). The criminality of women in eighteenth century England. In D.K. Weisberg (Ed.), *Women and the law: A social historical perspective*. Cambridge, MA: Schenkman.

Bélanger, A., Lanctôt, N. & Leblanc, M. (2005). *Is the predictive power of family risk factors on delinquent trajectories similar among adjudicated males and females?* Presented at the 57th annual meeting of the American Society of Criminology, Toronto, Ontario, Canada.

Belfrage, H. (1998). Implementing the HCR–20 scheme for risk assessment in a forensic psychiatric hospital: Integrating research and clinical practice. *Journal of Forensic Psychiatry*, **9**, 328–338.

Belfrage, H., Fransson, G. & Strand, S. (2000). Prediction of violence within the correctional system using the HCR–20 Risk Assessment Scheme. *Journal of Forensic Psychiatry*, **11** (1), 167–175.

Belknap, J. (2001). *The invisible woman: Gender, crime, and justice* (2nd edn). California: Wadsworth Publishing Company.

Belknap, J. & Holsinger, K. (1998). An overview of delinquent girls: How theory and practice have failed and the need for innovative changes. In R.T. Zaplin (Ed.), *Female offenders: Critical perspectives and effective interventions* (pp. 31–64). Gaithersburg, Maryland: Aspen Publishers.

Belknap, J. & Holsinger, K. (2006). The gendered nature of risk factors for delinquency. *Feminst Criminology*, **1** (1), 48–71.

Benda, B.B. (2005). Gender differences in life course theory of recidivism: A survival analysis. *International Journal of Offender Therapy and Comparative Criminology*, **49** (3), 325–342.

Blackwell, B.S. (2000). Perceived sanction threats, gender, and crime: A test and elaboration of power-control theory. *Criminology*, **38**, 439–488.

Blackwell, B.S. & Piquero, A.R. (2005). On the relationships between gender, power control, self-control, and crime. *Journal of Criminal Justice*, **33**, 1–17.

Blanchette, K. (1996). *The relationship between criminal history, mental disorder, and recidivism among federally sentenced female offenders*. Unpublished master's thesis, Carleton University, Ottawa, Ontario, Canada.

Blanchette, K. (1997a). *Risk and need among federally sentenced female offenders: A comparison of minimum-, medium-, and maximum-security inmates* (Research Report R-58). Ottawa, Ontario: Research Branch, Correctional Service Canada.

Blanchette, K. (1997b). *Maximum-security female and male federal offenders: A comparison* (Research Report R-53). Ottawa, Ontario: Research Branch, Correctional Service Canada.

Blanchette, K. (2005). *Field-test of a gender-informed security reclassification scale for female offenders*. Unpublished doctoral dissertation, Carleton University, Ottawa, Ontario, Canada.

Blanchette, K. & Dowden, C. (1998). A profile of federally sentenced women in the community: Addressing needs for successful reintegration. *Forum on Corrections Research*, **10** (1), 40–43.

Blanchette, K. & Eldjupovic-Guzina, G. (1998). *Results of a pilot study of the peer support program for women offenders* (Research Report R-73). Ottawa, Ontario: Research Branch, Correctional Service Canada.

Blanchette, K. & Motiuk, L.L. (1995, June). *Female offender risk assessment: The case management strategies approach*. Poster session presented at the Annual Convention of the Canadian Psychological Association, Charlottetown, Prince Edward Island.

Blanchette, K. & Taylor, K. (2005). *Development and field test of a gender-informed security reclassification scale for women offenders* (Research Report R-167). Ottawa, Ontario: Research Branch, Correctional Service Canada.

Blanchette, K. & Taylor, K. (in press). Development and field test of a gender-informed security reclassification scale for female offenders. *Criminal Justice and Behaviour*.

Blanchette, K., Verbrugge, P. & Wichmann, C.G. (2002). *The Custody Rating Scale, initial security level placement, and women offenders* (Research Report R-127). Ottawa, Ontario: Research Branch, Correctional Service Canada.

Bloom, B.E. (2000). Beyond recidivism: Perspectives on evaluation of programs for female offenders in community corrections. In: M. McMahon (Ed.), *Assessment to assistance: Programs for women in community corrections* (pp. 107–138). Arlington, VA: American Correctional Association.

Bloom, B.E. (2003). A new vision: Gender-responsive principles, policy, and practice. In B.E. Bloom (Ed.), *Gendered justice: Addressing female offenders* (pp. 267–288). Durham, North Carolina: Carolina Academic Press.

Bloom, B.E. & Covington, S. (2000, November). *Gendered justice: Programming for women in correctional settings*. Paper presented at the Annual Meeting of the American Society of Criminology, San Francisco, CA.

Bloom, B., Owen, B. & Covington, S.S. (2003). *Gender-responsive strategies for women offenders: Research, practice, and guiding principles for women offenders* (NIC Accession Number 018017). Retrieved August 15, 2005 from http://www.nicic.org.

Bloom, B., Owen, B. & Covington, S.S. (2004). Women offenders and the gendered effects of public policy. *Review of Policy Research*, **2** (1), 31–48.

Bloom, B., Owen, B. & Covington, S.S. (2005). *A summary of research, practice, and guiding principles for women offenders. The gender responsive strategies project: approach and findings* (Accession Number 020418). Retrieved August 15, 2005 from http://www.nicic.org.

Boe, R., Nafekh, M., Vuong, B., Sinclair, R. & Cousineau, C. (2003). *The changing profile of the federal inmate population: 1997 and 2002* (Research Report R-132). Ottawa, Ontario: Research Branch, Correctional Service Canada.

Bohman, M. (1996). Predisposition to criminality: Swedish adoption studies in retrospect. In G.R. Bock & J.A. Goode (Eds), *Genetics of criminal and antisocial behaviour* (pp. 99–114). Chichester, UK: John Wiley & Sons.

Boland, F., Henderson, K. & Baker, J. (1998). Case need domain: 'Substance abuse assessment review'. *Forum on Corrections Research*, **10** (3), 32–34.

Bolt, D.M., Hare, R.D., Vitale, J.E., & Newman, J.P. (2004). A multigroup item response theory analysis of the Psychopathy Checklist – Revised. *Psychological Assessment*, **16** (2), 155–168.

Bonta, J. (1995). The responsivity principle and offender rehabilitation. *Forum on Corrections Research*, **7**, 34–37.

Bonta, J. (1996). Risk-needs assessment and treatment. In A.T. Harland (Ed.), *Choosing correctional options that work: Defining the demand and evaluating the supply* (pp. 18–32). Thousand Oaks, CA: Sage.

Bonta, J. (2002). Offender risk assessment: Guidelines for selection and use. *Criminal Justice and Behavior*, **29** (4), 355–379.

Bonta, J. & Andrews, D.A. (2003). A commentary on Ward and Stewart's model of human needs. *Psychology, Crime and Law*, **9**, 215–218.

Bonta, J., Harman, W.G., Hann, R.G. & Cormier, R.B. (1996). The prediction of recidivism among federally sentenced offenders: A re-validation of the SIR scale. *Canadian Journal of Criminology*, **38**, 61–79.

Bonta, J., Law, M. & Hanson, K. (1998). The prediction of criminal and violent recidivism among mentally disordered offenders: A meta-analysis. *Psychological Bulletin*, **123** (2), 123–142.

Bonta, J., Pang, B. & Wallace-Capretta, S. (1995). Predictors of recidivism among incarcerated female offenders. *The Prison Journal*, **75**, 277–294.

Boritch, H. & Hagan, H. (1990). A century of crime in Toronto: Gender, class, and patterns of social control, 1859–1955. *Criminology*, **28**, 567–599.

Bowman, D., Scogin, F., Floyd, M. & Mckendree-Smith, N. (2001). Psychotherapy length of stay and outcome: A meta-analysis of the effect of therapist sex. *Psychotherapy*, **38**, 142–148.

Box, S. & Hale, C. (1984). Liberation/emancipation, economic marginalization, or less chivalry: The relevance of three arguments to female crime patterns in England and Wales, 1951–1980. *Criminology*, **22**, 473–498.

Brennan, T. (1987). Classification for control in jails and prisons. In D.M. Gottfredson & M. Tonry (Eds), *Prediction and classification: Criminal justice decision making* (pp. 323–366). Chicago: University of Chicago Press.

Brennan, T. (1998). Institutional classification of females: Problems and some proposals for reform. In R.T. Zaplin (Ed.), *Female offenders: Critical perspectives and effective interventions* (pp. 179–204). Gaithersburg, MD: Aspen Publishers.

Broidy, L. & Agnew, R. (1997). Gender and crime: A general strain theory perspective. *Journal of Research in Crime and Delinquency*, **34**, 275–306.

Brown, L.S. (1994). *Subversive dialogues: Theory in feminist therapy*. New York: Basic Books.

Brown, S.L. & Motiuk, L.L. (2005). *The Dynamic Factor Identification and Analysis (DFIA) component of the Offender Intake Assessment (OIA) process: A meta-analytic, psychometric and consultative review* (Research Report R-164). Ottawa, Ontario: Research Branch, Correctional Service Canada.

Brownstein, H.H., Spunt, B.J., Crimmins, S.M. & Langley, S.C. (1995). Women who kill in drug market situations. *Justice Quarterly*, **12**, 473–498.

Buchanan, R.A., Whitlow, K.L. & Austin, J. (1986). National evaluation of objective prison classification systems: The current state of the art. *Crime and Delinquency*, **32**, 272–290.

Bunch, B.J., Foley, L.A. & Urbina, S.P. (1983). The psychology of violent female offenders: A sex-role perspective. *The Prison Journal*, **63**, 66–79.

Burgess, R.L. & Akers, R.L. (1966). A differential association–reinforcement theory of criminal behaviour. *Social Problems*, **14**, 128–147.

Burke, P. & Adams, L. (1991). *Classification of women offenders in State correctional facilities: A handbook for practitioners*. Washington, D.C: National Institute of Corrections.

Burton, V.S., Cullen, F.T., Evans, T.D., Alarid, L.F. & Dunaway, R.G. (1998). Gender, self-control, and crime. *Journal of Research in Crime and Delinquency*, **35**, 123–147.

Byrne, M.K. & Howells, K. (2002). The psychological needs of women prisoners: Implications for rehabilitation and management. *Psychiatry, Psychology, and Law*, **9**, 34–43.

Cameron, M. (2001). *Women prisoners and correctional programs. Trends and issues in crime and criminal justice* (No. 194). Canberra, Australia: Australian Institute of Criminology.

Campbell, A. (1984). *The girls in the gang: A report from New York City*. Oxford, UK: Blackwell.

Campbell, A. (1995). A few good men: Evolutionary psychology and female adolescent aggression. *Ethnology and Sociobiology*, **16**, 99–123.

Campbell, A. (1999). Staying alive: Evolution, culture, and women's intrasexual aggression. *Behavioural and Brain Sciences*, **22**, 203–252.

Campbell, A. (2002). *A mind of her own: The evolutionary psychology of women*. Oxford: Oxford University Press.

Campbell, A., Muncer, S. & Bibel, D. (2001). Women and crime: An evolutionary approach. *Aggression and Violent Behavior*, **6**, 481–497.

Canadian Centre for Justice Statistics (2001). *Women in Canada* (Catalogue No. 85F0033MIE). Ottawa, Ontario, Canada: Statistics Canada.

Canadian Centre for Justice Statistics (2004). *Canadian crime statistics* (Catalogue No. 85-205-XIE). Ottawa, Ontario, Canada: Statistics Canada.

Canter, R. (1982). Sex differences in self-report delinquency. *Criminology*, **20**, 373–393.

Carey, G. & Goldman, D. (1997). The genetics of antisocial behaviour. In D.M. Stoff, J. Breiling & J.D. Maser (Eds), *Handbook of antisocial behaviour* (pp. 243–254). New York: John Wiley & Sons.

Carlen, P. (1988). *Women, crime and poverty*. Milton Keynes: Open University Press.

Caspi, A., Lynam, D., Moffitt, T.E. & Silva, P.A. (1993). Unraveling girls' delinquency: Biological, dispositional, and contextual contributions to adolescent misbehaviour. *Developmental Psychology*, **29**, 19–30.

Caspi, A., McClay, J., Moffitt, T.E., Mill, J., Martin, J., Craig, I.W., Taylor, A. & Poulton, R. (2002). Role of genotype in the cycle of violence in maltreated children. *Science*, **29**, 851–854.

Cernkovich, S.A. & Giordano, P.C. (1979). A comparative analysis of male and female delinquency. *Sociological Quarterly*, **20**, 131–145.

Champion, D. (2006). *Research methods for criminal justice and criminology* (3rd edn). Upper Saddle River, NJ: Pearson Prentice Hall.

Chapman, J.R. (1980). *Economic realities and the female offender*. Lexington, MA: Lexington Books.

Chesney-Lind, M. (1986). Women and crime: The female offender. *Signs: Journal of Women in Culture and Society*, **12** (1), 78–96.

Chesney-Lind, M. (1997). *The female offender: Girls, women and crime*. Sage Publications: Thousand Oaks.

Chesney-Lind, M. (1998, September). *What to do about girls? Promising perspectives and effective strategies*. Paper presented at the 6th Annual International Community Corrections Association (ICCA) Research Conference in Arlington, Virginia.

Chesney-Lind, M. (2000). What to do about girls? Thinking about programs for young women. In: M. McMahon (Ed.), *Assessment to assistance: Programs for women in community corrections* (pp. 139–170). Arlington, VA: American Correctional Association.

Chesney-Lind, M. (2001). Contexualizing women's violence and aggression: Beyond denial and demonization. *Behavioural and Brian Sciences*, **22**, 222–223.

Chesney-Lind, M. & Rodriguez, N. (1983). Women under lock and key. *Prison Journal*, **63**, 47–65.

Chesney-Lind, M. & Shelden, R.G. (1998). *Girls, delinquency, and juvenile justice* (2nd edn). Wadsworth Publishing Company: Belmont, CA.

Clark, D.A., Fisher, M.J. & McDougall, C. (1993). A new methodology for assessing level of risk in incarcerated offenders. *British Journal of Criminology*, **33** (3), 436–448.

Cloward, R.A. & Ohlin, L.E. (1960). *Delinquency and opportunity*. New York: Free Press.

Cohen, A.K. (1955). *Delinquent boys*. New York: Free Press.

Collie, R.M. (2003). Sorting women's risk: New Zealand women prisoners' misconducts and internal security risk. *New Zealand Journal of Psychology*, **32**, 101–109.

Comas-Diaz, L. & Greene, B. (1994). *Women of color*. New York: Guilford Press.

Cooke, D.J. (1995). Psychopathic disturbance in the Scottish prison population: The cross-cultural generalizability of the Hare Psychopathy Checklist. *Psychology, Crime, and the Law*, **2**, 101–118.

Copas, J. & Marshall, P. (1998). The Offender Group Reconviction Scale: A statistical reconviction score for use by probation officers. *Applied Statistics*, **47**, 159–171.

Corey, G. (2001). *Theory and practice of counseling and psychotherapy*. Belmont, CA: Brook/Cole-Thomson Learning.

Corrections Statistics Committee (2004). *Conditional release statistical overview* (Cat. No. PS4-12/20004E). Retrieved September 10, 2005 from http://www.sgc.gc.ca/corrections/publications_e.asp#2004.

Corulla, W.J. (1987). A psychometric investigation of the Eysenck Personality Questionnaire – Revised and I.7 Impulsiveness Questionnaire. *Personality and Individual Differences*, **8** (5), 651–658.

Coulson, G., Ilacqua, G., Nutbrown, V., Giulekas, D. & Cudjoe, F. (1996). Predictive utility of the LSI for incarcerated female offenders. *Criminal Justice and Behavior*, **23** (3), 427–439.

Covington, J. (1985). Gender differences in criminality among heroin users. *Journal of Research in Crime and Delinquency*, **22**, 329–353.

Covington, S.S. (1998). The relational theory of women's psychological development: Implications for the criminal justice system. In R.T. Zaplin (Ed.), *Female offenders: Critical perspectives and effective interventions* (pp. 113–128). Gaithersburg, Maryland: Aspen Publishers.

Covington, S.S. (2000). Helping women recover: Creating gender-specific treatment for substance-abusing women and girls in community corrections. In: M. McMahon (Ed.), *Assessment to assistance: Programs for women in community corrections* (pp. 171–234). Arlington, VA: American Correctional Association.

Covington, S.S. & Bloom, B.E. (2003). Gendered justice: Women in the criminal justice system. In B.E. Bloom (Ed.), *Gendered justice: Addressing female offenders* (pp. 3–23). Durham, North Carolina: Carolina Academic Press.

Crick, N.R., Ostrov, J.M., Appleyard, K., Jansen, E.A. & Casas, J.F. (2004). Relational aggression in early childhood: 'You can't come to my birthday party unless.' In M. Putallaz & K.L. Bierman (Eds), *Aggression, antisocial behaviour, and violence among girls* (pp. 71–89). New York: Guildford Press.

Daly, K. (1989). Gender and varieties of white-collar crime. *Criminology*, **27**, 77–92.

Daly, K. (1992). Women's pathways to felony court: Feminist theories of lawbreaking and problems of representation. *Review of Law and Women's Studies*, **2**, 11–52.

Daly, K. & Chesney-Lind, M. (1988). Feminism and criminology. *Justice Quarterly*, **5**, 497–538.

Daly, K. & Lane, R. (1999). Actuarial based online risk assessment in Western Australia. *Probation Journal*, **46** (3), 164–170.

Daly, M. & Wilson, M. (1988). *Homicide*. New York: Aldine De Gruyter.

Dauvergne-Latimer, M. (1995). *Exemplary community programs for federally sentenced women: A literature review*. Report submitted to Federally Sentenced Women Program. Ottawa, Ontario: Correctional Service Canada.

Dawes, R., Faust, D. & Meehl, P. (1989). Clinical versus actuarial judgment. *Science*, **243**, 1668–1674.

DeLange, J. (1995). Gender and communication in social work education. A cross-cultural perspective. *Journal of Social Work Education*, **311**, 75–81.

Dernevik, M. (1998). Preliminary findings on reliability and validity of the Historical-Clinical-Risk Assessment in a forensic psychiatric setting. *Psychology, Crime, and the Law*, **4**, 127–137.

Dobash, R.P., Dobash, R.E. & Gutteridge, S. (1986). *The imprisonment of women*. Oxford: Basil Blackwell.

Dougherty, J. (1998). Power-belief theory: Female criminality and the dynamics of oppression. In R.T. Zaplin (Ed.), *Female offenders: Critical perspectives and effective interventions* (pp. 133-160). Gaithersburg, Maryland: Aspen Publishers.

Douglas, K.S. (1999). *HCR–20 Violence Risk Assessment Scheme: Overview and annotated bibliography*. Unpublished manuscript.

Douglas, K. S., Klassen, C., Ross, D., Hart, S.D., Webster, C.D. & Eaves, D. (1998, August). *Psychometric properties of HCR–20 Violence Risk Assessment Scheme in insanity acquitees*. Poster session presented at the Annual meeting of the American Psychological Association, San Francisco, CA.

Douglas, K.S., Ogloff, J.R. & Nicholls, T.L. (1997, June). *Assessing the risk for inpatient psychiatric violence*. Paper presented at the Annual Convention of the Canadian Psychological Association, Toronto, Ontario, Canada.

Douglas, K.S., Ogloff, J.R., Nicholls, T.L. & Grant, I. (1999). Assessing risk for violence among psychiatric patients: The HCR–20 risk assessment scheme and the Psychopathy Checklist: Screening Version. *Journal of Consulting and Clinical Psychology*, **67** (6), 917–930.

Douglas, K.S. & Webster, C.D. (1999). The HCR–20 violence risk assessment scheme: Concurrent validity in a sample of incarcerated offenders. *Criminal Justice and Behavior*, **26** (1), 3–19.

Dowden, C. (2005, June). *What works for women offenders? A meta-analytic exploration of gender-responsive treatment targets and their role in the delivery of effective correctional intervention*.

Paper presented at What Works with Women Offenders: A cross-national dialogue about effective responses to female offenders, Prato, Italy.

Dowden, C. & Andrews, D.A. (1999). What works for female offenders: A meta-analytic review. *Crime and Delinquency*, **45** (4), 438–452.

Dowden, C. & Andrews, D.A. (2004). The importance of staff practice in delivering effective correctional treatment: A meta-analytic review of core correctional practice. *International Journal of Offender Therapy and Comparative Criminology*, **48** (2), 203–214.

Dowden, C. & Blanchette, K. (1998). Success rates of female offenders on discretionary versus statutory release: Substance abusers and non-abusers. *Forum on Corrections Research*, **10** (2), 27–29.

Dowden, C. & Blanchette, K. (1999). *An investigation into the characteristics of substance-abusing women offenders: Risk, need, and post-release outcome* (Research Report R-81). Ottawa, Ontario: Research Branch, Correctional Service Canada.

Dowden, C. & Brown, S.L. (2002). The role of substance abuse factors in predicting recidivism: A meta-analysis. *International Journal of Crime, Psychology, and Law*, 8, 243–264.

Eley, T.C. (1998). General genes: A new theme in developmental psychopathology. *Current Directions in Psychological Science*, **6**, 90–95.

Ellis, L. (1988). The victimful–victimless crime distinction, and seven universal demographic correlates of victimful criminal behaviour. *Personality and Individual Differences*, **9**, 525–548.

Enns, C.Z. (1997). *Feminist theories and feminist psychotherapies: Origins, themes and variations*. New York: Haworth Press.

Evans, K.M., Kincade, E.A., Marbley, A.F. & Seem, S.R. (2005). Feminism and feminist therapy: Lessons from the past and hopes for the future. *Journal of Counseling and Development*, **83**, 269–277.

Farr, K.A. (2000). Classification of female inmates: moving forward. *Crime and Delinquency*, **46** (1), 3–17.

Farrington, D.P. (1995). The development of offending and antisocial behaviour from childhood: Key findings from the Cambridge study in delinquent development. *Journal of Child Psychology and Psychiatry*, **36**, 929–964.

Farrington, D.P. (2005). Childhood origins of antisocial behaviour. *Clinical Psychology and Psychotherapy*, **12**, 177–190.

Farrington, D.P. & Painter, K.A. (2004). *Gender differences in offending: Implications for risk-focused prevention* (online report). Retrieved August 22, 2005 from http://www.homeoffice.gov.uk/rds/pdfs2/rdsolr0904.pdf.

Farrington, D.P. & West, D.J. (1995). Effects of marriage, separation, and children on offending by adult males. *Current Perspectives on Aging and the Life Cycle*, **4**, 249–281.

Fausto-Sterling, A. (1992). *Myths of gender: Biological theories about women and men* (2nd edn). New York: Basic Books.

Federal Bureau of Investigation (2002). *Crime in the United States 2002*. Uniform Crime Reporting Program. Retrieved September 15, 2005 from http://www.fbi.gov/ucr/cius_02/html/web/arrested/04-NC.html.

Feinman, C. (1983). A historical overview of the treatment of incarcerated women: Myths and realities of rehabilitation. *Prison Journal*, **63**, 12–26.

Feinman, C. (1986). *Women in the criminal justice system* (2nd edn). New York: Praeger Publishers.

Fergusson, D.M. & Horwood, L.J. (2002). Male and female offending trajectories. *Development and Psychopathology*, **14**, 159–177.

Finn, A., Trevethan, S., Carrière, G. & Kowalski, M. (1999). *Female inmates, Aboriginal inmates, and inmates serving life sentences: A one day snapshot* (Catalogue 85-002-XIE vol. 19, no. 5). Ottawa, Ontario: Canada: Ministry of Industry.

Forth, A.E., Brown, S.L., Hart, S. D. & Hare, R.D. (1996). The assessment of psychopathy in male and female noncriminals: reliability and validity. *Journal of Personality and Individual Differences*, **20**, 531–343.

Freud, S. (1953). *A general introduction to psychoanalysis*. New York: Permabooks.

Freyd, M. (1925). The statistical viewpoint in vocational selection. *Journal of Applied Psychology*, **9**, 349–356.

Funk, S.J. (1999). Risk assessment for juveniles on probation: A focus on gender. *Criminal Justice and Behavior*, **26** (1), 44–68.

Gates, M., Dowden, C. & Brown, S.L. (1998). Case need domain: 'Community Functioning'. *Forum on Corrections Research*, **10** (3), 35–37.

Gauthier, D.K. & Bankston, W.B. (1997). Gender equality and the sex ratio of intimate killing. *Criminology*, **35**, 577–600.

Gendreau, P. (1996). The principles of effective intervention with offenders. In A.T. Harland (Ed.), *Choosing correctional interventions that work: Defining the demand and evaluating the supply* (pp. 117–130). Newbury Park, CA: Sage.

Gendreau, P., French, S. & Gionet, A. (2004). What works (What doesn't work): The principles of effective correctional treatment. *Journal of Community Corrections*, **XIII** (Spring edition), 4–30.

Gendreau, P., Goggin, C., Cullen, F.T. & Paparozzi, M. (2002). The common-sense revolution and correctional policy. In J. McGuire (Ed.), *Offender rehabilitation and treatment: Effective programmes and policies to reduce re-offending* (pp. 359–386). Chichester, UK: John Wiley & Sons.

Gendreau, P., Goggin, C. & Gray, G. (2000). *Case needs review: Employment domain* (Research Report R-90). Ottawa, Ontario: Research Branch, Correctional Service Canada.

Gendreau, P., Goggin, C. & Smith, M. (1999, May). *Is there an actuarial measure that is demonstrably superior to all others?* Paper presented at the 60th Annual Convention of the Canadian Psychological Association. Halifax, Nova Scotia, Canada.

Gendreau, P., Goggin, C. & Smith, P. (2002). Is the PCL–R really the 'unparalled' measure of offender risk? A lesson in knowledge culmination. *Criminal Justice and Behavior*, **29** (4), 397–426.

Gendreau, P., Little, T. & Goggin, C. (1996). A meta-analysis of the predictors of adult offender recidivism: What works! *Criminology*, **34** (4), 575–607.

Gilfus, M. (1992). From victims to survivors to offenders: Women's routes of entry into street crime. *Women and Criminal Justice*, **4**, 63–89.

Gilligan, C. (1982). *In a difference voice: Psychological theory and women's development*. Cambridge, MA: Harvard University Press.

Giordano, P.C. & Cernkovich, S.A. (1979). On complicating the relationship between liberation and delinquency. *Social Problems*, **26**, 467–475.

Giordano, P.C., Cernkovich, S.A. & Rudolph, J.L. (2002). Gender, crime, and desistance: Toward a theory of cognitive transformation. *American Journal of Sociology*, **107**, 990–1064.

Glueck, S. & Glueck, E.T. (1934). *Five hundred delinquent women*. New York: Alfred A. Knopf, Inc.

Glueck, S. & Glueck, E.T. (1950). *Unraveling juvenile delinquency*. Cambridge, MA: Harvard University Press.

Glueck, S. & Glueck, E. (1968). *Delinquents and nondelinquents in perspective*. Cambridge, MA: Harvard University Press.

Goldstraw, J., Smith, R.G. & Sakurai, Y. (2005). Gender and serious fraud in Australia and New Zealand. *Trends and Issues in Crime and Criminal Justice, Australian Institute of Criminology*, **292**, 1–6.

Goggin, C., Gendreau, P. & Gray, G. (1998). Case need domain: Associates and social interaction. *Forum on Corrections Research*, **10** (3), 24–27.

Gottfredson, M.R. & Hirschi, T. (1990). *A general theory of crime.* Stanford, CA: Stanford University Press.

Grann, M. (2000). The PCL–R and gender. *European Journal of Psychological Assessment,* **16**, 147–149.

Grann, M., Belfrage, H. & Tengström, A. (2000). Actuarial assessment of risk for violence: Predictive validity of the VRAG and the Historical Part of the HCR–20. *Criminal Justice and Behavior,* **27**, 97–114.

Gray, T., Mays, G.L. & Stohr, M.K. (1995). Inmate needs and programming in exclusively women's jails. *The Prison Journal,* **75** (2), 186–202.

Greenfeld, L.A. & Snell, T.L. (1999). *Women offenders* (Special Report NCJ 175688). Bureau of Justice Statistics, US Department of Justice. Retrieved Sept 15, 2005 from http://www.ojp.usdoj.gov/bjs/abstract/wo.htm.

Grosser, G. (1952). Juvenile delinquency and contemporary American sex roles (Doctoral Dissertation, Harvard University, 1952). *Dissertation Abstracts International,* **17**, 2072.

Grove, W.M. & Meehl, P.E. (1996). Comparative efficiency of informal (subjective, impressionistic) and formal (mechanical, algorithmic) prediction procedures: The clinical–statistical controversy. *Psychology, Public Policy and Law,* **2** (2), 293–323.

Grove, W.M., Zald, D.H., Lebow, B.S., Snitz, B.E. & Nelson, C. (2000). Clinical versus mechanical prediction: A meta-analysis. *Psychological Assessment,* **12** (1), 19–30.

Hagan, J., Gillis, A.R. & Simpson, J. (1990). Clarifying and extending power-control theory. *American Journal of Sociology,* **95**, 1024–1037.

Hamburger, M.E., Lilienfeld, S.O. & Hogben, M. (1996). Psychopathy, gender, and gender roles: Implications for antisocial and histrionic personality disorders. *Journal of Personality Disorders,* **10**, 41–55.

Hanawalt, B. (1979). *Crime and conflict in English communities, 1300–1348.* Cambridge: MA: Harvard University Press.

Hann, R. & Harman, W. (1988). *Release risk prediction: A test of the Nuffield scoring system.* Ottawa, Ontario: Ministry of the Solicitor General of Canada.

Hann, R. & Harman, W. (1989). *Release risk prediction: A test of the Nuffield scoring system for native and female inmates.* Ottawa, Ontario: Ministry of the Solicitor General of Canada.

Hann, R. & Harman, W. (1992). *Predicting general release risk for Canadian penitentiary inmates* (User report #1992–07). Ottawa, Ontario: Ministry Secretariat, Solicitor General of Canada.

Hannah-Moffat, K. (1997). *From Christian maternalism to risk technologies: Penal powers and women's knowledges in the governance of female prisons.* Unpublished doctoral thesis, Centre of Criminology, University of Toronto, Ontario, Canada.

Hannah-Moffat, K. (1999). Moral agent or actuarial subject: Risk and Canadian women's imprisonment. *Theoretical Criminology,* **3** (1), 71–94.

Hannah-Moffat, K. (2000). Re-forming the prison: Re-thinking our ideals. In: K. Hannah-Moffat & M. Shaw (Eds), *An ideal prison? Critical essays on women's imprisonment in Canada* (pp. 30–40). Halifax, Nova Scotia: Fernwood Publishing.

Hannah-Moffat, K. (2004). Gendering risk at what cost: Negotiations of gender and risk in Canadian women's prisons. *Feminism and Psychology,* **14** (2), 243–249.

Hannah-Moffat, K. & Shaw, M. (2000a). (Eds) *An ideal prison: Critical essays on women's imprisonment in Canada.* Halifax, Nova Scotia, Canada: Fernwood Publishing.

Hannah-Moffat, K. & Shaw, M. (2000b). Thinking about cognitive skills? Think again! *Criminal Justice Matters,* **39**, 8–9.

Hannah-Moffat, K. & Shaw, M. (2001). *Taking risks: Incorporating gender and culture into classification and assessment of federally sentenced women in Canada.* Ottawa, Ontario: Status of Women Canada.

Hardyman, P.L. (2001). *Validation and refinement of objective prison classification systems for women: The experience of four states and common themes.* Washington, DC: The Institute on Crime, Justice and Corrections, National Institute of Corrections.

Hardyman, P.L. & Van Voorhis, P.V. (2004). *Developing gender-specific classification systems for women offenders.* National Institute of Corrections (NIC Accession Number 018931).

Hare, R.D. (1985). *The Psychopathy Checklist.* Vancouver, British Columbia: University of British Columbia Press.

Hare, R.D. (1991). *Manual for the Revised Psychopathy Checklist.* Toronto, Ontario: Multi-Health Systems.

Hare, R.D. (2003). *Hare Psychopathy Checklist – Revised (PCL-R)* (2nd edn). Toronto, Ontario: Multi-Health Systems.

Hare, R.D., Harpur, T.J., Hakstian, A.R., Forth, A.E., Hart, S.D. & Newman, J.P. (1990). The revised Psychopathy Checklist: Reliability and factor structure. *Psychological Assessment,* **2**, 338–341.

Harer, M.D. & Langan, N.P. (2001). Gender differences in predictors of prison violence: Assessing the predictive validity of a risk classification system. *Crime and Delinquency,* **47**, 513–536.

Harlow, C.W. (2003). *Education and Correctional Populations.* Special report, Bureau of Justice Statistics, US Department of Justice. Retrieved Sept. 25, 2005 from: http://www.ojp.usdoj.gov/bjs/pub/pdf/ecp.pdf

Harrison, P.M. & Beck., A.J. (2005). *Prison and jail inmates at midyear 2004* (NCJ 208801). Retrieved September 20, 2005 from http://www.ojp.usdoj.gov/bjs/abstract/pjim04.htm.

Hart, S.D., Forth, A.E. & Hare, R.D. (1991). The MCMI-II and Psychopathy. *Journal of Personality Disorders,* **5** (4), 318–327.

Hartnagel, T.F. (2000). Correlates of criminal behaviour. In R. Linden (Ed.), *Criminology: A Canadian perspective* (pp. 94–136). Toronto: Harcourt Brace Canada.

Hay, C. (2003). Family strain, gender, and delinquency. *Sociological Perspectives,* **46**, 107–135.

Heidensohn, F.M. (1985). *Women and crime: The life of the female offender.* New York: New York University Press.

Heney, J. (1990). *Report on self-injurious behaviour in the Kingston Prison for Women.* Ottawa, Ontario: Correctional Service Canada.

Henggeler, S.W. (1999). Multisystemic therapy: An overview of clinical procedures, outcomes, and policy implications. *Child Psychology and Psychiatry Review,* **4**, 2–10.

Her Majesty's Prison Service (2004). *Female prisoners.* Retrieved September 15, 2005 from: http://www.hmprisonservice.gov.uk/adviceandsupport/prison_life/femaleprisoners.

Hirschi, T. (1969). *Causes of delinquency.* Berkeley: University of California Press.

Hirschi, T. (2002). *Causes of delinquency.* New Brunswick, NJ: Transaction Publishers.

Hirschi, T. (2004). Self-control and crime. In R.F. Baumeister & K.D. Vohs (Eds), *Handbook of self-regulation: Research, theory, and applications* (pp. 537–552). New York: Guildford Press.

Hoffmann, J.P. & Su, S.S. (1997). The conditional effects of stress on delinquency and drug use: A strain theory assessment of sex differences. *Journal of Research in Crime and Delinquency,* **34** (1), 46–78.

Hoffman-Bustamante, D. (1973). The nature of female criminality. *Issues in Criminology,* **8**, 117–136.

Holtfreter, K., Reisig, M.D. & Morash, M. (2004). Poverty, state capital, and recidivism among women offenders. *Criminology and Public Policy,* **3** (2), 185–208.

Home Office. (2000). *Statistics on women and the criminal justice system: A home office publication under section 95 of the criminal justice act 1991.* Retrieved September 15, 2005 from http://www.homeoffice.gov.uk/docs/sect7.pdf.

Howden-Windell, J. & Clark, D. (1999). *Criminogenic needs of female offenders*. Her Majesty's Prison Service: unpublished report.

Howells, K., Heseltine, K., Sarre, R., Davey, L. & Day, A. (2004). *Correctional offender rehabilitation programs: The national picture in Australia*. Forensic Research Group, Centre for Applied Psychological Research: University of South Australia. Retrieved September 20, 2005 from http://www.aic.gov.au/crc/reports/200203–04.html.

Hunnicutt, G. & Broidy, L.M. (2004). Liberation and economic marginalization: A reformulation and test of (formerly?) competing models. *Journal of Research in Crime and Delinquency*, **41** (2), 130–155.

Inciardi, J., Lockwood, D. & Pottieger, A.E. (1993). *Women and crack-cocaine*. New York: Macmillan.

International Centre for Prison Studies (2004). *World prison brief* [database]. London: King's College. Retrieved September 15, 2005 from http://www.prisonstudies.org.

Izzo, R.L. & Ross, R.R. (1990). Meta-analysis of rehabilitation programs for juvenile delinquents: A brief report. *Criminal Justice and Behavior*, **17** (1), 134–142.

Jackson, P.G. & Stearns, C.A. (1995). Gender issues in the new generation jail. *The Prison Journal*, **75** (2), 203–221.

Jackson, R.L., Rogers, R., Neumann, C.S. & Lambert, P.L. (2002). Psychopathy in female offenders: An investigation of its underlying constructs. *Criminal Justice and Behavior*, **29** (6), 692–704.

James, J. & Thorton, W. (1980). Women's liberation and the female delinquent. *Journal of Research in Crime and Delinquency*, **20**, 230–244.

Johnson, R.E. (1979). *Juvenile delinquency and its origins: An integrative theoretical approach*. Cambridge, UK: Cambridge University Press.

Katz, R.S. (2000). Explaining girls' and women's crime and desistence in the context of their victimization experiences. *Violence Against Women*, **6**, 633–660.

Keane, C., Maxim, P. & Teevan, J. (1993). Drinking and driving, self-control, and gender. *Journal of Research in Crime and Delinquency*, **30**, 30–46.

Kelly, K. & Caputo, V. (1998). *Are federally sentenced women's experiences with family violence a factor in their contact with the criminal justice system? An exploratory study* (Technical Report TR19998-15e/x). Ottawa, Ontario: Department of Justice Canada.

Kempf-Leonard, K. & Sample, L. (March 2000). Disparity based on sex: Is gender-specific treatment warranted? *Justice Quarterly*, **17** (1).

Kendall, K. (1998). Evaluation of programs for female offenders. In R.T. Zaplin (Ed.), *Female offenders: Critical perspectives and effective interventions* (pp. 361–378). Gaithersburg, Maryland: Aspen Publishers.

Kendall, K. (2000). Psy-ence fiction: Governing female prisons through the psychological sciences. In K. Hannah-Moffat & M. Shaw (Eds), *An ideal prison: Critical essays on women's imprisonment in Canada* (pp. 82–93). Halifax, Nova Scotia: Fernwood Publishing.

Kendall, K. (2002). Time to think again about cognitive behavioural programmes. In P. Carlen (Ed.), *Women and punishment: The struggle for justice* (pp. 182–198). Cullompton, Devon: Willian Publishing.

Kendall, K. (2004). Dangerous thinking: A critical history of correctional cognitive behaviouralism. In G. Mair (Ed.), *What matters in probation* (pp. 53–89). Cullompton, Devon: Willian Publishing.

Kennedy, S.M. (2001). Treatment responsivity: Reducing recidivism by enhancing treatment effectiveness. In L.L. Motiuk & R.C. Serin (Eds), *Compendium 2000 on effective correctional treatment* (pp. 30–40). Ottawa, Ontario: Research Branch, Correctional Service Canada.

Kennedy, S.M. (2004). A practitioner's guide to responsivity: Maximizing treatment effectiveness. *Journal of Community Corrections*, **XIII** (7–9), 22–30.

Klassen, C. (1996). *Predicting aggression in psychiatric inpatients using 10 historical risk factors: Validating the 'H' of the HCR–20.* Unpublished honours thesis, Simon Fraser University, Burnaby, British Columbia, Canada.

Koons, B.A., Burrow, J.D., Morash, M. & Bynum, T. (1997). Expert and offender perceptions of program elements linked to successful outcomes for incarcerated women. *Crime and Delinquency*, **43** (4), 515–532.

Kratzer, L. & Hodgins, S. (1999). A typology of offenders: A test of Moffitt's theory among males and females from childhood to age 30. *Criminal Behaviour and Mental Health*, **9**, 57–73.

Kruttschnitt, C. (2001). Gender and violence. In C.M. Renzetti & L. Goodstein (Eds), *Women, crime, and criminal justice: Original feminist readings* (pp. 77–92). Los Angeles: Roxbury Publishing Company.

LaGrange, T.C. & Silverman, R.A. (1999). Low self-control and opportunity: Testing the general theory of crime as an explanation for gender differences in delinquency. *Criminology*, **37**, 41–72.

Lanctôt, N. & Leblanc, M. (2005). *Violent drug use trajectories: Their impact on adjudicated males' and females' quality of life in adulthood.* Presented at the 57th Annual Meeting of the American Society of Criminology, Toronto, Ontario, Canada.

Langan, P.A. & Levin, D.J. (2002). *Recidivism of prisoners released in 1994.* Special report, Bureau of Justice Statistics, US Department of Justice. Retrieved September. 25, 2005, from: http://www.ojp.usdoj.gov/bjs/pub/pdf/rpr94.pdf.

Langner, N., Barton, J., McDonagh, D., Noël, C. & Bouchard, F. (2002). Rates of prescribed medication use by women in prison. *Forum on Corrections Research*, **14**, 10–14.

Larivière, M. (1999). *The relationship between self-esteem, criminality, aggression, and violence: A meta-analysis.* Unpublished comprehensive examination, Carleton University, Ottawa, Ontario, Canada.

Laub, J.H., Nagin, D.S. & Sampson, R.J. (1998). Trajectories of change in criminal offending: Good marriages and the desistance process. *American Sociological Review*, **63**, 225–238.

Laub, S. & Sampson, R.J. (2003). *Shared beginnings, divergent lives: Delinquent boys to age 70!* Cambridge, MA: Harvard University Press.

Law, M.A. (2004). *A longitudinal follow-up of federally sentenced women in the community: Assessing the predictive validity of the dynamic characteristics of the Community Intervention Scale.* Unpublished doctoral dissertation, Carleton University, Ottawa, Ontario, Canada.

Leischied, A.W., Cummings, A., VanBrunschot, M., Cunningham, A. & Saunders, A. (2000). *Female adolescent aggression: A review of the literature and the correlates of aggression.* Ottawa, Ontario: Public Works and Government Services Canada.

Lemgruber, J. (2001). Women in the criminal justice system. In N. Ollus & S. Nevala (Eds), *Proceedings of the workshop held at the Tenth United Nations Congress on the preventions of crime and the treatment of offenders: Volume 336. Women in the criminal justice system: International examples and national responses* (pp. 59–67). Helsinki, Finland: European Institute for Crime Prevention and Control.

Leonard, E. (1982). *Women, crime and society.* New York: Longman.

Lex, B.W. (1995). Alcohol and other psychoactive substances dependence in women and men. In M.V. Seeman (Ed.), *Gender and psychopathology* (pp. 311–357). Washington, DC: American Psychiatric Press.

Lightfoot, L. & Lambert, L. (1992). *Substance abuse treatment needs of federally sentenced women* (Technical Report #2). Ottawa, Ontario: Correctional Service of Canada.

Linehan, M.M. (1993). *Cognitive behavioral therapy for borderline personality disorder.* New York: Guilford Press.

Lipsey, M.W. (1995). The efficacy of correctional treatment: A review and synthesis of meta-evaluations. In J. McGuire (Ed.), *What works: Reducing reoffending* (pp. 79–111). Chichester, UK: John Wiley & Sons.

Lipton, D.S., Pearson, F.S., Cleland, C.M. & Yee, D. (2002). The effectiveness of cognitive-behavioural treatment methods on offender recidivism. In J.M. McGuire (Ed.), *Offender rehabilitation and treatment: Effective programmes and policies to reduce re-offending* (pp. 79–112). Chichester, UK: John Wiley & Sons.

Lodhi, P.H. & Thakur, S. (1993). Personality of drug addicts: Eysenckian Analysis. *Personality and Individual Differences*, **15** (2), 121–128.

Loeber, R. (1982). The stability of antisocial and delinquent child behaviour: A review. *Child Development*, **53**, 1431–1446.

Loeber, R. & LeBlanc, M. (1990). Toward a developmental criminology. In M. Tonry & N. Morris (Eds), *Crime and justice: A review of research* (vol. 12; pp. 375–473). Chicago, IL: University of Chicago Press.

Lombroso, C. & Ferrero, W. (1895). *The female offender*. London: T. Fisher Unwin.

Lösel, F. (1995). The efficacy of correctional treatment: A review and synthesis of meta-evaluations. In J. McGuire (Ed.), *What works: Reducing re-offending: Guidelines from research and practice* (pp. 79–111). Chichester, UK: John Wiley & Sons.

Lösel, F. (1996). Effective correctional programming: What empirical research tells us and what it doesn't. *Forum on Corrections Research*, **8** (3), 33–37.

Loucks, A.D. (1995). *Criminal behaviour, violent behaviour, and prison maladjustment in federal female offenders*. Unpublished doctoral dissertation, Queen's University, Kingston, Ontario, Canada.

Loucks, A.D. & Zamble, E. (1994). Some comparisons of female and male serious offenders. *Forum on Corrections Research*, **6** (1), 22–24.

Loucks, A.D. & Zamble, E. (2000). *Predictors of criminal behavior and prison misconduct in serious female offenders*. Unpublished manuscript, Queen's University, Kingston, Ontario, Canada.

Lowenkamp, C.T., Holsinger, A.M. & Latessa, E.J.(2001). Risk/need assessment, offender classification, and the role of childhood abuse. *Criminal Justice and Behavior*, **28** (5), 543–563.

Lundberg, G.A. (1926). Case work and the statistical prediction. *Social Forces*, **5**, 61–65.

Lytton, H. & Romney, D. (1991). Parents' differential treatment of boys and girls: A meta-analysis. *Psychological Bulletin*, **109**, 267–296.

Maccoby, E.E. (2004). Aggression in the context of gender development. In M. Putallaz & K.L. Bierman (Eds), *Aggression, antisocial behaviour, and violence among girls* (pp. 3–22). New York: Guildford Press.

Maccoby, E.E. & Jacklin, C.N. (1974). *The psychology of sex differences*. Stanford, CA: Stanford University Press.

Maher, L. (1995). Women and the initiation to illicit drugs. In R.E. Dobash, R.P. Dobash & L. Noaks (Eds), *Gender and crime* (pp. 132–166). Cardiff: University of Wales Press.

Mann, C.R. (1996). *When women kill*. Albany: State University of New York Press.

Marchese, M.C. (1992). Clinical versus actuarial prediction: A review of the literature. *Perceptual and Motor Skills*, **75**, 583–594.

Mauer, M., Potler, C. & Wolf, R. (1999). *Gender and justice: Women, drugs and sentencing policy*. Washington, DC: The sentencing project.

McClellan, D.S., Farabee, D. & Crouch, B.M. (1997). Early victimization, drug use, and criminality: A comparison of male and female prisoners. *Criminal Justice and Behavior*, **24** (4), 455–476.

McConnell, B. (1996). *The prediction of female federal offender recidivism with the Level of Supervision Inventory*. Unpublished honours thesis, Queen's University, Kingston, Ontario, Canada.

McCord, J. & Otten, L. (1983). A consideration of sex roles and motivations for crime. *Criminal Justice and Behaviour*, **10**, 3–12.

McDonagh, D., Noël, C. & Wichmann, C. (2002). Mental health needs of women offenders: Needs analysis for the development of the intensive intervention strategy. *Forum on Corrections Research*, **14**, 32–35.

McDonagh, D., Taylor, K. & Blanchette, K. (2002). Correctional adaptation of Dialectical Behaviour Therapy (DBT) for federally sentenced women. *Forum on Corrections Research*, **14**, 36–39.

McGuire, J. (Ed.) (1995). *What works: Reducing re-offending – Guidelines from research and practice*. Chichester, UK: John Wiley & Sons.

McGuire, J. (Ed). (2002). *Offender rehabilitation and treatment: Effective programmes and policies to reduce re-offending*. New York: John Wiley & Sons.

McLanahan, S.S., Sorensen, A. & Watson, D. (1989). Sex differences in poverty, 1950–1980. *Signs*, **15**, 102–123.

McLean, H. (1998). Psychological assessment of women offenders. In T.A. Leis, L.L. Motiuk & J.R.P. Ogloff (Eds), *Forensic psychology: Policy and practice in corrections* (pp. 43–51). Ottawa, Ontario: Correctional Service Canada.

McMahon, M. (Ed.) (2000). *Assessment to assistance: Programs for women in community corrections*. Arlington, VA: American Correctional Association.

McMurran, M., Tyler, P., Hogue, T., Cooper, K., Dunseath, W. & McDaid, D. (1998). Measuring motivation to change in offenders. *Psychology, Crime and Law*, **4**, 43–50.

Meehl, P.E. (1954). *Clinical versus statistical prediction: A theoretical analysis and a review of the evidence*. Minneapolis: University of Minnesota Press.

Meehl, P.E. (1965). Seer over sigh: The first good example. *Journal of Experimental Research in Personality*, **1**, 27–32.

Merton, R. (1938). Social structure and anomie. *American Sociological Review*, **3**, 672–682.

Messina, N. & Grella, C. (2005). *Childhood trauma and women's physical and mental health: a prison population*. Presented at the 57th Annual Conference of the American Society of Criminology, Toronto, Ontario, Canada.

Miller, E. (1986a). *Street woman*. Philadelphia: Temple University Press.

Miller, J.(1998). Up it up: Gender and the accomplishment of street robbery. *Criminology*, **36**, 37–66.

Miller, J.B. (1976). *Toward a new psychology of women*. Boston: Beacon Press.

Miller, J.B. (1986b). *What do we mean by relationships?* Work in Progress No. 33. Wellesley, MA: Stone Center, Working Paper Series.

Miller, S.L. & Burack, C. (1993). A critique of Gottfredson and Hirschi's general theory of crime: Selective (in)attention to gender and power positions. *Women and Criminal Justice*, **4**, 115–134.

Miller, W.B. (1958). Lower class culture as a generating milieu of gang delinquency. *Journal of Social Issues*, **14**, 5–19.

Moffitt, T.E. (1993). 'Life-course-persistent' and 'adolescence-limited' antisocial behaviour: A developmental taxonomy. *Psychological Review*, **100**, 674–701.

Moffitt, T.E. (1994). Natural histories of delinquency. In E. Weitekamp & H. J. Kerner (Eds), *Cross-national longitudinal research on human development and criminal behaviour* (pp. 3–61). Dordrecht, Netherlands: Kluwer Academic Press.

Moffitt, T.E. & Caspi, A. (2001). Childhood predictors differentiate life-course persistent and adolescence-limited antisocial pathways among males and females. *Development and Psychopathology*, **13**, 355–375.

Moffitt, T.E., Caspi, A., Rutter, M. & Silva, P.A. (2001). *Sex difference in antisocial behaviour: Conduct disorder, delinquency, and violence in the Dunedin Longitudinal Study*. Cambridge: Cambridge University Press.

Morash, M. (1986). Gender, peer group experiences, and seriousness of delinquency. *Journal of Research in Crime and Delinquency*, **23**, 43–67.

Morash, M. (1999). A consideration of gender in relation to social learning and social structure: A general theory of crime and deviance. (Symposium on Ronald L. Aker's social learning and social structure: A general theory of crime and deviance). *Theoretical Criminology*, **3** (4), 451–461.

Morash, M., Bynam, T.S. & Koons, B.A. (1998). *Women Offenders: Programming needs and Promising approaches*. Research in Brief. Washington, DC: National Institute of Justice.

Morash, M., Haar, R.N. & Rucker, L. (1994). A comparison of programming for women and men in US prisons in the 1980s. *Crime and Delinquency*, **40** (2), 197–221.

Morris, E.K. & Braukmann, C.J. (1987). *Behavioural approaches to crime and delinquency. A handbook of application, research and concepts*. New York: Plenum Press.

Morris, R. (1964). Female delinquency and relational problems. *Social Forces*, **43**, 82–89.

Morris, R.R. (1987). *Women, crime and criminal justice*. Oxford: Basil Blackwell.

Motiuk, L.L. (1997). Classification for correctional programming: The Offender Intake Assessment (OIA) process. *Forum on Corrections Research*, **9** (1), 18–22.

Motiuk, L.L. (1998). Profiling federal offenders on conditional release. *Forum on Corrections Research*, **10** (2), 11–14.

Motiuk, L.L. & Blanchette, K. (2000). *Assessing female offenders: What works*. In M. McMahon (Ed.), *Assessment to assistance: Programs for women in community corrections* (pp. 235–266). Arlington, VA: American Correctional Association.

Motiuk, L.L. & Brown, S.L. (1993). *The validity of Offender Needs Identification and Analysis in community corrections* (Research Report R–34). Ottawa, Ontario: Correctional Service Canada.

Motiuk, L.L. & Porporino, F. (1989). *Offender Risk/Needs Assessment: A study of conditional releases* (Research Report R–01). Ottawa, Ontario: Correctional Service Canada.

Motiuk, L.L. & Serin, R.C. (Eds). (2001). *Compendium 2000 on effective correctional programming*. Ottawa: Research Branch, Correctional Service Canada.

Murray, L. & Fiti, R. (2004). *Arrests for notifiable offences and the operation of certain police powers under PACE: England and Wales, 2003/2004*. London: Home Office. Retrieved September 15, 2005 from www.homeoffice.gov.uk/rds/arrests1.html.

Nafekh, M. & Motiuk, L. (2002). *The Statistical Information on Recidivism – Revised 1 (SIR–R1) Scale: A psychometric examination* (Research Report R-126). Ottawa, Ontario: Correctional Service Canada.

Naffine, N. (1987). *Female crime: The construction of women in criminology*. Sydney: Allen and Unwin.

Naffine, N. (1996). *Feminism and criminology*. Philadelphia: Temple University Press.

Nagin, D.S. & Paternoster, R. (1993). Enduring individual differences and rational choice theories of crime. *Law and Society Review*, **27**, 467–496.

Neary, A. (1990). *DSM-III and Psychopathy Checklist assessment of antisocial personality disorder in black and white female felons*. Unpublished doctoral dissertation, University of Missouri, St. Louis, Mo.

Nicholls, T.L., Ogloff, J.R. & Douglas, K.S. (1997, June). *Comparing risk assessments with female and male psychiatric inpatients: Utility of the HCR–20 and Psychopathy Checklist: Screening Version*. Paper presented at the 57th Annual Convention of the Canadian Psychological Association, Toronto, Ontario, Canada.

Nuffield, J. (1982). *Parole decision-making in Canada: Research toward decision guidelines*. Ottawa, Ontario, Canada: Communications Division.

Nye, F.I. (1958). *Family relationships and delinquent behaviour*. New York: John Wiley & Sons.

O'Connor, D.A. (2003). *The female psychopath: Validity and factor structure of the Revised Psychopathy Checklist (PCL–R) in women inmates*. Dissertation Abstracts International: Section B: the Sciences and Engineering, Vol. 63 (12-B), p. 6101.

Oddone Paolucci, E., Violato, C. & Schofield, M. (1998). Case need domain: 'Marital and Family'. *Forum on Corrections Research*, **10** (3), 20–23.

Ogloff, J.R. & Davis, M.R. (2004). Advances in offender assessment and rehabilitation: Contributions of the risk–needs–responsivity approach. *Psychology, Crime and Law*, **10**, 229–242.

Olson, D.E., Alderden, M. & Lurigio, A.J. (2003). Men are from Mars, women are from Venus, but what role does gender play in probation recidivism? *Justice Research and Policy*, **5** (2), 33–54.

Owen, B. (2001). Perspectives on women in prison. In C. M. Renzetti & L. Goodstein (Eds), *Women, crime, and criminal justice: Original feminist readings* (pp. 243–254). Los Angeles: Roxbury.

Owen, B. & Bloom, B. (1995). *Profiling the needs of California's female prisoners: A needs assessment*. Washington, DC: National Institute of Corrections.

Patterson, G.R. (1992). Developmental changes in antisocial behaviour. In R. De V. Peters, R.J., McMahon & V.L. Quinsey (Eds), *Aggression and violence throughout the life span* (pp. 2–82). Newbury Park, CA: Sage.

Patterson, G.R., Reid, J.B., Jones, R.Q. & Conger, R.E. (1975). *A social learning approach to family intervention. Vol. 1*. Eugene, OR: Castalia Publishing Co.

Patterson, G.R. & Yoerger, K. (1997). A developmental model for late onset delinquency. In D.W. Osgood (Ed.), *Motivation and delinquency: Nebraska Symposium on Motivation* (Vol. 44; pp. 119–177). Lincoln: University of Nebraska Press.

Peters, R.H., Strozier, A.L., Murrin, M.R. & Kearns, W.D. (1997). Treatment of substance abusing jail inmates: Examination of gender differences. *Journal of Substance Abuse Treatment*, **14**, 339–349.

Piquero, N.L., Gover, A.R., MacDonald, J.M. & Piquero, A.R. (2005). The influence of delinquent peers on delinquency: Does gender matter? *Youth and Society*, **36** (3), 251–275.

Pollack, O. (1950). *The criminality of women*. Philadelphia: University of Philadelphia Press.

Pollack, J. (1986). *Sex and supervision: Guarding male and female inmates*. New York, NY: Greenwood Press.

Pollack, S. (2005). Taming the shrew: Regulating prisoners through women-centered mental health programming. *Critical Criminology*, **13**, 71–87.

Pratt, T.C. & Cullen, F.T. (2000). The empirical status of Gottfredson and Hirschi's General Theory of Crime: A meta-analysis. *Criminology*, **38**, 931–964.

Prendergast, M.L., Wellisch, J. & Falkin, G.P. (1995). Assessment of and services for substance-abusing women offenders in community and correctional settings. *The Prison Journal*, **75** (2), 240–256.

Prendergast, M.L., Wellisch, J. & Wong, M.M. (1996). Residential treatment for women parolees following prison-based drug treatment: Treatment experiences, needs and services, outcomes. *The Prison Journal*, **76** (3), 253–274.

Putallaz, M. & Bierman, K.L. (Eds) (2004). *Aggression, antisocial behaviour, and violence among girls*. New York: Guildford Press.

Quinsey, V.L., Skilling, T.A., Lalumière, M.L. & Craig, W.M. (2004). *Juvenile delinquency: Understanding the origins of individual differences*. Washington DC: American Psychological Association.

Reckless, W.C. (1967). *The crime problem* (4th edn). New York: Appleton-Century-Crofts.

Reiss, A.J. (1951). Delinquency as the failure of personal and social controls. *American Sociological Review*, **16**, 196–207.

Rettinger, J.L. (1998). *A recidivism follow-up study investigating risk and need within a sample of provincially sentenced women.* Unpublished doctoral dissertation, Carleton University, Ottawa, Ontario, Canada.

Rice, M.E. & Harris, G.T. (1995). Violent recidivism: Assessing predictive validity. *Journal of Consulting and Clinical Psychology,* **63,** 737–748.

Richards, H.J., Casey, J.O. & Lucente, S.W. (2003). Psychopathy and treatment response in incarcerated female substance abusers. *Criminal Justice and Behavior,* **30,** 251–276.

Richie, B.(2001). Challenges incarcerated women face as they return to their communities: Findings from life history interviews. *Crime and Delinquency,* **47,** 368–389.

Robinson, D., Porporino, F. & Beal, C. (1998). *A review of the literature on personal/emotional need factors* (Research Report R-76). Ottawa, Ontario: Research Branch: Correctional Service of Canada.

Ross, D.J., Hart, S.D. & Webster, C.D. (1998). *Aggression in psychiatric patients: Using the HCR–20 to assess risk for violence in hospital and in the community.* Unpublished manuscript.

Ross, R.R. & Fabiano, E.A. (1985a). *Correctional afterthoughts: Programs for female offenders* (User Report #1985–18). Ottawa, Ontario: Programs Branch, Ministry of the Solicitor General of Canada.

Ross, R.R. & Fabiano, E.A. (1985b). *Time to think: A cognitive model of delinquency prevention and offender rehabilitation.* Johnson City, Tennessee: Institute of Social Sciences and Arts.

Ross, R.R. & Fabiano, E.A. (1986). *Female offenders: Correctional afterthoughts.* Jefferson, North Carolina: McFarland.

Rowe, D.C. (1986). Genetic and environmental components of antisocial behaviour: A study of 265 twin pairs. *Criminology,* **24,** 513–532.

Rowe, D.C. (2002). *Biology and crime.* Los Angeles, CA: Roxbury.

Rutherford, M.J., Cacciola, J.S., Alterman, A.I. & McKay, J.R. (1996). Reliability and validity of the revised Psychopathy Checklist in women methadone patients. *Assessment,* **3,** 43–54.

Salekin, R.T., Rogers, R. & Sewell, K.W. (1997). Construct validity of psychopathy in a female offender sample: A multitrait-multimethod evaluation. *Journal of Abnormal Psychology,* **106,** 576–585.

Salekin, R.T., Rogers, R., Ustad, K.L. & Sewell, K.W. (1998). Psychopathy and recidivism among female inmates. *Law and Human Behavior,* **22,** 109–127.

Sampson, R.J. & Laub, J.H. (1990). Crime and deviance over the life course: The salience of adult social bonds. *American Sociological Review,* **55,** 609–627.

Sampson, R.J. & Laub, J.H. (1993). *Crime in the making: Pathways and turning points through life.* Cambridge, MA: Harvard University Press.

Sellers, C.S., Cochran, J.K. & Winfree, L.T. Jr (2003). Social learning theory and courtship violence: An empirical test. In R.L. Akers & G.F. Jensen (Eds), *Social learning theory and the explanation of crime* (pp. 109–127). New Brunswick, NJ: Transaction Publishers.

Serin, R.C. (1996). Violent recidivism in criminal psychopaths, *Law and Human Behaviour,* **20,** 207–217.

Serin, R.C. (2001). Treatability, treatment responsivity, and risk management. In K.S. Douglas, C.D. Webster, S.D. Hart, D. Eaves & J.R.P. Ogloff (Eds), *HCR–20: Violence Risk Management Companion Guide* (pp. 109–118). Burnaby, British Columbia, Canada: Mental Health, Law and Policy Institute, Simon Fraser University.

Serin, R.C. & Kennedy, S. (1997). *Treatment readiness and responsivity: Contributing to effective correctional programming* (Research Report R-54). Ottawa, Ontario: Research Branch, Correctional Service Canada.

Severiens, S. & ten Dam, G.T.M. (1994). Gender differences in learning styles: A narrative review and quantitative meta-analysis. *Higher Education,* **27,** 487–501.

Sharf, R. (2003). *Theories of psychotherapy and counseling: Concepts and cases.* Pacific Grove, CA: Wadsworth.

Shaw, M. (1991a). *Survey of federally sentenced women: Report to the Task Force on Federally Sentenced Women on the prison survey* (User Report #1991–4). Ottawa, Ontario: Ministry Secretariat, Solicitor General Canada.

Shaw, M. (1991b). *The release study: Survey of federally-sentenced women in the community* (User Report #1991–5). Ottawa, Ontario: Ministry Secretariat, Solicitor General Canada.

Shaw, M. & Hannah-Moffat, K. (2000). Gender, diversity, and risk assessment in Canadian corrections. *Probation Journal*, **47** (3), 163–173.

Shaw, M. & Hannah-Moffat, K. (2004). How cognitive skills forgot about gender and diversity. In G. Mair (Ed.), *What matters in probation* (pp. 90–121). Cullompton, Devon: Willian Publishing.

Shaw, M., Rodgers, K., Blanchette, J. Hattem, T., Seto Thomas, L. & Tamarack, L. (1991). *Paying the price: Federally sentenced women in context* (User Report No. 1991–5). Ottawa, Ontario: Ministry of the Solicitor General Canada.

Silver, E. & Miller, L.L. (2002). A cautionary note on the use of actuarial risk assessment tools for social control. *Crime and Delinquency*, **48**, 138–161.

Silverthorn, P. & Frick, P.J. (1999). Developmental pathways to antisocial behaviour: The delayed-onset pathway in girls. *Development and Psychopathology*, **11**, 101–126.

Simon, R.J. (1975). *Women and crime*. Lexington, MA: Lexington Books.

Simon, R.J. & Landis, J. (1991). *The crimes women commit, the punishment they receive*. Lexington, MA: Lexington Books.

Simons, R.L., Miller, R.L. & Aigner, S.M. (1980). Contemporary theories of deviance and female delinquency: An empirical test. *Journal of Research in Crime and Delinquency*, **17**, 42–57.

Simourd, L. & Andrews, D.A. (1994). Correlates of delinquency: A look at gender differences. *Forum on Corrections Research*, **6** (1), 26–31.

Simourd, D. & Hoge, R. (2000). Psychopathy: a risk–need perspective. *Criminal Justice and Behavior*, **27** (2), 256–272.

Sinclair, R.L. & Boe, R. (2002). *Canadian federal women offender profiles: Trends from 1981 to 2002 (revised)* (Research Report R-131). Ottawa, Ontario: Research Branch, Correctional Service Canada.

Smart, C. (1976). *Women, crime and criminology: A feminist critique*. London: Routledge & Kegan Paul.

Smart, C. (1982). The new female offender: Reality or myth? In B.R. Price & N. Sokoloff (Eds), *The criminal justice system and women* (pp. 105–116). New York: Clark Boardman.

Solicitor General Canada. (1987). *Development of a security classification model for Canadian federal offenders*. Ottawa, Ontario: Author.

Sommers, I. & Baskin, D.R. (1993). The situational context of violent female offending. *Journal of Research in Crime and Delinquency*, **30**, 136–162.

Sorbello, L., Eccleston, L., Ward, T. & Jones, R. (2002). Treatment needs of female offenders: A review. *Australian Psychologist*, **37**, 196–205.

Spencer, D.L. & MacKenzie, D.L. (2003). The gendered effects of adult social bonds on the criminal activities of probationers. *Criminal Justice Review*, **28** (2), 278–298.

Steffensmeier, D. (1978). Crime and the contemporary woman: An analysis of changing levels of female property crime, 1960–75. *Social Forces*, **57**, 566–584.

Steffensmeier, D. (1980). Sex differences in patterns of adult crime, 1965–1977. *Social Forces*, **58** (4), 1080–1109.

Steffensmeier, D. (1993). National trends in female arrests, 1960–1990: Assessment and recommendations for research. *Journal of Quantitative Criminology*, **9**, 411–441.

Steffensmeier, D. (2001a). Sex differences in patterns of adult crime, 1965–77: A review and assessment. *Social Forces*, **58**, 1080–1108.

Steffensmeier, D. (2001b). Female crime trends, 1960–1995. In C.M. Renzetti & L. Goodstein (Eds), *Women, crime and criminal justice: Original feminist readings* (pp. 191–211). Los Angeles: Roxbury Publishing Company.

Steffensmeier, D. & Allan, E. (1996). Gender and crime: Toward a gendered theory of female offending. *Annual Sociological Review*, **22**, 459–487.

Steffensmeier, D. & Haynie, D. (2000). Gender, structural disadvantage, and urban crime: Do macrosocial variables also explain female offending rates? *Criminology*, **38**, 403–427.

Strachan, C.E. (1993). *The assessment of psychopathy in female offenders*. Unpublished doctoral dissertation, University of British Columbia, Vancouver, British Columbia, Canada.

Strand, S. & Belfrage, H. (2001). Comparison of HCR–20 scores in violent mentally disordered men and women: gender differences and similarities. *Psychology, Crime, and Law*, **7**, 71–79.

Susman, E.J. & Pajer, K. (2004). Biology-behaviour integration and antisocial behaviour in girls. In M. Putallaz & K.L. Bierman (Eds), *Aggression, antisocial behaviour, and violence among girls* (pp. 23–47). New York: Guildford Press.

Sutherland, E.H. (1947). *Principles of criminology* (4th edn). Philadelphia: Lippincott.

Swets, J.A., Dawes, R.M. & Monahan, J. (2000). Psychological science in the public interest: psychological science can improve diagnostic decisions. *Journal of the American Psychological Society*, **1**, 1–26.

Task Force on Federally Sentenced Women (1990). *Creating choices: Report of the Task Force on Federally Sentenced Women*. Ottawa, Ontario: Ministry of the Solicitor General Canada.

Taylor, N. & Bareja, M. (2002). *2002 National Police Custody Survey*. Canberra: Australian Institute of Criminology. Retrieved September 15, 2005 from http://www.aic.gov.au/publications/tbp/tbp013/.

Thomas, W.I. (1923). *The unadjusted girl*. Boston: Little, Brown and Company.

Tien, G., Lamb, D., Bond, L., Gillstom, B. & Paris, F. (1993). *Report on the needs assessment of women at the Burnaby Correctional Centre for Women*. Burnaby, British Columbia, Canada: BC Institute on Family Violence.

Tittle, C.R., Ward, D.A. & Grasmick, H.G. (2003). Gender, age, and crime/deviance: A challenge to self-control theory. *Journal of Research in Crime and Delinquency*, **40** (4), 426–453.

Trickett, P.K. & Gordis, E.B. (2004). Aggression and antisocial behaviour in sexually abused females. In M. Putallaz & K.L. Bierman (Eds), *Aggression, antisocial behaviour, and violence among girls* (pp. 162–185). New York: Guildford Press.

Van Dusen, K.T. & Mednick, S.A. (Eds) (1983). *Prospective studies of crime and delinquency*. Boston: Kluwer–Nijhoff.

Van Voorhis, P.V. & Presser, L. (2001). *Classification of women offenders: A national assessment of current practices*. Washington, D.C: US Department of Justice, National Institute of Corrections.

Van Wormer, K. (2001). *Counseling female offenders and victims: A strengths-restorative approach*. Springer: New York.

Vazsonyi, A.T. & Crosswhite, J.M. (2004). A test of Gottfredson and Hirschi's general theory of crime in African-American adolescents. *Journal of Research in Crime and Deliqnuency*, **41** (4), 407–432.

Vitale, J.E. & Newman, J.P. (2001). Using the Psychopathy Checklist – Revised with female samples: Reliability, validity, and implications for clinical utility. *Clinical Psychology: Science and Practice*, **8** (1), 117–132.

Vitale, J.E., Smith, S.S., Brinkley, C.A. & Newman, J.P. (2002). The reliability and validity of the Psychopathy Checklist – Revised in a sample of female offenders. *Criminal Justice and Behaviour*, **29**, 202–231.

Viteles, M.S. (1925). The clinical viewpoint in vocational psychology. *Journal of Applied Psychology*, **9**, 131–138.

Walters, G.D. (1995). The Psychological Inventory of Criminal Thinking Styles part 1: Reliability and preliminary validity. *Criminal Justice and Behavior*, **22** (3), 307–325.

Walters, G.D. & Elliott, W.N. (1999). Predicting release and disciplinary outcome with the Psychological Inventory of Criminal Thinking Styles: Female data. *Legal and Criminological Psychology*, **4**, 15–21.

Walters, G.D., Elliott, W.N. & Miscoll, D. (1998). Use of the Psychological Inventory of Criminal Thinking Styles in a group of female offenders. *Criminal Justice and Behavior*, **25** (1), 125–134.

Ward, T. & Brown, M. (2004). The Good Lives model and conceptual issues in offender rehabilitation. *Psychology, Crime and Law*, **10**, 243–257.

Ward, T. & Eccleston, L. (2004). Risk, responsivity, and the treatment of offenders: Introduction to the special issue. *Psychology, Crime and Law*, **10**, 223–227.

Ward, T. & Stewart, C. (2003a). Criminogenic needs and human needs: A theoretical model. *Psychology, Crime and Law*, **10** (3), 125–143.

Ward, T. & Stewart, C. (2003b). The relationship between human needs and criminogenic needs *Psychology, Crime and Law*, **9** (3), 219–224.

Warren, J.I., Burnette, M.L., South, S.C., Chauhan, P., Bale, R., Friend, R. & Van Patten, I. (2003). Psychopathy in women: Structural modeling and comorbidity. *International Journal of Law and Psychiatry*, **26** (3), 223–242.

Webster, C.D., Douglas, K.S., Eaves, D. & Hart, S.D. (1997). *HCR–20: Assessing risk for violence (Version 2)*. Unpublished document, Simon Fraser University, Burnaby, British Columbia, Canada.

Webster, C.D., Eaves, D., Douglas, K.S. & Wintrup, A. (1995). *The HCR–20 Scheme: The assessment of dangerousness and risk.* Unpublished document, Simon Fraser University, Burnaby, British Columbia, Canada.

Webster, C.M. & Doob, A.N. (2004). Classification without validity or equity: An empirical examination of the Custody Rating Scale for federally sentenced women offenders in Canada. *Canadian Journal of Criminology and Criminal Justice*, **46**, 395–421.

Wellisch, J. Anglin, M.D. & Prendergast, M.L. (1993). Treatment strategies for drug-abusing women offenders. In J.A. Inciardi (Ed.), *Drug treatment and criminal justice* (pp. 5–25). Newbury Park, CA: Sage Publications.

Wexler, H.K., Falkin, G.P. & Lipton, D.S. (1990). Outcome evaluation of a prison therapeutic community for substance abuse treatment. *Criminal Justice and Behaviour*, **17** (1), 71–92.

White, J.L., Moffitt, T.E., Caspi, A., Bartusch, B.J., Needles, D.J. & Stouthamer-Loeber, M.D. (1994). Measuring impulsiveness and examining its relationship to delinquency. *Journal of Abnormal Psychology*, **103**, 192–205.

Widom, C.S. (1989). The cycle of violence. *Science*, **244**, 160–166.

Widom, C.S. (2000). Child victimization: Early adversity, later psychopathology (NCJ 180077). *National Institute of Justice Journal*. Retrieved September 28, 2005 from: www.nij.ncjrs.org/publications.

Widom, C.S. (2003). Understanding child maltreatment and juvenile delinquency: The research. In J. Wiig, C.S. Widom & J.A. Tuell (Eds), *Understanding child maltreatment and juvenile delinquency: From research to effective program, practice and systemic solutions* (pp. 1–10). Washington, DC: Child Welfare League of America. Retrieved September 28, 2005 from: www.cwla.org/programs/juvenilejustice/ucmjd.htm.

Wilczynski, A. (1995). Child-killing by parents. In R.E. Dobash, R.P. Dobash & L. Noaks (Eds) *Gender and crime* (pp.167–180). Cardiff: University of Wales Press.

Willis, K. & Rushforth, C. (2003). The female criminal: An overview of women's drug use and offending behaviour. *Trends and Issues in Crime and Criminal Justice*. Australian Institute of Criminology, Canberra, No. 264, 1–6.

Wilson, D.B., Gallagher, C.A. & MacKenzie, D.L. (2000). A meta-analysis of corrections-based education, vocation, and work programs for adult offenders. *Journal of Research in Crime and Delinquency*, **37** (4), 347–368.

Wilson, M.I. & Daly, M. (1992). Who kills whom in spouse killings? On the exceptional sex ratio of spousal homicides in the United States. *Criminology*, **30**, 189–215.

Worell, J. (2001). Feminist interventions: Accountability beyond symptom reduction. *Psychology of Women Quarterly*, **25**, 335–343.

Worell, J. & Remer, P. (1992). *Feminist perspectives in therapy: An empowerment model for women*. Chichester, UK: John Wiley & Sons.

Worell, J. & Remer, P. (2003). *Feminist perspectives in therapy: Empowering diverse women* (2nd edn). Hoboken, NJ: John Wiley & Sons.

Wormith, J.S. & Goldstone, C.S. (1984). The clinical and statistical prediction of recidivism. *Criminal Justice and Behavior*, **11** (3), 3–34.

Wright, R. (1995). *The moral animal: Evolutionary psychology and everyday life*. New York: Vintage Books.

Zahn-Waxler, C. & Polanichka, N. (2004). All things interpersonal. Socialization and female aggression. In M. Putallaz & K.L. Bierman (Eds), *Aggression, antisocial behaviour, and violence among girls* (pp. 48–68). New York: Guildford Press.

Zaplin, R.T. (1998). Female offenders: A systems perspective. In R.T. Zaplin (Ed.), *Female offenders: Critical perspectives and effective interventions* (pp. 65–78). Gaithersburg, MD: Aspen Publishers.

Zietz, D. (1981). *Women who embezzle or defraud: A study of convicted felons*. New York: Praeger.

Zinger, I. (2004). Actuarial risk assessment and human rights: A commentary. *Canadian Journal of Criminology and Criminal Justice*, **46**, 607–621.

Zinger, I. & Forth, A.E. (1998). Psychopathy and Canadian criminal proceedings: The potential for human rights abuses. *Canadian Journal of Criminology*, **40** (3), 237–276.

INDEX

Aboriginal people 6–7, 125, 134, 142
abuse
 against women 108–9, 129–30
 by women 107
 in childhood 28–9, 35–6, 108, 109, 145
 incarceration trends 8
 responsivity principle 129–30
accomplices 12–13
actuarial assessment 45–6, 50, 51, 52, 140
 Historical Clinical Risk Scheme 78–9, 80
 Level of Service/Case Management
  Inventory 74–8, 79–80, 140
 need principle 83–4, 141
 Psychopathy Checklist-Revised 59–74,
  79–80
 recommendations 81–2, 144–5
 risk principle 55–6
 Statistical Information on Recidivism
  56–9, 79–80
adolescent offenders see girls
advocacy brokerage 128
aggression
 family factors 89
 gender differential 2–3, 13
 overt 138
 relational 3, 138
 socialization theories 33
 see also violent crime
alcohol abuse 97–101, 122, 134
antisocial associates 92–4, 101
antisocial attitudes 94–7, 101
antisocial personality disorder (APD)
 68–9, 71
anxiety 69, 124

assault 10, 13
assessment see actuarial assessment;
  criminogenic needs (dynamic risk
  factors), assessment; offender classification, assessment for; recidivism,
  assessment of risk for
associates 92–4, 101
attachment 18, 19, 20, 90, 91
attitudes
 antisocial 94–7, 101
 of staff 133, 134

behavioural genetics 27–8
behavioural interventions 116–17, 127–30,
  136, 141
biological theories of offending 27–9, 139, 145
borderline personality disorder (BPD) 70,
  71, 73, 124

California Psychological Inventory (CPI-So)
  65, 66, 67
Canada, corrections service 133–4
CARE programme 136
caregivers, incarceration 8
child abuse
 by women 107
 survivors 28–9, 35–6, 108, 109, 145
childcare 122
child-killings 9–10
child-rearing practices
 criminogenic needs and 89–91
 socialization 32–3, 34
 see also developmental (life-course)
  theories of offending

Choices, Actions, Relationships and Emotions (CARE) 136
classification of offenders, assessment for *see* offender classification, assessment for
client-centred counselling 130
clinical assessment method 45, 46, 51
cognitive ability 105–7, 125
cognitive behavioural therapy 116, 117, 127–33, 141
cognitive restructuring 116
communication styles 121–2
community functioning 101–4, 111
community supervision 135
connection principle 120, 129
control theories 16–20, 138–9, 146
correctional afterthoughts 83, 137
correctional interventions *see* treatment
Correctional Service of Canada (CSC) 133–4
criminogenic needs (dynamic risk factors) 43, 44–6, 48, 147
  assessment 83–113, 140–1
    associates 92–4, 101
    attitudes 94–7, 101
    community functioning 101–4, 111
    education 85–9
    emotional domain 104–7
    employment 85–9, 101, 104
    family 89–92, 113, 141
    need principle 83, 84–5, 110–11, 140–1
    parasuicide 110
    personal domain 104–7
    personal victimization 108–9, 144
    recommendations 144
    review conclusions 110–13
    self-esteem 107–8
    self-harm 110
    substance abuse 97–101, 109
  poverty 102–4, 111, 139–40, 144
cultural diversity 125, 134, 142, 147
dehumanization of women 131–2
demographics 125
developmental (life-course) theories of offending 18–19, 24–6, 39, 138
see also child-rearing practices
differential association 20, 21
differential reinforcement 20–1
diversity issues 125, 134, 142, 147

drug abuse 97–101, 134, 135
drug-related crime 7, 12
dynamic risk factors *see* criminogenic needs

economic equality 30, 32
economic marginality 78
  see also poverty
economic marginalization theory 31, 32, 139
education needs 85–9
emancipation theory *see* liberation/emancipation theory
embezzlement 11
emotional problems 104–7
employment needs 85–9, 101, 104
employment-related interventions 121, 129–30, 135
empowerment 120–1, 126–7, 129, 130, 134
England, corrections service 136
enhancement approaches *see* strengths-based assessment/treatment
environments for treatment 117, 118, 134, 135
evolutionary theory of offending 26–7, 40, 121, 139
extinction 116
Eysenck Personality Questionnaire (EPQ) 65, 66, 67

familial female violence 9–10, 138
  see also physical abuse
family factors 89–92, 113, 141
  gender-responsive corrections 135
  parental substance abuse 98, 99, 100
  responsivity principle 129–30
  see also parenting
female-centred theories of offending 15, 29–36, 37–40, 121, 138, 139
female offenders *see* girls; women
female-specific treatment 122, 133–6, 141, 142, 147
feminist criticisms of responsivity principle 127–33, 136, 141
feminist pathways research 35–6, 38, 130, 139
feminist theories of offending 35–6, 38, 40, 121, 139
feminist therapy 119–20, 127–8, 136
financial problems 102–4, 135
  see also poverty
fraud 12
future research 146–7

gender difference
  criminogenic needs   84–5, 140–1
    associates 92, 94
    attitudes   94
    education 85, 89
    employment   85–6, 89
    family factors 91, 92
    personal victimization   108
    review conclusions   112–13
    self-esteem   107
    self-harm   110
    socio-economic factors   102–4
    substance abuse   100
  future research   146
  incarceration rates 6, 7, 8, 137–8, 142
  need principle   84–5
    see also gender difference, criminogenic
      needs
  offending patterns   1–5, 13
    gestalt of   8–13, 14, 137–8
  risk principle   55–6
  theories of offending
    feminist   36
    gendered   39
    general strain   37–8
    genetic   28–9, 145
    life-course   25–6
    power control   34
    relational   33–4, 113, 138
    self-control   16–17
    social control   19–20, 146
    social learning   21–2
    socialization   32–3, 34
  treatment and
    cognitive ability   125
    communication styles   121–2
    learning styles   121
    mental health   124
    motivation   125–6
    personality disorders   124
    physical health   125
    psychopathy   124
    substance abuse   122
    therapist-client matching   126
gender equality theory see liberation/
    emancipation theory
gender inequality (economic
    marginalization) theory 31, 32, 1
    39
gender-informed assessment   48–52, 112,
    113, 143, 144–5

gender-informed responsivity princi-
    ple   126–7, 129, 145
gender-informed theories of offending 40,
    143
gender-informed treatment 122, 133–6, 141,
    142, 147
gender-neutral theories of offending 15,
    16–29, 37–40, 138–9, 143, 146
gender-responsive corrections   133–6
gender-specific theories of offending 15,
    29–36, 37–40, 121, 138, 139
gendered theory of offending   38–9, 139
general responsivity principle   116–17,
    118–19, 120, 126, 129, 136
general strain theory (GST)   37–8, 139
general theory of crime (self-control
    theory)   16–18, 40
genetic theories of offending   27–9, 145
gestalt of offending patterns   8–13, 14,
    137–8
girls
  assessment models   51–2, 144–5
  needs assessment   144
    associates 93, 94
    attitudes   97
    employment/education 87, 88, 89
    family factors 89, 90, 91, 92, 141
    socio-economic factors   102–4
  offending patterns   1–2, 3–5, 138
  recommendations   143–6, 147
  relational aggression 3, 138
  theories of offending
    biological   28–9, 145
    feminist   35–6
    life-course   25–6
    socialization   32–3, 34
    'What Works'   142
good lives model see strengths-based
    assessment/treatment

health care 122, 125
Her Majesty's Prison Service   136
Historical Clinical Risk Scheme
    (HCR-20)   78–9, 80
histrionic personality disorder (HPD) 70,
    71, 73
holistic treatment 122, 133–6, 141
homicides   8–10, 13, 138

incarceration trends   5–8, 13–14, 137–8, 142
indigenous peoples   6–7, 125, 134, 142

infanticide 9–10
intellectual functioning 105–7, 125
inter-agency collaboration 135
inter-agency communication 128
interdisciplinary research 147
Interpersonal Reactivity Index (IRI)
    66, 67
interventions see treatment

juvenile offenders see girls

learning styles 121, 136
Level of Service/Case Management
    Inventory (LS/CMI) 74–8, 79–80,
    140
liberation/emancipation theory 4, 5, 29–31,
    32, 139
life-course (developmental) theories of
    offending 18–19, 24–6, 39, 139

Machiavellianism-IV scale (MACH-IV)
    65
marital relationships 89, 90, 91, 92, 101, 138
mathematical assessment tools see actuarial
    assessment
men, role in female crime 12–13
    see also gender difference
mental ability 105–7, 125
mental health
    criminogenic needs 106, 107, 109,
        110
    incarceration trends 8
    treatment 122, 124, 135, 136
meta-analyses 130–1
minority groups 6–7, 125, 134, 142
molecular genetics 27, 28–9, 145
motivation to change 125–6
murder 8–10, 13, 138
mutuality 120, 121

Narcissism Personality Inventory (NPI) 66,
    67–8
National Institute of Corrections
    (NIC) 135
need principle 23, 24, 43–4, 83, 84–5, 110–11,
    140–1
    applicability to women see criminogenic
        needs (dynamic risk factors),
        assessment
non-criminogenic needs (static risk
    factors) 44–6, 101, 122, 144

offender classification, assessment for
    41–52, 140
    actuarial see actuarial assessment
    applicability of standard tools 46–8, 51,
        79–82, 140, 146
        see also recidivism, assessment of risk for
    clinical 45, 46, 51
    dynamic risk factors 43, 44–6, 48, 84, 144
    function 42
    future research 146
    gender-informed models 48–52, 112,
        113, 143, 144–5
    history of 42
    principles of 42–4, 51, 54–6, 116, 143–4
    recommendations 51–2, 143–4
    static risk factors 44–6, 144
offending, theories of see theories of
    offending
offending patterns 1–5, 13
    gestalt of 8–13, 14, 137–8
    incarceration trends 7
operant conditioning 116

paranoid personality disorder 70, 71, 73
parasuicide 110
parenting
    criminogenic needs 89–91
    theories of offending 32–3, 34
    see also family factors
peers, antisocial 92–4
personal, interpersonal, community-
        reinforcement (PIC-R) theory 23–4,
        39, 40, 138
    see also need principle; risk principle;
        treatment, responsivity principle
personal problems 104–7
personal victimization 108–9, 129–30, 144
personality disorders 68–71, 73, 124
physical abuse
    against women 108–9, 129–30
    in childhood 108, 109
    incarceration trends 8
    responsivity principle 129–30
physical health 122, 125
positive reinforcement 116
post-traumatic stress 109
poverty
    assessing risk for recidivism 78
    criminogenic needs 102–4, 111, 139–40,
        144

gestalt of offending   138
responsivity principle 127, 129–30
theories of offending 27, 31, 32, 139–40
power belief theory 35, 139
power control theory 34, 139
prison, incarceration trends   5–8, 13–14,
    137–8
professional override principle   43–4
property crime
    gender difference 3,   4–5, 10–12, 13, 138
    substance abuse   97
    theories of offending   26–7, 30
prosocial modelling 116, 117
prosocial skills acquisition   116
prostitution   12
protective factors   145
psychiatric health *see* mental health
Psychological Inventory of Criminal
        Thinking (PICTS) 94, 95, 96, 105
psychology, biases in 131, 142–3
psychopathy
    assessment   59–74
    treatment and   124
Psychopathy Checklist-Revised
        (PCL-R)   59–74, 79–80
    concurrent validity   63–4
    construct validity   61–3
    convergent validity   64–9
    discriminant validity   69–71
    predictive validity   71–4
    reliability   60–1
    treatment progress   124

racism   127
recidivism
    assessment of risk for   53–82, 140
        Historical Clinical Risk Scheme   78–9,
            80
        Level of Service/Case Management
            Inventory   74–8, 79–80, 140
        Psychopathy Checklist-Revised
            59–74, 79–80
        recommendations   81–2, 144–5
        risk principle   54–6, 80, 140
        Statistical Information on
            Recidivism   56–9, 79–80
    criminogenic needs and   84–5, 140–1
        associates   92–4
        attitudes   94–7
        community functioning   101–4, 111
        employment/education 86, 87–9, 104

family factors   89–92
    mental health   107
    personal victimization   108–9, 144
    personal/emotional   104–5
    recommendations   144
    review conclusions   111–13
    self-harm   110
    substance abuse   97–101
non-criminogenic needs and   144
responsivity principle   116
    see also treatment, responsivity principle
recommendations   81–2, 143–6, 147
relational theory   33–4, 38, 113, 120–1, 129,
        135, 136, 138, 139
relational violence   3–4, 138
research methodologies   130–1, 142–3,
        146
research recommendations   146–7
responsivity principle *see* treatment,
        responsivity principle
risk assessment
    for offender classification *see* offender
        classification, assessment for
    of risk to recidivate *see* recidivism
risk management 41, 42, 81–2, 83, 140
risk principle   23–4, 43–4, 54–6, 80, 140,
        143–4
RNR approach   23–4, 143
    feminist criticisms   127–33
    see also need principle; risk principle;
        treatment, responsivity principle
robbery 10, 13
role convergence theory *see* liberation/
        emancipation theory

science, biases in 131, 142–3
self-control theory   16–18, 40
self-efficacy 121, 129, 130
self-esteem   107–8, 124, 130, 134
self-harm
    CARE programme   136
    criminogenic needs   110
    incarceration trends   8
Self-Report Psychopathy Checklist
        (SRP-II)   63–4
Self-Report Psychopathy Scale (SRPS)   64
sexual abuse
    in childhood 36, 108,   109
    incarceration trends   8
social control theories   18–20, 39, 40, 146
social learning interventions 116, 128, 129

social learning theories (SLTs) 20–2, 39,
    121, 128, 139
socialization theories 32–3, 34, 139
specific responsivity principle 116, 117,
    123–6, 136, 141
staff attitudes 133, 134
static risk factors (non-criminogenic
    needs) 44–6, 101, 122, 144
Statistical Information on Recidivism -
    Revised (SIR-R1) scale 56–9, 79–80
strain theory 37–8
strengths-based assessment/treat-
    ment 49–51, 112, 113, 123, 126, 132,
    141, 145
structured behavioural interventions
    116–17, 127–30, 136, 141
substance abuse 97–101, 109
    treatment 122, 134, 135, 136, 140
suicidal behaviour 110

theories of offending 15–40, 138–40
    female-centred 15, 29–36, 39–40, 138,
        139
    gender-informed 40, 143
    gender-neutral 15, 16–29, 39–40, 138–9,
        143, 146
    hybrid 37–9, 40, 138, 139
    recommendations 40, 143
    responsivity principle 120–1
therapists 117, 118, 123, 126, 132–3
thinking styles 94, 96, 130
treatment
    Canada 133–4
    England 136
    environments for 117, 118, 134, 135
    need assessment and 83–4
        see also criminogenic needs (dynamic
            risk factors), assessment
    need principle 23, 24, 43, 83, 84–5,
        110–11, 140, 144
    responsivity principle 23, 24, 43–4,
        115–36, 141
        applicability to women 118–19, 123–6
        classes of interventions 116–17
        client strengths 123, 126, 132
        cognitive ability 125
        communication styles 121–2
        criticisms of 127–33, 136, 141
        defining 116–17
        demographics 125
        empowerment 120–1, 126–7, 129, 130, 134

external responsivity factors
    117, 126
feminist therapy 119–20, 127–8, 136
gender-informed reformulation
    126–7, 129, 141, 145
general 116–17, 118–19, 120, 126, 129,
    136, 141
holistic approaches 122, 133–6, 141
internal responsivity factors 117, 126
learning styles 121, 136
mental health 122, 124
motivation 125–6
personality 124
physical health 122, 125
relational theory 120–1, 129, 136
self-efficacy 121, 129, 130
specific 116, 117, 123–6, 136, 141
therapist characteristics 117, 118, 123,
    126, 132–3
therapist-client matching 126
treatment environment 117, 118
women-specific targets 122, 133–6, 141,
    147
risk assessment and 41, 143–4
    see also offender classification,
        assessment for
risk principle 23–4, 43, 54–6, 80, 140,
    143–4
strengths-based 49–51, 123, 126, 132
substance abuse 122, 134, 135, 136, 141
USA 135
Wales 136
'What Works' 142

unemployment 86
USA, women-centred corrections 135

victimization 108–9, 129–30, 144
violence, relational 3–4, 138
violent crime
    CARE programme 136
    criminogenic needs
        associates 92, 93
        attitudes 94, 95
        community functioning 102, 103, 104
        employment/education needs 87, 88
        family factors 90, 91
        personal victimization 108, 109
        self-esteem 107
        self-harm 110
        substance abuse 97

gender difference 2, 3–4, 8–10, 13, 14, 138
offender classification 47–8, 140
recidivism
   assessing risk for 76, 78–9, 80, 140
   criminogenic needs *see* violent crime, criminogenic needs
theories of offending 22, 27, 30
see also physical abuse

Wales, corrections service 136
weapons, use of 10
'What Works' 142
white-collar crime 11–12, 30

women
   assessing needs of 83–113
   assessing for offender classification 41–52, 140, 143–4
   assessing risk to recidivate 53–82
   as correctional afterthoughts 83, 137
   corrections *see* treatment
   future research 146–7
   incarceration trends 5–8, 13–14, 137–8, 142
   offending patterns 1–5, 7, 8–13, 14, 137–8
   recommendations 81–2, 143–6, 147
   theories of offending by 15–40, 138–40, 143